VOLUME FIFTY SIX

ADVANCES IN
THE STUDY OF BEHAVIOR

VOLUME FIFTY SIX

Advances in
THE STUDY OF BEHAVIOR

Edited by

JEFFREY PODOS
Department of Biology
Morrill Science Center
University of Massachusetts Amherst
United States

SUSAN HEALY
School of Biology
Centre for Biological Diversity
University of St Andrews
United Kingdom

ACADEMIC PRESS
An imprint of Elsevier

Academic Press is an imprint of Elsevier
125 London Wall, London, EC2Y 5AS, United Kingdom
50 Hampshire Street, 5th Floor, Cambridge, MA 02139, United States
525 B Street, Suite 1650, San Diego, CA 92101, United States

First edition 2024

Copyright © 2024 Elsevier Inc. All rights are reserved, including those for text and data mining, AI training, and similar technologies.

Publisher's note: Elsevier takes a neutral position with respect to territorial disputes or jurisdictional claims in its published content, including in maps and institutional affiliations.

No part of this publication may be reproduced or transmitted in any form or by any means, electronic or mechanical, including photocopying, recording, or any information storage and retrieval system, without permission in writing from the publisher. Details on how to seek permission, further information about the Publisher's permissions policies and our arrangements with organizations such as the Copyright Clearance Center and the Copyright Licensing Agency, can be found at our website: www.elsevier.com/permissions.

This book and the individual contributions contained in it are protected under copyright by the Publisher (other than as may be noted herein).

Notices
Knowledge and best practice in this field are constantly changing. As new research and experience broaden our understanding, changes in research methods, professional practices, or medical treatment may become necessary.

Practitioners and researchers must always rely on their own experience and knowledge in evaluating and using any information, methods, compounds, or experiments described herein. In using such information or methods they should be mindful of their own safety and the safety of others, including parties for whom they have a professional responsibility.

To the fullest extent of the law, neither the Publisher nor the authors, contributors, or editors, assume any liability for any injury and/or damage to persons or property as a matter of products liability, negligence or otherwise, or from any use or operation of any methods, products, instructions, or ideas contained in the material herein.

ISBN: 978-0-443-29440-2
ISSN: 0065-3454

For information on all Academic Press publications
visit our website at https://www.elsevier.com/books-and-journals

Publisher: Zoe Kruze
Acquisition Editor: Mariana Kuhl
Editorial Project Manager: Devwart Chauhan
Production Project Manager: Abdulla Sait
Cover Designer: Matthew Limbert

Typeset by MPS Limited, India

Contents

Contributors	*vii*
Preface	*ix*

1. Wall-following behavior: Its ultimate and proximate explanations, prevalence, and implications   1
Inon Scharf and Alejandro Farji-Brener

1.	Introduction	2
2.	Anxiety, stress, and predation-avoidance behavior	6
3.	Exploration	12
4.	Favorable biotic and abiotic conditions	14
5.	The test arena's size, shape, and structure	17
6.	Development, aging, carryover effects, and parental effects	21
7.	Sex, population, and other intraspecific and interspecific differences	25
8.	Behavioral repeatability and correlations with other behaviors	26
9.	Future research on wall-following behavior	28
10.	Concluding comments	32
	Acknowledgments	33
	References	33

2. Quiet but not forgotten: Insights into adaptive evolution and behavior from 20 years of (mostly) silent Hawaiian crickets   51
Nathan W. Bailey, Marlene Zuk, and Robin M. Tinghitella

1.	Introduction	52
2.	Behavior's role in adaptive evolution	62
3.	Behavior links signal, form, and function	66
4.	Rapid convergent adaptation: Causes and consequences	71
5.	Synthesis: The value of long-term insect studies in nature	78
	Acknowledgements	79
	References	79
	Further readings	87

3. Patterns of host specificity in interactions involving behavioral manipulation of spiders by Darwin wasps
89

Marcelo O. Gonzaga, Rafael R. Moura, Alexander Gaione-Costa, and Thiago G. Kloss

1. Introduction	90
2. Methods	101
3. State-of-art and trends in studies of polysphinctine-host interactions	105
4. Patterns of host specificity	107
5. Parasitoid-spider networks	115
6. Factors influencing specificity patterns	127
7. Conclusions	143
Acknowledgements	145
Appendix A. Supporting information	145
References	145

4. Orb web construction in a new generation of behavioral analysis: A user's guide
155

William G. Eberhard

1. Introduction	156
2. A brief introduction to orb construction behavior	157
3. Additional decisions during sticky spiral construction	175
4. Uniformity of cues used in different families of orb weavers	176
5. Learning and maturation	184
6. Coordination and independence of flexible adjustments of web variables	186
7. Do spiders have expectations regarding the sites and orientations of web lines?	193
8. Conclusion: The promise of orbs for new directions of behavioral research	204
Acknowledgements	206
References	206
Further reading	211

Contributors

Nathan W. Bailey
School of Biology, University of St Andrews, St Andrews, United Kingdom

William G. Eberhard
Smithsonian Tropical Research Institute, Balboa, Panama; Escuela de Biologia, Universidad de Costa Rica, Ciudad Universitaria, Costa Rica; Museum of Natural Science, Louisiana State University, Baton Rouge, Louisiana, USA

Alejandro Farji-Brener
LIHO (Laboratorio de Investigaciones en Hormigas), INIBIOMA-CONICET y CRUB, Universidad Nacional Del Comahue, Bariloche, Argentina

Alexander Gaione-Costa
Programa de Pós-graduação em Ecologia, Universidade Federal de Viçosa, Viçosa, MG, Brazil

Marcelo O. Gonzaga
Instituto de Biologia, Universidade Federal de Uberlândia,Uberlândia, MG, Brazil

Thiago G. Kloss
Departamento de Biologia Geral, Universidade Federal de Viçosa, Viçosa, MG, Brazil

Rafael R. Moura
Núcleo de Extensão e Pesquisa em Ecologia e Evolução (NEPEE), Departamento de Ciências Agrárias e Naturais, Universidade do Estado de Minas Gerais, Ituiutaba, MG, Brazil

Inon Scharf
School of Zoology, The George S. Wise Faculty of Life Sciences, Tel Aviv University, Tel Aviv, Israel

Robin M. Tinghitella
Department of Biological Sciences, University of Denver, Denver, CO, United States

Marlene Zuk
Department of Ecology, Evolution and Behavior, University of Minnesota, St. Paul, MN, United States

Preface

Volume 56 of *Advances in the Study of Behavior* offers up a feast of Tinbergian delights, covering all four of his famous questions, spanning evolution to mechanisms

Chapter 1, by Scharf and Farji-Brener, reviews a topic that might be of particular interest to our shyest readers: wall-following. The tendency to move along walls, be they human-constructed or natural, is widely distributed across taxa and habitats, yet much of our knowledge about this behaviour has been gleaned mainly from four readily available model species (lab mice and rats, zebrafish, and *Drosophila melanogaster*). Scharf and Farji-Brener first review the wide range of potential functions for wall following – including anxiety reduction, forming trails or spatial maps, hiding from predators – and then offer suggestions for future research. Notably, the authors call for more attention to field studies, and the costs and benefits of this fascinating, understudied behaviour.

Chapter 2, by Bailey, Zuk, and Tinghitella, reviews two decades of research on a species of Hawaiian cricket, *Teleogryllus oceanicus*, reflecting on a wonderful, field-based case study regarding how animals can evolve rapidly in response to parasitoidism. The parasitoids in this case, a fly (*Ormia ochracea*), detect their hosts by sound, which has favored in the crickets a diversity of mutations to their sound-producing wing elements ("adaptive breakage") that has rendered them silent or near silent, and thus cryptic to the flies. Incredibly, the crickets are able to accommodate the loss of their acoustic mating signals and still mate, through other means. The wealth of data on this system has allowed the authors to document fast-moving changes in behaviour, how those changes map onto evolving patterns of genetic architecture and demography, and most generally the power of behavioral plasticity and accommodation

Host–parasitoid relationships are also central to Chapter 3, by Gonzaga, Moura, Gaione-Costa, and Kloss. These authors focus on a group of diverse, fascinating wasps called Polysphinctines which lay their eggs on unwitting spider hosts. The wasp larvae not only feed on spiders (eventually) but also manipulate spider hosts' behavior to their favor, in part by inducing them to alter the structure of their webs – more specifically to use materials and patterns that favor the wasp larvaes' capacity to build cocoons and thus metamorphize. A main goal of the chapter is to offer comprehensive, original analyses of spider host x wasp parasitoid interaction networks, based on data culled from a deep dive into the literature including from traditionally overlooked localities. The authors' analyses reinforce the supposition that many wasp species specialize onto distinct spider host species, and further show that the wasps' behaviors, such as in how they attack their hosts, evolve in response to their hosts' particular defense strategies

In Chapter 4, Eberhard continues the focus on spiders and their web constructions, but draws our attention more directly to the the process of web construction itself. Of particular interest here is the phenomenon of "sticky spiral" construction, in which silk lines covered with liquid or fibrous adhesive are overlaid, in a continuous inwards spiral, atop a pre-woven base of anchor, frame, radius, and auxiliary lines. Eberhard walks us through the various decision rules that spiders use (or don't use) regarding the task itself and the positioning of their bodies and body parts, as they space and repair lines in the inward spiral. Overall, this review provides a case study for a series of concepts of broad interest in our field including behavioral precision, repeatability, flexibility, and attention; cue assessment; insight as a means for problem solving; mental representations; and algorithms for converting mental representations into actions.

A common theme across these chapters is that the authors all provide a wealth of suggestions for future work. This is a volume rich in data, questions for testing, and inspiration for all of us fascinated by the behaviour of the animals around us. Enjoy!

CHAPTER ONE

Wall-following behavior: Its ultimate and proximate explanations, prevalence, and implications

Inon Scharf[a,]* and Alejandro Farji-Brener[b]

[a]School of Zoology, The George S. Wise Faculty of Life Sciences, Tel Aviv University, Tel Aviv, Israel
[b]LIHO (Laboratorio de Investigaciones en Hormigas), INIBIOMA-CONICET y CRUB, Universidad Nacional Del Comahue, Bariloche, Argentina
*Corresponding author. e-mail address: scharfi@tauex.tau.ac.il

Contents

1. Introduction — 2
2. Anxiety, stress, and predation-avoidance behavior — 6
3. Exploration — 12
4. Favorable biotic and abiotic conditions — 14
5. The test arena's size, shape, and structure — 17
6. Development, aging, carryover effects, and parental effects — 21
7. Sex, population, and other intraspecific and interspecific differences — 25
8. Behavioral repeatability and correlations with other behaviors — 26
9. Future research on wall-following behavior — 28
10. Concluding comments — 32
Acknowledgments — 33
References — 33

Abstract

Wall-following behavior is the movement along a wall exhibited by various animals. It is a conserved behavior among taxa, from unicellular organisms to humans, prone to selection pressure, and it is energetically cheap since it provides a homogenous trail and can help animals to follow the shortest distance between two points. There are three sets of explanations for this behavior. The first is that it is a defensive behavior meant to lead the animal to shelter or reduce predation risk, and which, at least in vertebrates, is a proxy of anxiety. The second explanation suggests it is an exploratory behavior, helping an animal either to exit an enclosed space or to orient in a novel (unfamiliar) environment, especially when vision is limited. As novel environments often induce stress, these two explanations are not mutually exclusive. Finally, the wall itself may offer some desired biotic or abiotic conditions, such as a higher prey availability moving along it or favorable microclimate conditions. Wall following is a variable behavior, easily affected by the test conditions, such as the test arena size (e.g., more in smaller arenas), shape, and illumination level. Standardization of its measurement is required to facilitate comparison among studies and species. The timing of examination plays a role too: Wall following often changes along development and with aging. Generally, females follow walls more often than do males. Furthermore, certain conditions experienced at a young age affect wall-following later, so the behavioral changes may be long-lasting. Wall following is correlated with a few other behaviors, such as a negative correlation with phototaxis and activity. We end our review by presenting some future research directions, such as examining wall-following behavior in predator-prey systems, examining whether and when wall-following is adaptive, and studying it in the context of urban ecology. Finally, there is a need to examine how common this behavior is in the wild as most studies have been conducted in the lab.

1. Introduction

Wall-following behavior is a concept in animal behavior referring to the movement along a wall or staying next to it, either close to the wall or by touching it. It should also refer to cases in which animals move or stay on the wall itself. It is phylogenetically conserved and requires little skill, just following a wall using touch or vision (Kallai et al., 2007; Lebreton & Martin, 2009). We use the term 'wall' to refer to any vertical surface and not only the dictionary definition of a wall. Although it has been most often documented in the laboratory, it can take place in nature too. Urban habitats comprise many walls, and animals follow walls in order to find shelter or to dwell (Mammola, Isaia, Demonte, Triolo, & Nervo, 2018; Winchell et al., 2020). Fences can function similarly to walls if animals cannot go through the gaps in the fences (Bojarska et al., 2017; Van Dyk & Slotow, 2003). Clearly, animals have evolved under more natural conditions, where the wall can be easily replaced with any type of barrier, such as logs, rocks, or cave walls, making wall-following behavior relevant also in more natural settings, such as caves, cliff rocks, and woody trunks in forests, on land or in water (Fišer, Prevorčnik, Lozej, & Trontelj, 2019; Jethva, Liversage, & Kundu, 2022; Douglass & Reinert, 1982). Walls or barriers need not, actually, be vertical: If animals move vertically, such as ants moving on a tree trunk, barriers can be horizontal (Forbes & Northfield, 2017; Islam, Deeti, Mahmudah, Kamhi, & Cheng, 2023; Qin et al., 2019). Wall-following behavior is not, however, a universal response when walls are encountered. Another possible response is bouncing back from the wall at the same angle or another angle. For example, canines, such as dogs and foxes, jump at walls and bounce back, which might be an indicator of stress and is negatively correlated with cage size (Korhonen, Niemelä, & Jauhiainen, 2001; Stephen & Ledger, 2005). Another example is the barrier-avoidance behavior of ants: Some species do not move along barriers but rather learn how to change their routes to avoid encountering them (Islam et al., 2023; McCreery, Dix, Breed, & Nagpal, 2016).

Wall following is a behavior that crosses taxa and habitats (Fig. 1). It has been observed in most animal taxa, from unicellular animals, through worms, insects, fish, and rodents, to medium-sized mammals, like humans (Akiyama, Agata, & Inoue, 2015; Dussutour, Deneubourg, & Fourcassié, 2005; Kallai, Karadi, & Feldmann, 2009; Schnörr, Steenbergen, Richardson, & Champagne, 2012; Sikora, Baranowski, & Zajaczkowska, 1992; Valle, 1970). However, the majority of studies have been conducted on only three model species: lab mice, rats, and zebrafish with several studies on wall-following

Fig. 1 Four reptiles moving along or on natural or artificial walls. (A) *Stellagama stellio* on rocks in northwest Tel Aviv, Israel; (B) *Podarcis muralis* on rocks next to Baden Baden, Germany; (C) *Ptyodactylus guttatus* on a staircase at Tel Aviv University; and (D) an *Uromastyx ornata* on its terrarium wall in Antwerp Zoo, Belgium. Photos by IS.

behavior in cavefish. The most studied invertebrate is *Drosophila melanogaster* but otherwise, only a few species have been studied more than four-five times (but see, for example, American cockroaches or humans: e.g., Creed & Miller, 1990; Wang, Liu, Liu, & Chai, 2023). Wall-following behavior has been found in animals occurring in terrestrial, aquatic, and marine habitats. For instance, crustaceans in all three habitats have been observed to follow walls (Devigne, Broly, & Deneubourg, 2011; McGaw, 2001; McMahon, Patullo, & Macmillan, 2005).

Wall-following behavior has several synonyms (or near-synonyms) in the scientific literature. The most common one is "Thigmotaxis", defined in this context as "the tendency to remain close to walls" or "vertical surfaces" (Lamprea, Cardenas, Setem, & Morato, 2008; Martinez & Morato, 2004; Simon, Dupuis, & Costentin, 1994). Note that this is quite a narrow definition for thigmotaxis, and broader ones exist too, such as "contact-oriented behavior of organisms… that is associated with the movement toward or away from a mechanical stimulus" (Masarovič, Zvaríková, Fedorová, & Fedor, 2017) or "the way in which an organism organizes behavior relative to tactile stimuli" (Kallai et al., 2007). Thus, when using this term, one should be aware of its exact definition in the studied context. Interestingly, "taxis" means to move toward (or away from) a stimulus gradient, like light or certain chemicals (phototaxis and chemotaxis; Adler, 1975; Jékely, 2009). In contrast, walls do not necessarily have a gradient, and wall following occurs after an animal reaches the wall (so there is no longer movement toward the wall). Furthermore, thigmotaxis (from Greek, thigma = touch, taxis = movement) hints that movement along walls takes place by touch, whereas it does not always hold, as many animals use other senses, such as vision or a mixture of senses (Doria, Morand-Ferron, & Bertram, 2019; Dussutour et al., 2005; Filgueiras, Carvalho-Netto, & Estanislau, 2014; Martínez, Cardenas, Lamprea, & Morato, 2002; Pratt, Brooks, & Franks, 2001).

Wall following or wall hugging are two additional synonyms. Both wall following and wall hugging suggest some movement, although animals may just seek walls and stop moving when a wall is reached (Iwatsuki & Hirano, 1995; Scharf, Silberklang, Avidov, & Subach, 2020). "Wall seeking" (as in Kvist, Selander, & Viemerö, 1995; for example) is a more general term, which is neutral towards the outcome once the wall is reached. Another synonym is centrophobism, which does not emphasize contact with walls but rather the avoidance of open areas in the test arena's center (coined by Götz & Biesinger, 1985a; Götz & Biesinger, 1985b). However, while the wall serves as a stimulus or a "home base" in wall-following behavior or thigmotaxis (Kallai et al., 2007; Lebreton & Martin, 2009; Stewart et al., 2010), it is not very clear what the 'central' stimulus is when referring to centrophobism. Finally, although such phenomena are similar, attention should be given to what exactly is measured—whether it is the proportion of time animals remain close to walls with or without movement, their tendency to start moving along walls after encountering them, or the tendency to leave the wall and enter the arena's center. Less common synonyms are wall or edge preference, wall seeking, wall clinging, and perimeter patrolling (Avni & Eilam, 2008; Costanzo, 1989; Kjær, Jørgensen, Hageman, Miskowiak, & Wörtwein, 2020; Ramlan et al., 2017). A possible explanation for the different synonyms depends on the species studied. For example, centrophobism is mostly used concerning fruit flies (Besson & Martin, 2005; Soibam et al., 2012), whereas the majority of studies on humans use either wall following or thigmotaxis (Fridolf, Ronchi, Nilsson, & Frantzich, 2013; Walz, Mühlberger, & Pauli, 2016). In the rest of this review, we will use wall-following behavior and refer to it and all its synonyms and near-synonyms. When the behavior we discuss is essentially different, for example, when the animal stops once it attaches to a wall further without movement, we will mention it explicitly. Some authors differentiate between "active" and "passive" wall following. The former term refers to being highly thigmotactic and following the wall independent of its shape, whereas the latter means that only certain wall types (e.g., concave) are followed (Creed & Miller, 1990; Patton, Windsor, & Coombs, 2010). These two are probably just endpoints of a spectrum.

In this review, we will discuss wall-following behavior from a broad perspective. Although there are no reviews of wall-following behavior as a single behavior, it has been partially surveyed in reviews focusing on related themes. For example, quantifying wall-following behavior is often used as a proxy for anxiety in rodents and zebrafish (Maximino et al., 2010; Simon et al., 1994; Treit & Fundytus, 1988). Thigmotaxis is often mentioned in papers presenting or summarizing specific methodologies used to assess stress levels, such as open-field tests or elevated-plus mazes (e.g., Devan, McDonald, & White, 1999; Prut & Belzung, 2003; Telonis & Margarity, 2015; Zhang, Vollert, Sena, Rice, & Soliman, 2021). Thigmotaxis is also extensively used for determining the impacts of the deleterious effects of different chemicals, such as organic pollutants, on animal behavior, or as a proxy of the sedative effects of anxiolytic drugs and is often discussed in such contexts (e.g., Bose, Brodin, Cerveny, & McCallum, 2022; Harris, 2021; Muniandy, 2018).

The first question we wish to answer is why animals follow walls. This question has been discussed extensively, with several possible, non-mutually exclusive explanations, and like other behaviors, both ultimate and proximate explanations have been suggested. Most studies, and especially those on vertebrates, suggest that wall following is an "anxiety-like behavior" (Grillon & Ernst, 2016; Maximino, Carvalho, & Morato, 2014; Ou et al., 2015; Pellow & File, 1986; Yang et al., 2017), which is a proximate explanation. Much more commonly for invertebrates, this behavior is suggested to be indicative of "exploration". Walls are then used to navigate in the habitat (Grosslight & Harrison, 1961; McMahon et al., 2005) or to direct animals to suitable shelters (Laurent Salazar, Planas-Sitjà, Sempo, & Deneubourg, 2018; McGaw, 2001). Wall-following behavior may often be a behavior used to reduce predation risk (Chen, Li, Wang, Lin, & Yang, 2022; Kotrschal et al., 2014; Lebreton & Martin, 2009), which in vertebrates can be a proxy of anxiety, and is an ultimate explanation. The second question we ask is how wall-following behavior differs based on the test conditions. If, for example, walls are followed much more frequently in smaller than in larger arenas, what is measured is not the natural tendency of the studied animal to follow walls but rather its interaction with the specific test arena. The third question we discuss is variability in wall-following behavior either within the same animal (e.g., differences between juveniles and adults and between the sexes), between individuals of the same species, or among species, and how it correlates with other behaviors. This is done to understand whether wall-following behavior is part of a known behavioral axis, such as that of activity and exploration. Our final goal is to suggest gaps in the existing literature and future research directions for wall-following behavior.

2. Anxiety, stress, and predation-avoidance behavior

Animals follow walls for different reasons, which depend greatly on the studied organism but also the discipline of research. In brief, such reasons include anxiety, stress, seeking shelter, an attempt to avoid predation, habitat exploration, or an attempt to search for an exit from a bounded habitat, seeking suitable locations to ambush prey, and seeking certain favorable abiotic conditions (Table 1). Psychologists working mostly with mice and rats have interpreted wall-following behavior as "anxiety-related behavior". There are two lines of support for this interpretation. First, treating insects, snails, fish, or rodents with anxiolytic drugs, like Benzodiazepines, typically reduce wall-following behavior (Baiamonte, Parker, Vinson, & Brennan, 2016; Bose et al., 2022; Choleris, Thomas, Kavaliers, & Prato, 2001;

Table 1 Why do animals follow walls?.

Explanation	Representative taxa	Comments	References
Anxiety/fear	Fish, small rodents, humans	Anxiety elevates wall-following behavior, which is later moderated by habituation.	Herrero et al. (2006); Schnörr et al. (2012); Walz et al. (2016)
Stress	Fish, small rodents	Stress elevates wall-following behavior; the effect of chronic and acute exposure may differ.	Morland et al. (2015); Alfonso et al. (2020); Dean et al. (2020)
Shelter/predation avoidance	Arthropods	Wall-following behavior is a means to find suitable shelters.	Antonelli et al. (1999); Laurent Salazar et al. (2018); Mosquera and Lorenzo (2020)
Exploration	Fish, small rodents, insects	Exploration in novel environments, often when visibility is low.	Avni et al. (2008); Tan et al. (2011); Endlein and Sitti (2018)
Exit	Humans, insects, fish	Following the wall in search of an exit from a confined area.	Isobe et al. (2004); Champagne et al. (2010); Soibam et al. (2012)
Ambushing prey	Snakes, canines, spiders	Predators take advantage of the prey's wall-following behavior and ambush it along walls.	Reinert et al. (1984); Van Dyk and Slotow (2003); Mammola et al. (2018)
Abiotic factors	Arthropods	Favorable temperature or humidity along the wall or in wall crevices.	Lorenzo and Lazzari (1999); Voss et al. (2007); Scharf, Gilad et al. (2021)

Mohammad et al., 2016; Richendrfer, Pelkowski, Colwill, & Creton, 2012; Treit & Fundytus, 1988). In contrast, treating them with known anxiogenic drugs or hormones, like caffeine or corticosteroids in rodents and fish, elevates wall-following behavior (Abu Bakar et al., 2022; de Carvalho et al., 2019; Snihur, Hampson, & Cain, 2008; Thompson & Vijayan, 2020). In some studies, a change in behavior, like elevated wall following, interpreted as anxiety, is accompanied by a documented increase in stress hormones, such as corticosteroids, or higher activity in the amygdala (Beiko, Lander, Hampson, Boon, & Cain, 2004; Huang, Zhou, & Zhang, 2012; Kapoor & Matthews, 2005; Morland, Novejarque, Spicer, Pheby, & Rice, 2016), which supports such an interpretation. These cases are quite straightforward. Most cases are unfortunately more complex when, for example, the exposure to certain drugs/chemicals is dose-dependent (Deng et al., 2023; Li et al., 2015; Maciąg et al., 2020; Table 2). A good example is a study on zebrafish, which showed an increase followed by a decrease in wall-following behavior with increasing doses of ethanol (Tsang, Ansari, & Gerlai, 2019). In other cases, there is a considerable difference between acute and chronic exposure to the same drug. An example is the effect of nicotine provision in zebrafish, which at first decreases wall-following behavior, but repeated exposures elevate it, perhaps as a withdrawal effect (Dean et al., 2020). Another example is the increase in wall-following behavior after acute exposure to chemicals that cause bladder inflammation in rats, an increase that is not evident under chronic bladder inflammation (Morland et al., 2015). Finally, terpene (a phytochemical also found in cannabis) reduces wall-following behavior in the short term, but after a seven-day exposure, the effect vanishes (Szaszkiewicz, Leigh, & Hamilton, 2021).

When animals are exposed to some chemicals, such as environmental toxins, there may be changes in wall-following behavior (Table 2). For example, the change in wall-following behavior after exposure of zebrafish to insecticides is both chemical- and dose-dependent (Hutton et al., 2023; Mundy et al., 2021), and an increase in CO_2 concentration in water leads to a mixed effect on wall-following behavior in fish (Hamilton, Radke, Bajwa, Chaput, & Tresguerres, 2021; Hamilton et al., 2023; Ou et al., 2015; Vossen, Jutfelt, Cocco, Thörnqvist, & Winberg, 2016). Changes in wall-following behavior following exposure to environmental toxins are difficult to predict in advance and interpret. This is in contrast to the effects of drugs, which effects can be expected based on prior knowledge of human reaction to such drugs. Anyhow, wall-following behavior should not be interpreted strictly as "anxiety" but rather more generally as a "stress-induced response", with anxiety being only one possible type of a stress response.

Table 2 Drugs and chemicals affecting wall-following behavior.

Drug/chemical	Taxa	Comments	References
Ethanol	Fish, small rodents	Mixed; it depends on dose, acute vs. chronic exposure, and social interactions. Withdrawal effects usually increase wall-following behavior.	Santucci et al. (2008); Ramlan et al. (2017); Dean et al. (2021)
Nicotine	Fish, small rodents	Little effect; usually decreases wall-following behavior, or interaction with social interactions. Withdrawal effects increase it.	Tzavara, Monory, Hanoune, and Nomikos (2002); Dean et al. (2020); Harris (2021)
Caffeine	Fish, protozoa	Usually an increase in wall-following behavior	Iwatsuki and Hirano (1996); Thompson and Vijayan (2020); Abu Bakar et al. (2022)
Cannabis	Fish, small rodents	Usually a decrease in wall-following behavior, but it depends on the test platform and timing.	Acheson et al. (2011); Breit et al. (2019); Carty et al. (2019)
Benzodiazepines	Fish, small rodents, insects	A decrease in wall-following behavior.	Choleris et al. (2001); Baiamonte et al. (2016); Mohammad et al. (2016)
Seizure-inducing/ preventing drugs	Fish	Seizure-inducing drugs increase wall-following behavior, while anti-seizure drugs usually decrease it.	Ou et al. (2015); Liu et al. (2016); Peng et al. (2016); Ji et al. (2017)
SSRI drugs[a]	Fish, small rodents	Usually a decrease in wall-following behavior.	Ansai et al. (2016); Nielsen et al. (2018); Furukawa et al. (2021)
Pesticides	Fish	Mixed, depending on material and dose.	Mundy et al. (2021); Hutton et al. (2023); Mathiron, Gallego, and Silvestre (2023)
Other pollutants[b]	Fish	Mixed, depending on the material.	Faria et al. (2018); Rowsey et al. (2019); Roberts et al. (2020)

[a]Or serotonin-releasing drugs.
[b]Pollutants such as oil or other organic pollutants.

There are a few examples of changes in wall-following behavior with stress, as defined above, which are often inconsistent. For example, higher water salinity can make freshwater fish more active and less thigmotactic, more thigmotactic, or can have no effect (cf. Cheng, Tan, Chua, Tan, & Wee, 2022; Hamilton et al., 2022; Segarra et al., 2021). CO_2-induced water acidification either reduced, had an inverse U-shaped effect, or had no effect on wall-following behavior in three fish species (cf. Hamilton et al., 2021; Hamilton et al., 2023; Ou et al., 2015; Vossen et al., 2016). Wall-following behavior, in the context of stress, refers in most studies to exposure to chemical compounds, such as drugs and environmental toxins. However, it is important to remember that stress has many manifestations. Strong light might be stressful for nocturnal animals leading to more wall following when lights are on (small rodents: Garcia, Cardenas, & Morato, 2005; Huang et al., 2012; Valle, 1970; Zadicario, Avni, Zadicario, & Eilam, 2005). In addition, specific wavelengths might trigger more wall following. Older fruit flies follow walls less than do younger flies. However, when exposed to red light they resume wall following as if they were younger (Weinrich, Hogg, & Jeffery, 2018). Changing illumination levels abruptly may either increase or decrease wall following (Schnörr et al., 2012). Here, one should consider whether the animal under study is typically diurnal or nocturnal in order to make a firm prediction regarding the effect of change.

A good practice may be to compare the wall-following behavior of the tested drug/chemical to known drugs affecting wall-following behavior or to examine "anxiety" or "stress" in several methods, such as using several arena types, backing it up with physiological measurements, and test whether the emerging patterns are consistent. Regarding "stress", it is defined as a situation in which organisms are pushed near the edges or out of their ecological niche or optimal conditions (Van Straalen, 2003). Such deviations from optimal conditions induce stress, which in turn affects behavior. Such changes are either adaptive, intended to improve coping with stress, usually when stress levels are moderate or when exposure is short, or maladaptive, simply as a byproduct of prolonged exposure to stress or when stress is too high (Dhabhar, 2000; Salehi, Cordero, & Sandi, 2010).

Another source of stress is "social isolation", or the shortage of interactions with conspecifics compared to a desired level (Hawkley & Capitanio, 2015). Social isolation is relevant mostly for social animals, and it leads to an array of behavioral changes, such as increased anxiety, a decrease in risk-taking, learning impairment, and lower interest in social interactions

(Grippo, Wu, Hassan, & Carter, 2008; Hewlett, Wareham, & Barron, 2018; Ichikawa & Sasaki, 2003; Pan, Liu, Young, Zhang, & Wang, 2009). In most cases, social isolation leads to no change in wall-following behavior (Daniel & Bhat, 2022; Martinez & Morato, 2004; Scharf, Stoldt et al., 2021; Shams, Amlani, Buske, Chatterjee, & Gerlai, 2018; Tamilselvan & Sloman, 2017; Wang et al., 2023) but both decreases (Dalesman, 2018; Faraday, Scheufele, Rahman, & Grunberg, 1999; Newton, 1982; Shams, Chatterjee, & Gerlai, 2015) and increases in wall-following behavior with social isolation (least often) have been described (Koto, Mersch, Hollis, & Keller, 2015). Social isolation interacts with other stressors. For instance, the increase in wall-following behavior is moderated following exposure to ethanol in groups compared to isolated zebrafish (Dean, Radke, Velupillai, Franczak, & Hamilton, 2021). In a related manner, increasing conspecific density above a threshold led to proportionally less wall-following behavior (Bartels, 2000; Broly, Mullier, Deneubourg, & Devigne, 2012; Suzuki, Takagi, & Hiraishi, 2003). The reason may be a negative density-dependent effect on peripheral positions making central positions more likely to be held (similar to ideal-free distribution). Finally, hunger is a common stressor, experienced by most animals at some point(s), which leads to multiple behavioral changes (reviewed in Scharf, 2016). Hunger usually decreases wall-following behavior and/or increases exploration (Barcay & Bennett, 1991; Hansen, Schaerf, & Ward, 2015; Hughson et al., 2018; but see Clift, Richendrfer, Thorn, Colwill, & Creton, 2014 for an increase in wall-following behavior with hunger or Depickère, Fresneau, Deneubourg, & Detrain, 2008 for no short-term effect).

The key to understanding the inconsistent effect of some stressors on wall-following behavior is perhaps the dependency of the outcome on stress level and duration. In addition to differences due to acute or chronic exposure (Dean et al., 2020; Morland et al., 2015; Szaszkiewicz et al., 2021), stress can be induced by withdrawal of some chemicals (Bravo et al., 2020; Löfgren, Johansson, Meyerson, Lundgren, & Bäckström, 2006). These effects on wall-following behavior are system- and drug-specific. For example, whereas withdrawal from nicotine usually does not affect wall-following behavior, withdrawal from ethanol more often elevates it (cf. Hamilton, Berger, Perry, & Grunberg, 2009; Harris, 2021; Tan et al., 2019; with Krook, Duperreault, Newton, Ross, & Hamilton, 2019; Santucci, Cortes, Bettica, & Cortes, 2008; Swartzwelder et al., 2014).

In invertebrates, wall-following is rarely described as "anxiety-like behavior" (but see, e.g., Bath, Thomson, & Perry, 2020; Chen, Wilburn, Hao, & Tully, 2014). Rather, it is interpreted as anti-predation behavior, meant to either minimize encounters with predators or capture by them or increase the likelihood of arriving at a shelter (Hess et al., 2019; Laurent Salazar et al., 2018; Mosquera & Lorenzo, 2020). For example, during sensitive life stages, such as diapause or aestivation, invertebrates are likely to require shelter, and thigmotaxis may help them to reach a suitable, protected shelter (Domingue, Scheff, Arthur, & Myers, 2021; Yamana, Hamano, & Goshima, 2009). Two examples of predation-risk-induced responses are the increase in wall-following behavior following the exposure of zebrafish to alarm signal of conspecifics or a solution of injured individuals (Borba et al., 2022) and the same response in meadow vole males in response to a predator (fox) odor (Perrot-Sinal, Heale, Ossenkopp, & Kavaliers, 1996). Both could be an indication of a predator nearby. In addition, a predator-mimicking robot induces wall-following in a Mosquitofish, and the better the robot imitates the predator's movement, the stronger the wall-following behavior is (Polverino, Karakaya, Spinello, Soman, & Porfiri, 2019). As one can imagine, animals under predation risk naturally get anxious and there is a strong link between predation risk and anxiety. Thus, we believe that interpreting wall-following behavior either as anxiety or anti-predation are related, perhaps an ultimate vs. a more proximate explanation.

As most behavioral studies on animals monitor the animal's behavioral responses rather than their emotions, state of mind, or any physiological/ neural response, one should be careful with the common interpretation of "anxiety-like behavior". Regarding anti-predation behavior, one can put it to the test if it indeed assists against predators. This has been done very rarely but could be tested in predator-prey systems, in which both are free to adapt their behavior (e.g., a spider-fly system or a fish-zooplankton system; Uiterwaal, Dell, & DeLong, 2019; Rowsey et al., 2019). As we will detail below, walls can have a deleterious effect on potential prey by making prey more easily detected by predators.

3. Exploration

Walls are sometimes followed as a means of exploration since they are prominent landmarks against the habitat background. A wall/barrier can help, for example, to form a "home base" in the habitat, which is often along a wall (Kallai et al., 2007; Stewart et al., 2010), serves as a means to explore a novel, unfamiliar area with some boundaries (e.g., Lai & Chao, 2021), or help ants to form a trail and discover food faster (Farji-Brener et al., 2007;

Freeman & Chaves-Campos, 2016). Wall following may enable the forming of some "basic cognitive map" and help to capture the geometry and size of the habitat (Eilam, 2014). This is supported by the fact that "boundary cells"—a special type of place neurons that are active when the animal is at the boundary of an area—have "an additional firing field" next to walls (Stewart, Jeewajee, Wills, Burgess, & Lever, 2014). When animals are enclosed in some enclosure, the walls can be followed and lead to an exit if it exists (Isobe, Helbing, & Nagatani, 2004; Simon et al., 1994). Movement along the wall can also be a useful means of reaching a shelter (Broly et al., 2012; Burger, Boylan, & Aucone, 2007; Champagne, Hoefnagels, De Kloet, & Richardson, 2010; Laurent Salazar et al., 2018). One example is the wall-following behavior of humans during a forced evacuation under limited visibility (e.g., a fire simulation). In such scenarios, people usually search for walls using their hands. When they reach the wall, they turn to one side and follow the wall until leaving the room (Cao, Song, Lv, & Fang, 2015; Fridolf et al., 2013; Guo, Huang, & Wong, 2012; Xue et al., 2020). Exploring a habitat under limited visibility is not unique to humans, and a series of experiments on blind cavefish and a paper on blind mole rats suggest these animals do something similar (Avni, Tzvaigrach, & Eilam, 2008; Sharma, Coombs, Patton, & De Perera, 2009; Tan, Patton, & Coombs, 2011; Teyke, 1985). However, low visibility does not universally lead to wall-following. For example, blinded fruit flies followed walls less than do intact flies, blinded crickets decreased or increased wall-following behavior depending on the angle between the wall and the floor, American cockroaches showed no to little difference in their wall-following after blinding, and sighted mice moved faster in the wall's direction than did blind mice (Besson & Martin, 2005; Creed & Miller, 1990; Horev, Benjamini, Sakov, & Golani, 2007; Kastberger, 1982).

In laboratory assays, walls can be successfully used to solve mazes, as when animals follow the walls (and turn consistently in one direction) they often increase their likelihood of reaching the reward or the exit at the maze's end (Hunt et al., 2014; McMahon et al., 2005). Following walls is used in robotics and is a known maze-solving algorithm (e.g., Mishra & Bande, 2008; Saman & Abdramane, 2013). The contribution of wall following to solving mazes might differ among maze types. For example, wall following might be less common when animals are presented with T-mazes than Y-mazes owing to the sharper turn in T-mazes than in Y-mazes: sharp turns hinder wall following (Czaczkes, 2018).

Unsurprisingly, wall-following behavior is often higher in novel than in familiar environments (Pinheiro-da-Silva, Agues-Barbosa, & Luchiari, 2020;

Sharma et al., 2009; Wang et al., 2023; see also below). Two possible interpretations for this pattern are possible. First, if wall-following behavior is a means of exploring a novel environment, after reaching a certain level of familiarity, other movement patterns should be used for different purposes (end of exploration). An alternative explanation is habituation to perceived danger, as animals are first defensive or anxious and move along the walls but then decide that the environment is not dangerous (habituation to perceived danger). A way to separate the two may be to examine whether wall-following behavior is correlated with exploratory behavior and whether it indeed leads to covering more sections of the environment: both are not expected if habituation is taking place. That said, the link between exploration and wall-following is inconsistent and both positive and negative correlations exist suggesting that exploration is not a universal explanation of wall-following (cf. Dalesman, 2018; Rowsey, Johansen, Khursigara, & Esbaugh, 2019; Webster & Laland, 2015). Another way to examine the trigger for wall following, perhaps, is to measure typical anxiety-like behaviors (e.g., freezing, seeking shelter, or changes in interactions with conspecifics) and examine whether they correlate with wall-following behavior. Thus, correlating wall following with other behaviors typical for exploration or under anxiety may shed light on what best explains wall following in the studied system. It would be useful to find further ways to separate the two explanations, which may depend on species and context. A good example is the change in movement speed after reaching the wall, which can suggest whether the trigger for wall following is exploration or anxiety/avoiding predation. If the wall is used as a means of exploration, then movement speed should perhaps increase after reaching it (Camhi & Johnson, 1999; Cao et al., 2015; van den Berg et al., 2023; but see Sikora et al., 1992). Alternatively, if anxiety, predation, or stress avoidance is responsible for wall following, movement speed should decrease when reaching the wall, which is perceived as a safer place (Alzogaray, Fontán, & Zerba, 1997; Hassan, Huang, Xu, Wu, & Mehmood, 2021). This occurs in rats: An electrical shock causes movement toward the wall followed by freezing (Grossen & Kelley, 1972). Finally, human participants can simply be asked why they followed the wall: under low visibility conditions, the answer was related to exploration and orientation (Fridolf et al., 2013).

4. Favorable biotic and abiotic conditions

While the two main reasons for wall following seem to be either defensive behavior or exploration, a wall itself may provide better conditions rather than being used by animals as a guide to shelter or for exploration. Wall lizards, for instance, use small gaps or crevices between rocks or on walls as a refuge (Martín & López, 1999). Pit-building wormlions prefer digging their pitfall traps adjacent to walls in Mediterranean habitats because walls provide shade, and shade is a clear indicator of lower temperatures in summer (Scharf et al., 2020; Scharf, Gilad, Taichman, & Subach, 2021). Similarly, wall spiders (*Oecobius* spp.) take advantage of cracks and crevices when building small webs on city walls. Sites on walls protect against extreme temperatures, low humidity, and direct sunlight and rainfall (Voss, Main, & Dadour, 2007). A blood-sucking bug (*Triatoma infestans*) prefers shelters in adobe walls, which moderate thermal variation and provide better abiotic conditions (Lorenzo & Lazzari, 1999). Finally, urban birds prefer to nest on walls with climbing plants than on bare walls (Chiquet, Dover, & Mitchell, 2013). Urban walls, as a habitat analog of natural rocks and cliffs, serve as a suitable habitat for a variety of plants and animals (Francis, 2011; Lundholm & Richardson, 2010). While the full survey of walls as a suitable habitat for plants and animals is out of the scope of the current review, it is important to note that animals may follow walls in search of suitable habitats. Stopping along the wall rather than moving along suggests that the wall provides some favorable conditions. In some animals, there is even a better indication for the preference of positions along/on walls. Trap-building predators, like web-building spiders or pit-building antlions/wormlions, construct or dig traps to hunt prey. Trap construction is energetically expensive, which makes their initial site selection important (Lucas, 1985; Tanaka, 1989). When their traps are constructed along/on walls, this should be a good indication that walls are a suitable habitat for hunting (e.g., Scharf et al., 2020; Scharf, Gilad et al., 2021). Clearly, it is recommended to examine whether such positions along walls are indeed more successful over the long run than those at more central positions either in prey capture, avoiding predation, or avoiding extreme abiotic conditions.

Some animals may not use walls due to favorable abiotic factors. Rather, if animals tend to move along walls, such walls may serve as meeting points for conspecifics (Boulay, Devigne, Gosset, & Charabidze, 2013; Farine & Lobreau, 1984; Gruszka et al., 2020; Hansen et al., 2015). Aggregation in such cases may have various purposes, such as dilution of predation risk as a 'selfish herd'. As prey spend more time along walls, sit-and-wait predators could use walls to ambush prey as well to increase their encounter probability with prey. This has been suggested for pit-building antlions along rocks/roots ambushing ants and other small arthropods, snakes along logs waiting for small mammals, and wild dogs or wolves along fences seeking antelopes and deer because prey may be more abundant next to such barriers or easier to capture (Bojarska et al., 2017; Douglass & Reinert, 1982; Hayashi, Hayashi, Hayashi, & Hayashi, 2023; Jingu & Hayashi, 2018; Reinert, Cundall, & Bushar, 1984; Van Dyk & Slotow, 2003). If there is a wall next to artificial light in cities (or when walls are intentionally lit at night), it may attract prey at night to the wall, leading to spiders ambushing prey next to/ on it (Frank, 2009; Mammola et al., 2018). In human-modified habitats, one could create an 'ecological trap' for prey species that follow fences or walls. Finally, humans in the Middle East have used "desert kite traps" since the 7th century BC to hunt wild ungulates. The trap comprises two stone walls in a funnel shape ending in an enclosure (Holzer, Avner, Porat, & Horwitz, 2010). The shape of the enclosure takes advantage of the prey's tendency to follow walls after encountering them.

Prey can also react to a predator's habitat use and its ability to hunt along walls. A possible case study is that of desert rodents and their snake/owl predators. A common defense tactic in the field against owls is to move next to bushes, which forms a "penetrated wall" and reduces predation. This tactic fails when snakes are present because they hunt equally well in open microhabitats and next to bushes (Bouskila, 1995, 2001). Australian lizards appear to do something similar to rodents: they approach trunks of thorny bushes that protect against predators (Kerr, Bull, & Burzacott, 2003).

Spatially explicit simulation models suggest some conditions favor the success of predators along barriers compared to those at random positions. For example, predators along barriers are more successful in low densities, when prey is abundant, and when prey moves more directionally (Scharf, Gilad et al., 2021). Ambushing prey along walls is sensitive to shadow competition, that is, the interception of prey by another predator closer to the arrival source of the prey (Linton et al., 1991). Thus, not all positions along a barrier are equally profitable, and those in a barrier's center in particular might receive the fewest prey (Scharf & Ruxton, 2023).

Similar to predators, people can take advantage of some animals' tendency to follow walls. One applied consequence of wall-following behavior is the choice of where to place pesticides. If the targeted pest follows walls, then spraying along walls may be effective (Kells & Hymel, 2017). Similarly, capturing small rodents or cockroaches inside buildings could rely on their wall-following behavior, and thus traps should be placed along walls (Durier & Rivault, 2003; Stryjek & Modlińska, 2013). Both applications are not very different from predators taking advantage of a prey animal's wall-following behavior.

5. The test arena's size, shape, and structure

Whenever touch is the main mechanism to follow walls, the wall structure or texture may change wall-following behavior (Iwatsuki et al., 1996; Patullo & MacMillan, 2006). For instance, a smoother wall triggered less wall following than did a coarser wall in a crayfish (bubble wrap vs. sandpaper; Patullo & MacMillan, 2006). Whenever vision is responsible, the wall height or the shadow it casts may affect wall-following behavior (Graham & Collett, 2002; Pratt et al., 2001; Street, 1968). For example, wall following by ants decreased with wall height, perhaps because the shadow indicated that the area along the wall was larger and the more distant mice were from the wall the less parallel their movement with respect to the wall was (Horev et al., 2007; Pratt et al., 2001). Furthermore, transparent walls may be followed more strongly than opaque walls or wall transparency level may interact with wall height to affect wall-following behavior (Martínez et al., 2002; Soibam et al., 2012; but see Filgueiras et al., 2014). As noted above, many animals are more likely to follow concave walls than convex ones, which can be used as a means to separate "active" from "passive" wall followers, as only "active" wall followers do not leave a convex wall (Creed & Miller, 1990; Dussutour et al., 2005; Hänzi & Straka, 2018).

The arena size and shape are both meaningful to wall-following behavior (Table 3). Walls are followed more frequently in smaller than in larger arenas (Hänzi & Straka, 2018; Henry et al., 2022; Kohler, Parker, & Ford, 2018a; Scharf, Hanna, & Gottlieb, 2024; but see Eilam, 2003; Patton et al., 2010). There is often no standardization in the test arena size even when a single type, round, is used and a single species, *D. melanogaster*, is tested (e.g., a radius of 2, 3, 3.5, 4.4, or 9 cm; Götz & Biesinger, 1985a; Götz & Biesinger, 1985b; Ismail et al., 2015; White, Humphrey, & Hirth, 2010), which may lead to variation in the animals' responses. There is a difference between smaller round arenas created by reducing their radius and smaller arenas designed by blocking the center of the circle with a smaller inaccessible circle. Whereas in the former case, animals move more frequently along the arena's walls, in the second case, there is no effect (Scharf, Hanna, & Gottlieb, 2024; Uiterwaal, Dell, & DeLong, 2019; but see Sato & Sato, 2022). If most movement is already along the wall, changes in the arena's center have probably little effect, whereas movement along the wall is probably affected by the curvature level of the wall. There are also differences between round and rectangular arenas, but the effect of shape is less clear than that of size (stronger wall-following behavior in

Table 3 Studies examining wall-following behavior in more than a single platform.

Platforms	Taxa	Comments	References
Open field, water maze, elevated-plus maze	Small rodents	Often (but not always) correlated responses in all platforms.	Herrero et al. (2006); Bonito-Oliva et al. (2014); Breit et al. (2019)
Round vs. rectangular arenas	Arthropods; small rodents	Increase, decrease, or no effect.	Yaski, Portugali, and Eilam (2011); Kohler et al. (2018a); Scharf, Hanna, & Gottlieb, 2024
Arena size	Arthropods, amphibians	More wall-following behavior in smaller arenas.	Kohler et al. (2018a); Scharf, Hanna, & Gottlieb, 2024; Hänzi and Straka (2018); Henry et al. (2022)
Increasing the number of walls or corners	Arthropods; small rodents	Preference for higher numbers of adjacent walls/corners.	Martinez and Morato (2004); Lamprea et al. (2008); Soibam et al. (2012)
Wall height	Insects; small rodents	Mixed; interaction with the wall's shadow and transparency.	Street (1968); Pratt et al. (2001); Martínez et al. (2002)
Wall structure/texture	Small rodents	Mixed effect of transparent walls; rough substrates are followed more.	Soibam et al. (2012); Martínez et al. (2002); Filgueiras et al. (2014); Patullo and Macmillan (2006)

round than in rectangular arenas: Yaski et al., 2011; Scharf, Hanna, & Gottlieb, 2024; stronger wall-following behavior in rectangular arenas: Kohler et al., 2018a; no difference: Akiyama et al., 2015; Grabovskaya & Salyha, 2014). In cases where wall following is greater in round arenas, the reason could be the gradual decrease in wall-following from concave to straight to convex walls. In rectangular arenas, however, the corners may be a source of attraction, probably because some animals prefer two walls over one, because corners are darker, or because corners act as salient landmarks when navigating in the environment (Choleris et al., 2001; Lamprea et al., 2008; Liu, Davis, & Roman, 2007; Martinez & Morato, 2004; Soibam et al., 2012; Zadicario et al., 2005). Using round vs. rectangular arenas has been suggested as the reason behind some mismatches among studies in *D. melanogaster* perhaps because fruit flies are attracted to dark corners perceived as shelters, which are present only in rectangular arenas (Bath et al., 2020; Soibam et al., 2012). Preference for corners matches the predation–avoidance or anxiety explanation of wall-following behavior rather than exploration and if this behavior is observed it may be a way to separate between the two.

Both round and rectangular arenas are simple "open-field" structures, but animals are often examined in more complex structures, such as the elevated-plus maze and the light–dark arena (e.g., Acevedo, Nizhnikov, Molina, & Pautassi, 2014; Rodgers & Shepherd, 1993). In the former, an animal is placed in the center of a horizontal cross, with two arms being open and the other two bordered with walls. In the latter, the arena is split into two, a dark/shaded and an open/lit side. If significant differences are already known between round and rectangular arenas, it is no surprise that wall-following differs based on the test arena here too, such as examining wall following in an open field, an elevated plus maze, or a water maze, all of which are common test arenas to examine exploration, activity, and often also anxiety. Several studies conducted a similar examination of wall-following behavior in more than one arena structure, and the results sometimes but not always match (Table 3). More specifically, if we measure the same behavioral response, wall following in an open field or a water maze test should positively correlate with one another and negatively correlate with entries to the open arms of the elevated plus maze. This is sometimes the case (Bonito-Oliva, Masini, & Fisone, 2014; Branchi et al., 2006; Herrero, Sandi, & Venero, 2006; Löfgren et al., 2006; Ramos, Correia, Izídio, & Brüske, 2003) but not always. For example, mice expressing Parkinson's disease symptoms followed walls more frequently in an open-field test but entered the open arms of an elevated–plus maze more compared to the control (George et al., 2008). Ethanol and a cannabinoid receptor agonist decreased wall-following behavior in an open-field test but increased wall-following behavior in a Morris water maze (Breit, Zamudio, & Thomas, 2019). All such known and potential effects of the arena size, shape, and structure should be considered when conducting experiments involving a treatment vs. control. It could be that some treatments would be significant in some tested arenas but will not be so in others. Indeed, Bertotto, Catron, and Tal (2020) suggest that the lack of a standardized method for measuring thigmotaxis is responsible for some contradictions among studies in zebrafish.

Another source of confusion comes from the way in which wall-following behavior is measured. In an open arena, the most obvious difference is between studies in which the wall is the point of reference and those in which the arena's center is the point of reference (e.g., cf. White et al., 2010 and Bath et al., 2020). This is not a trivial difference, as animals may move far from the center but still not along the wall, but it clearly depends on the animal size relative to that of the arena. In some studies, the arena is divided into a central and a peripheral zone. Even in studies on a single species, the two zones could be similar in size or not (e.g., cf. Besson & Martin, 2005; Topic et al., 2005; Tower et al., 2019) even though it is not clear whether this quite arbitrary definition can affect the experiment outcome.

The studies in which the wall is the point of reference also vary based on whether movement distances along the wall or time spent along the wall is measured (distance: e.g., Barcay & Bennett, 1991; Durier & Rivault, 2003; time: e.g., Kozlovsky, Poirier, Hermer, Bertram, & Morand-Ferron, 2022; Vossen, Nilsson, Jansson, & Roman, 2023). This difference is meaningful too: More movement along the wall may indicate exploration, whereas standing still does not and may indicate stress.

Even when the movement along the wall is documented, there is variation among studies regarding what "along the wall" is. Some studies use the body size of the studied animal to define it (e.g., distance from the wall equals one mean body length; Merola, Lucon-Xiccato, Bertolucci, & Perugini, 2021; Schnörr et al., 2012). Some use a fixed distance, which may be somewhat arbitrary (e.g., 1 mm vs ~2.65 cm in mosquito larvae; cf. Gonzalez, Alvarez Costa, & Masuh, 2017; Zuharah, Fadzly, Yusof, & Dieng, 2015; or 6 vs 10.7 cm in two salmon species; cf. Hamilton et al., 2022; Ou et al., 2015). Others use a percentage of the studied arena (d'Isa, Brambilla, & Fasano, 2014; Wexler, Wertheimer, Subach, Pruitt, & Scharf, 2017), but then it is not clear how to compare data from arenas that differ in size. In some studies, the measure requires a direct touch of the wall (Camhi & Johnson, 1999; Mongeau, Demir, Lee, Cowan, & Full, 2013). Perhaps a good factor to consider is the movement direction compared to the wall. For instance, a movement parallel to the wall may suggest that the animal is aware of the wall and uses it by touch or vision, for example, to guide movement. Movement in other directions, irrespective of the exact distance from the wall, may be related less to the wall.

Finally, measurement times are important, as many animals habituate with time to the test arena conditions and follow the wall less frequently (a type of habituation; see below). Thus, if averaged over the whole measurement, longer studies might wrongly indicate that animals follow the wall less than shorter studies. In short, standardization of arenas and measurement methods across experiments will facilitate inter-study and interspecific comparisons.

6. Development, aging, carryover effects, and parental effects

There is accumulating evidence that animals differ in wall-following behavior according to life stage (Table 4). If wall-following behavior is a defensive behavior, one might expect more sensitive stages, such as juveniles, to follow walls more than adults, as shown in rats and mice (Acheson, Moore, Kuhn, Wilson, & Swartzwelder, 2011; Bishnoi, Ossenkopp, & Kavaliers, 2021; Harris, 2021; Harris, D'eath, & Healy, 2008; Sparling, Baker, & Bielajew, 2018). Zebrafish juveniles may also be more sensitive to some tested drugs/chemicals, making them follow more walls after exposure than adults (Peng et al., 2016). However, again there seems to be variation according to species and context as there are also examples of juveniles following walls less often than do adults (Lucon-Xiccato, Conti, Loosli, Foulkes, & Bertolucci, 2020). For example, young frog larvae did not follow walls, whereas older stages did (Hänzi & Straka, 2018). In crayfish, juveniles of one species preferred dark shelters over walled shelters and adults preferred to follow walls even when bright, whereas, in another species, juveniles are both more thigmotactic and photophobic than adults (Alberstadt, Steele, & Skinner, 1995; Antonelli, Steele, & Skinner, 1999). In insects, there are only sporadic comparisons between larvae and adults or younger and older larvae (but see Tomczak, Schweiger, & Müller, 2016; Wexler, Subach, Pruitt, & Scharf, 2016). In short, there is no clear pattern here, or the pattern is taxon specific.

Table 4 Intra-/inter-specific causes of variance.

Source of variation	Taxa	Comments	References
Sex	Fish, insects, small rodents	Females usually follow walls more than males.	Martin (2004); Leppänen et al. (2006); Snihur et al. (2008); Brand et al. (2023)
Development	Fish, small rodents, echinoderms	Mixed or no effect.	Harris et al. (2008); Yamaguchi, Masuda, and Yamashita (2018); Lucon-Xiccato et al. (2020)
Aging	Insects, small rodents	Insects: mostly decreasing with age; small rodents: mostly increasing with age.	Harati et al. (2011); Wexler et al. (2016); Tower et al. (2019); Bishnoi et al. (2021)
Test duration	Fish, amphibians, small rodents, humans	Less wall following with habituation within and between days.	Newton (1982); Perrot-Sinal et al. (1996); Bilbo et al. (2000); Kallai et al. (2009)
Carryover effects	Fish, small rodents	Eggs→juveniles, juveniles→adults.	Wexler et al. (2016); Branchi et al. (2006); Facciol et al. (2022)
Parental effects	Fish, small rodents, reptiles	Wall-following behavior is influenced by maternal exposure to stressful conditions.	Kapoor and Matthews (2005); Rozen-Rechels et al. (2018); Carty et al. (2019)
Populations	Crustaceans, gastropods, fish	Differences among populations, a possible effect of natural conditions.	Dalesman (2018); Fišer et al. (2019); Agues-Barbosa et al. (2023)
Related species	Protozoa, insects, crustaceans	Differences among related species, a possible effect of natural conditions.	Kitamura (1986); Gonzalez et al. (2017); Kohler et al. (2018b)

Aging, the decline in fitness components and performance with age (Rose, 1991), affects a variety of movement-related traits, such as exploration level, the distance traveled, or movement directionality (e.g., Le Bourg, 1983; Shukitt-Hale, Casadesus, Cantuti-Castelvetri, & Joseph, 2001). Thus, aging is expected to affect wall-following behavior as well. In fruit flies and flour beetles, wall-following behavior decreases with age (Ismail et al., 2015; Tower et al., 2019; Wexler et al., 2016; but see White et al., 2010 for no aging effect). As reduced wall-following behavior was accompanied by a lower activity level in these cases, it is unclear whether aging itself led to reduced wall-following behavior or whether it was mediated through the change in activity. If we refer to wall-following as a defensive behavior, one could suggest that lower wall-following in older ages is a result of lower predation risk or alternatively taking higher risks due to a decreasing probability of future reproduction (Magnhagen & Borcherding, 2008; Magnhagen, 1990; Tallamy, 1982). In contrast to flies and fruit flies, rodents in a water maze are more likely to follow walls at advanced age than earlier (Harati et al., 2011; Schulz, Topic, Silva, & Huston, 2004). Aging may also interact with other factors, such as social dominance or enrichment. For instance, dominant mice are less thigmotactic than subordinate ones, but only in mid-age (Francia et al., 2006), and aged rats are more thigmotactic than young ones but only without environmental enrichment (Harati et al., 2011).

In addition to aging, wall following can change throughout life owing to carryover effects. We use a broad definition of carryover effects as exposure to certain conditions earlier in life affects phenotype and performance later (O'Connor, Norris, Crossin, & Cooke, 2014). Similar effects are parental effects or transgenerational effects, in which conditions experienced by the parents, usually by the mother but not only, affect their offspring phenotype (Uller, 2008). First, as the simplest case of carryover effects, there is strong evidence for the decrease in wall-following behavior with exposure time or successive tests in the same arena (Ansai, Hosokawa, Maegawa, & Kinoshita, 2016; Kallai et al., 2009; Lei et al., 2022; Newton, 1982), although there are a few exceptional cases of no change (Carlson & Langkilde, 2013; Doria et al., 2019) or a u-shaped pattern of a decrease followed by an increase (Daniel & Bhat, 2022; Maximino et al., 2010). More wall following often takes place in novel environments or new spatial situations (Durier & Rivault, 2003; Kallai et al., 2007). For example, in a virtual reality game, humans under low visibility follow walls in novel environments more than in known ones (Wang et al., 2023). The reason is perhaps to explore new environments when vision is limited or to construct a spatial representation of the new environment (Avni et al., 2008; Sharma et al., 2009).

The decline in wall-following behavior with exposure is a type of habituation (Thiel, Müller, Huston, & Schwarting, 1999). Habituation is also evident between days (Acheson et al., 2011; Labaude, O'Donnell, & Griffin, 2018; Perrot-Sinal et al., 1996; Snihur et al., 2008). It is not a trivial outcome, as repeated exposure to the same stressor may not lead only to habituation but also to sensitization, at least in the short term (Blumstein, 2016). Indeed, retesting mice in a water maze led to lower wall-following (habituation) at dim light but no change or even a minor increase with exposure to bright light (Huang et al., 2012). It is probable that the longer the interval between exposures, the closer the level of wall following to the original level is. Thus, one may apply a treatment, use repeated exposure to the same environment in different time intervals, and the return of wall-following behavior to its original levels to examine how long the treatment effects persist.

Second, exposure to some conditions at one life stage can affect wall-following behavior at a later stage (e.g., juveniles to adults or fish embryos to juveniles). This pattern is evident under isolation/social enrichment, physical enrichment, environmental pollutants, or drugs (Branchi et al., 2006; Facciol, Marawi, Syed, & Gerlai, 2022; Harati et al., 2011; but see Sparling et al., 2018). Such effects vary in their duration and may be quite long. For example, exposure to ethanol for at least a week may affect wall-following behavior by juvenile zebra fish for as long as six months post-exposure (Baiamonte et al., 2016; Santucci et al., 2008).

Finally, there is accumulating evidence for parental effects, or conditions experienced by the parents, on the wall-following behavior of offspring (Kapoor & Matthews, 2005; Redfern et al., 2017). For instance, exposure of zebrafish parents to an active component of cannabis reduced the wall-following of their offspring (Carty et al., 2019), while parents with limited water access produced offspring with increased wall-following (Rozen-Rechels et al., 2018). That said, not all parental exposures affect the behavior of their offspring. For example, only one of two studies on zebra fish that examined parental effects of exposure to ethanol detected such effects on wall-following behavior (cf. Collier et al., 2020; Suresh, Abozaid, Tsang, & Gerlai, 2021). Best, Kurrasch, and Vijayan (2017) injected cortisol into zebra fish eggs, which reduced wall-following behavior in the resulting young offspring. In comparison, Kapoor and Matthews (2005) exposed stressed guinea pig mothers to strobe light, which led to elevated wall-following by the offspring. They also had higher levels of plasma cortisol, suggesting that the mechanism here is anxiety rather than exploration, but future studies should further examine the mechanisms behind such parental effects.

7. Sex, population, and other intraspecific and interspecific differences

One of the most general patterns in the literature is that females follow walls more often than do males (Brand et al., 2023; Leppänen, Ravaja, & Ewalds-Kvist, 2006; Martin, 2004; Perrot-Sinal et al., 1996; Snihur et al., 2008; Wexler et al., 2016; but see Bath et al., 2020; Daniel & Bhat, 2022). There are several possible reasons for this pattern, such as the tendency of males to take higher risks (Byrnes, Miller, & Schafer, 1999; Jolles, Boogert, & van den Bos, 2015), lower levels of stress hormones in males (e.g., corticosterone; Beiko et al., 2004), or their better spatial orientation (Svoboda, Telenský, Blahna, Bures, & Stuchlik, 2012). Females often perform less well in a Morris water maze, which is correlated with more frequent wall following because the target is never along the wall (Beiko et al., 2004; Harris, D'Eath, & Healy, 2009; Liu, Day, Summers, & Burmeister, 2019; Perrot-Sinal et al., 1996). Perhaps due to the originally higher wall-following behavior levels of females, SSRI drugs more strongly decrease wall-following behavior levels in females than males (Ansai et al., 2016; Nielsen et al., 2018). Furthermore, as females may have already higher wall-following levels than males, factors elevating such levels, such as exposure to predator cues, may have a stronger effect on males than females (Perrot-Sinal et al., 1996). The inter-sexual differences are often minor when young and increase in adulthood (Harris et al., 2008), and sometimes the differences increase when females are gravid (Webster & Laland, 2011). Finally, a different stage in the reproductive cycle or mating can affect wall-following behavior: In mice, females are more thigmotactic during estrus than later after mating and having pups elevates wall-seeking, and flour beetles are also less thigmotactic after mating (Kvist & Selander, 1994; Kvist et al., 1995; Wexler et al., 2017). The reason for these differences may be related to higher vulnerability or a higher demand for exploration of specific life stages.

Differences in wall-following behavior are common between populations (Agues-Barbosa, de Souza, de Lima, & Luchiari, 2023; Dalesman, 2018; Götz & Biesinger, 1985a) or related species (Gonzalez et al., 2017; Kitamura, 1986; Kohler, Parker, & Ford, 2018b) and probably depend on the selective local forces (Table 4). Even within the same population, differences sometimes exist. For instance, *D. melanogaster* individuals differ in their foraging strategies: 'rovers' are more active, moving in straight lines, and 'sitters' are less active, using more tortuous movement (de Belle & Sokolowski, 1987;

Nagle & Bell, 1987). These strains also exhibit differences in wall-following behavior, with 'sitters' being stronger wall followers than 'rovers' (Hughson et al., 2018).

Another variation source, unrelated to sex, population, or species, affecting wall-following behavior is caste. In eusocial insects, there are several morphological or behavioral castes, such as soldiers, foragers, and nurses. In the ant *Lasius niger*, foragers follow walls less than do inner-nest workers (Depickère et al., 2008), which probably fits the foragers' exploratory role and the nest workers' defensive behavior. However, among foragers, there are no differences between scouts, patrollers, and recruits (Detrain, Pereira, & Fourcassié, 2019). In the dimorphic ant *Pheidole pallidula*, small workers ('minors') comprise the main worker force and are responsible for the colony routine, while larger ones ('majors') are fewer in number and less active. Minors follow walls more than majors and are less aggregative (Sempo, Depickere, & Detrain, 2006). Similarly, in a cavity-dwelling ant, more active ants are wall followers, whereas less active ones stick to the center (Sendova-Franks & Franks, 1994). In small rodents, dominant individuals are less thigmotactic than subordinate individuals, which may be also more often bitten (Choi et al., 2006; Francia et al., 2006). Thus, wall-following here is probably related to fear.

Finally, wall-following behavior has, in some species, a strong genetic background, and it differs among populations, probably due to distinct selective pressures (Fišer et al., 2019; Leppänen et al., 2006). This suggests that artificial selection on wall-following behavior is possible. Indeed, artificially created strains or mutants can differ in their wall-following levels compared to the wild type, which may enable the determination of the mechanism behind wall-following. Fruit flies, mice, and rats expressing specific genes, which are involved in Parkinson's and Alzheimer's diseases, two degenerative human brain disorders, or with induced brain damage similar to these two diseases, follow walls more, especially as they age (Bonito-Oliva et al., 2014; Chen et al., 2014; Lin et al., 2021; Mayagoitia et al., 2021; but see George et al., 2008; for a more complex pattern).

8. Behavioral repeatability and correlations with other behaviors

Wall-following behavior is reported to be moderately repeatable over at least a few days (Brand et al., 2023; Carlson & Langkilde, 2013;

Labaude et al., 2018; Vossen et al., 2023) and sometimes even weeks (Rajput, Parikh, & Kenney, 2022; Webster & Laland, 2015). Several studies, however, have found that such repeatability within life stages fails to hold between life stages (the larval to adult stage in holometabolous insects or juveniles to yearlings in fish: Rozen-Rechels et al., 2018; Wexler et al., 2016). One possible key to understanding behavioral repeatability is to look at the behavior's physiological mechanisms (e.g., the metabolic rate; Biro & Stamps, 2010), particularly, and especially in vertebrates, changes in stress hormones. It may also be that certain morphological traits make individuals more or less prone to follow walls, leading to variation in behavioral repeatability. For instance, large snails follow walls more than do smaller snails (Bose et al., 2022), and since size changes slowly, wall following happens to be repeatable. If arthropods use their antennae to follow walls (e.g., crayfish or cockroaches; Basil & Sandeman, 2000; Camhi & Johnson, 1999), then it could be that wall following is affected by antenna length or sensitivity. In crickets, wall following is greater when relying on touch than vision (Doria et al., 2019), and inter-individual differences in such a tendency are possible.

Wall-following behavior seems to be correlated, either positively or negatively, with several other behaviors, like phototaxis, exploration, activity, and boldness. Examining these cases enables a better understanding of both the mechanisms behind wall following and its consequences. For example, wall following is often correlated with negative phototaxis, or moving away from light (Alberstadt et al., 1995; Bartels, 2000; Brand et al., 2023; Street, 1968) or seeking shelter (Burger et al., 2007; Domingue et al., 2021; McGaw, 2001). In earthworms, however, contact with a wall decreased negative phototaxis (Doolittle, 1971). Activity, as well as exploration and foraging, are usually negatively correlated with wall following (Brand et al., 2023; Hess et al., 2019; Labaude et al., 2018; Tower et al., 2019; Webster & Laland, 2015; Wexler et al., 2017). When this holds, it is suggesting wall-following is not a mechanism of exploration. This negative activity-wall following association can also be morph-specific (e.g., only cichlid males of a specific color/morph show it; Seaver & Hurd, 2017). In mice, wall following is negatively correlated with rearing (standing on two legs; Leppänen et al., 2006; Leppänen, Ravaja, & Ewalds-Kvist, 2008; but see a positive correlation between walls and rearing in rats; Lamprea et al., 2008). With aging, fruit flies become less active and also follow walls less often (Ismail et al., 2015), suggesting a positive link here of wall following and activity. In zebrafish, wall following is positively correlated with both activity and the tendency to leave shelter (boldness; Alfonso, Peyrafort, Cousin, & Bégout, 2020; but see Dos Santos, de Oliveira, Silva, & Luchiari, 2023). These two examples are opposite to the former examples, suggesting a negative link between wall following and activity. In contrast, boldness, exploration, and wall following are uncorrelated in crickets (Doria et al., 2019). Regarding boldness, it might be a problematic umbrella term for several behaviors, which are not necessarily inter-correlated (Carter, Marshall, Heinsohn, & Cowlishaw, 2012; Watanabe et al., 2012). One paper on zebrafish used thigmotaxis as a proxy of boldness (Nielsen et al., 2018). This suggests that the negative correlation between 'boldness' and wall following is simply the expression of a similar behavior under different contexts, such as fish that spend more time along walls in an open-field test are also more reluctant to move from the black side to the white one in a white-black test (Dos Santos et al., 2023). Anyhow, the link between wall following and boldness is not often documented and is still debated (Alfonso et al., 2020).

In several studies, wall following has been negatively correlated with spatial learning or memory (Bilbo, Day, & Wilczynski, 2000; Dalesman, 2018; Doria et al., 2019; Kallai et al., 2007; Kozlovsky et al., 2022). When wall following is correlated with impaired spatial performance, it is important to examine whether the experimental setup is responsible for this outcome. The clearest case is the Morris water maze, in which rodents swim in search of a platform. This is a particularly stressful apparatus and rodents swimming in it nearly always begin by wall following. As the platform is somewhere in the center and never along the walls, wall following inherently impedes performance (e.g., Herrero et al., 2006; Huang et al., 2012; Liu et al., 2019). Later, once the rodents habituate to the apparatus, they are more likely to find the platform. However, wall following would have been an excellent tactic if the platform had been located along one wall, so the link between wall following and spatial performance here is heavily affected by the setup.

9. Future research on wall-following behavior

As described above, a large body of research on wall-following behavior used it as a proxy for stress or anxiety, examining how drugs, pollutants, and other chemicals affect wall-following behavior. We believe that wall-following behavior is an interesting behavior. First, it can serve as a proxy for other behaviors or states, such as exploration or anxiety.

Second, it is a means by which animals interact with their immediate habitat and with conspecifics. Third, it has implications for the spatial distribution patterns of animals in the wild, and their interactions with lower and higher trophic levels, that is, their prey and predators. We will offer a few research directions worthwhile taking in order to better understand wall-following behavior.

First, wall-following behavior is almost always measured in the laboratory. Measuring it in natural habitats may shed light on its adaptive value, origin, and prevalence. It may also explain why related species or distinct populations vary in their use of wall-following behavior. We are currently not aware of how prevalent wall-following behavior in nature is, and it could be that wall-following behavior is exaggerated in the laboratory because animals are tested in too small arenas. Linking habitat complexity (surface irregularities) with wall-following behavior is also an interesting direction.

Second, wall-following behavior is proposed to be a defensive or exploratory behavior. If wall following is adaptive, then a cost-benefit analysis should show this to be the case. To date, neither the benefits nor the costs of wall following have been well studied. For example, if walls are not shelters in their own right, does wall following help animals find suitable shelter? Does it help to reduce predation? The costs could be diverse and include energetic and missed-opportunity costs. Costs can be translated to slower growth, for example (Seaver & Hurd, 2017), and the long-term consequences of wall-following behavior have been rarely studied.

Pit-building antlions/wormlions may be a productive system for cost-benefit analysis (Fig. 2), as they often try to avoid either direct sunlight, rain, or plant debris falling on their pits (Farji-Brener & Amador-Vargas, 2020; Gotelli, 1993; Scharf et al., 2018; Scharf et al., 2020). Walls can help to protect from all three, at least partially. If ants or other prey follow walls (Dussutour et al., 2005), some positions along the wall may also be more profitable for antlions/wormlions than are other positions. However, walls might have several disadvantages. They may restrict a key behavior of antlions: pit cleaning. Pit-cleaning behavior consists of rapid jerks of the head and mandibles, expelling sand, prey carcasses, and debris outside the trap (Büsse, Büscher, Heepe, Gorb, & Stutz, 2021; Franks, Worley, Falkenberg, Sendova-Franks, & Christensen, 2019). The adjacent wall may interfere with maintenance activities because what the antlion throws outside the pit can bounce off the walls and fall back. If walls restrict the direction in which debris can be thrown, they may also limit the orientation of the antlion inside the pit, that is, where its mandibles point, which

Fig. 2 Antlion larvae (Neuroptera: Myrmeleontidae) often build their pits near walls (artificial A, C; and natural, B) to protect them from rain and litterfall. (A) La Selva Biological Station, humid forest of Costa Rica, (B) a semi-deciduous forest in Yucatán peninsula, México, and (C) Palo Verde Biological Station, a seasonal dry forest in Nicoya, Costa Rica. Photos by AGFB. (D) Wormlion larvae (Diptera: Vermileonidae) next to a wall at Tel Aviv University, Israel. Photo by IS.

can play a role in prey capture success. Finally, if there is much arthropod traffic along walls, they might damage the pit and require high investment in reconstruction activity (Hayashi et al., 2023). In sum, walls probably provide both advantages and disadvantages, and the balance point between the two should dictate the optimal distance from the wall (Fig. 3).

Third, as mentioned above, not only potential prey can follow walls, but also predators can adjust their behavior and wait along walls/fences (Bojarska et al., 2017; Van Dyk & Slotow, 2003). This makes wall-following costly as a defensive tactic. Studying wall-following behavior as a tactic of both predators and prey in a combined system is rare (but see Uiterwaal et al., 2019; Rowsey et al., 2019) but seems to be a worthwhile direction both empirically and theoretically. Predator-prey dynamics should take into account the behavior of both players rather than assuming that one of the two is fixed (Lima, 2002; Scharf, 2021). Therefore, one may expect specific dynamics, such as prey following walls, predators ambushing prey along walls, prey stopping following walls, predators quitting ambushing prey along walls, prey returning to move along walls, and so on.

Fourth, as walls are a common feature in human-designed environments (Antrop, 2000), understanding adaptations or pre-adaptations to

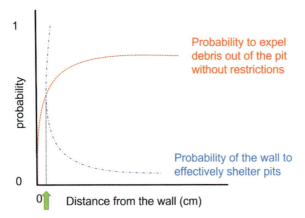

Fig. 3 A scheme of a suggested trade-off between two opposing constraints operating on pit-building predators when locating their pits: The probability of expelling debris out of the pit without restrictions increases with the distance from the wall, whereas its protective effect on pits (e.g., against direct sunlight, rain, and debris) drops with the distance from the wall. The cross-point of the two functions is the optimal location. Clearly, the exact cross-point location, as well as the shape of each function, are system-specific.

urban habitats is important in predicting which animals should cope well with this increasing habitat change. One possible direction, for example, would be to compare animal populations in urban and more natural habitats regarding their wall-following behavior (Magura et al., 2021). There is a large body of research on urban ecology, and integrating wall-following behavior here will benefit both.

Fifth, we recommend taking advantage of the tendency of many animals to follow walls in applied studies. Moving along walls makes animal movement more predictable, and animals use a lower proportion of their habitat. This can enable appropriate choices for placing pesticides and traps along walls (Kells & Hymel, 2017; Stryjek & Modlińska, 2013). If pests move along walls only under certain conditions, such as under light, one could apply such conditions, which will help to figure out where to place traps. One could also apply the "desert kite traps" (two walls in a funnel shape ending in an enclosure) to concentrate pests in a designated place, where they can be more easily dealt with.

Sixth, the interaction between wall-following behavior and learning is not fully known. Wall-following indeed decreases with time in novel environments and impairs learning under specific maze designs, such as the water maze, perhaps owing to high anxiety in such a maze. But it can also contribute to learning in other maze types, such as Y-mazes, as a means of exploration. Its interactions with social behavior are understudied too. On the one hand, the wall can serve as a meeting point for conspecifics. On the other hand, lower proportions follow walls when densities get high. In short, the link between tactics like wall following and the animal's score in maze solving is not fully known.

Finally, perhaps the four questions of Tinbergen (1963) can be a good platform to further investigate wall-following behavior. Many more studies deal with the proximate questions of the neurological/physiological mechanism and the effect of ontogeny on wall-following behavior than the two ultimate questions on the function of this behavior as well as its evolution.

10. Concluding comments

Wall-following behavior is a widespread behavior. Although the expression of this behavior can seem similar across systems and contexts, the explanations and triggers for it may greatly differ. Different animals move along walls for different reasons. It can be explained as a defensive strategy owing to anxiety or fear or a means of exploration. The wall itself may also provide better biotic conditions, such as higher prey availability, or abiotic ones, like shade, shelter, or a suitable substrate. The wall may guide substances in nature, such as water in a river or sand in a desert wadi. Moving along the wall may simply be energetically cheaper because it provides a homogenous trail and because it can help animals follow the shortest distance between two points. It is widely used as a proxy of induced behavioral changes by different stressors. The vast majority of studies thus far have documented it in the laboratory, with only a few examples from nature. Therefore, it is difficult to reach a solid conclusion regarding its role. It is also difficult to determine which natural situations trigger it, how common it is, and whether it is adaptive. Behavioral responses in the laboratory might differ greatly between the laboratory and field (e.g., desert gerbils forage more efficiently and respond more weakly to predation risk in the field compared to laboratory/enclosure conditions; Abramsky, Strauss, Subach, Riechman, & Kotler, 1996; Ovadia, Ziv, Abramsky, Pinshow, & Kotler, 2001). The necessary next steps are to examine wall-following behavior in nature as well as its consequences for various fitness components of the animals employing it.

Acknowledgments

We are grateful to David Eilam, Sue Healy, and Aziz Subach for fruitful discussions and helpful comments on an earlier version of the manuscript. We are also grateful to Glauco Machado for the invitation to write this review.

References

Abramsky, Z., Strauss, E., Subach, A., Riechman, A., & Kotler, B. P. (1996). The effect of barn owls (*Tyto alba*) on the activity and microhabitat selection of *Gerbillus allenbyi* and *G. pyramidum*. *Oecologia, 105*, 313–319.

Abu Bakar, N., Wan Ibrahim, W. N., Che Abdullah, C. A., Ramlan, N. F., Shaari, K., Shohaimi, S., & Mohd Faudzi, S. M. (2022). Embryonic arsenic exposure triggers long-term behavioral impairment with metabolite alterations in zebrafish. *Toxics, 10*, 493.

Acevedo, M. B., Nizhnikov, M. E., Molina, J. C., & Pautassi, R. M. (2014). Relationship between ethanol-induced activity and anxiolysis in the open field, elevated plus maze, light-dark box, and ethanol intake in adolescent rats. *Behavioural Brain Research, 265*, 203–215.

Acheson, S. K., Moore, N. L., Kuhn, C. M., Wilson, W. A., & Swartzwelder, H. S. (2011). The synthetic cannabinoid WIN 55212-2 differentially modulates thigmotaxis but not spatial learning in adolescent and adult animals. *Neuroscience Letters, 487*, 411–414.

Adler, J. (1975). Chemotaxis in bacteria. *Annual Review of Biochemistry, 44*, 341–356.

Agues-Barbosa, T., de Souza, A. M., de Lima, J. N. G., & Luchiari, A. C. (2023). Long-term behavioral alterations following embryonic alcohol exposure in three zebrafish populations. *Neurotoxicology, 96*, 174–183.

Akiyama, Y., Agata, K., & Inoue, T. (2015). Spontaneous behaviors and wall-curvature lead to apparent wall preference in planarian. *PLoS One, 10*, e0142214.

Alberstadt, P. J., Steele, C. W., & Skinner, C. (1995). Cover-seeking behavior in juvenile and adult crayfish, *Orconectes rusticus*: Effects of darkness and thigmotactic cues. *Journal of Crustacean Biology, 15*, 537–541.

Alfonso, S., Peyrafort, M., Cousin, X., & Bégout, M. L. (2020). Zebrafish Danio rerio shows behavioural cross-context consistency at larval and juvenile stages but no consistency between stages. *Journal of Fish Biology, 96*, 1411–1421.

Alzogaray, R. A., Fontán, A., & Zerba, E. N. (1997). Evaluation of hyperactivity produced by pyrethroid treatment on third instar nymphs of *Triatoma infestans* (Hemiptera: Reduviidae). *Archives of Insect Biochemistry and Physiology, 35*, 323–333.

Ansai, S., Hosokawa, H., Maegawa, S., & Kinoshita, M. (2016). Chronic fluoxetine treatment induces anxiolytic responses and altered social behaviors in medaka, *Oryzias latipes*. *Behavioural Brain Research, 303*, 126–136.

Antonelli, J., Steele, C., & Skinner, C. (1999). Cover-seeking behavior and shelter use by juvenile and adult crayfish, *Procambarus clarkii*: Potential importance in species invasion. *Journal of Crustacean Biology, 19*, 293–300.

Antrop, M. (2000). Changing patterns in the urbanized countryside of Western Europe. *Landscape Ecology, 15*, 257–270.

Avni, R., & Eilam, D. (2008). On the border: Perimeter patrolling as a transitional exploratory phase in a diurnal rodent, the fat sand rat (*Psammomys obesus*). *Animal Cognition, 11*, 311–318.

Avni, R., Tzvaigrach, Y., & Eilam, D. (2008). Exploration and navigation in the blind mole rat (*Spalax ehrenbergi*): Global calibration as a primer of spatial representation. *Journal of Experimental Biology, 211*, 2817–2826.

Baiamonte, M., Parker, M. O., Vinson, G. P., & Brennan, C. H. (2016). Sustained effects of developmental exposure to ethanol on zebrafish anxiety-like behaviour. *PLoS One, 11*, e0148425.

Barcay, S. J., & Bennett, G. W. (1991). Influence of starvation and lighting on the movement behavior of the German cockroach (Blattodea: Blattellidae). *Journal of Economic Entomology, 84,* 1520–1524.

Bartels, D. (2000). Dispersion behaviour of *Oryzaephilus mercator* (Fauvel) (Coleoptera: Silvanidae) in a preferendum arena for phototaxis, geotaxis and thigmotaxis. *Integrated Protection of Stored Products, 23,* 227–232.

Basil, J., & Sandeman, D. (2000). Crayfish (*Cherax destructor*) use tactile cues to detect and learn topographical changes in their environment. *Ethology: Formerly Zeitschrift fur Tierpsychologie, 106,* 247–259.

Bath, E., Thomson, J., & Perry, J. C. (2020). Anxiety-like behaviour is regulated independently from sex, mating status and the sex peptide receptor in *Drosophila melanogaster. Animal Behaviour, 166,* 1–7.

Beiko, J., Lander, R., Hampson, E., Boon, F., & Cain, D. P. (2004). Contribution of sex differences in the acute stress response to sex differences in water maze performance in the rat. *Behavioural Brain Research, 151,* 239–253.

Bertotto, L. B., Catron, T. R., & Tal, T. (2020). Exploring interactions between xenobiotics, microbiota, and neurotoxicity in zebrafish. *Neurotoxicology, 76,* 235–244.

Besson, M., & Martin, J. R. (2005). Centrophobism/thigmotaxis, a new role for the mushroom bodies in *Drosophila. Journal of Neurobiology, 62,* 386–396.

Best, C., Kurrasch, D. M., & Vijayan, M. M. (2017). Maternal cortisol stimulates neurogenesis and affects larval behaviour in zebrafish. *Scientific Reports, 7,* 40905.

Bilbo, S. D., Day, L. B., & Wilczynski, W. (2000). Anticholinergic effects in frogs in a Morris water maze analog. *Physiology & Behavior, 69,* 351–357.

Biro, P. A., & Stamps, J. A. (2010). Do consistent individual differences in metabolic rate promote consistent individual differences in behavior? *Trends in Ecology & Evolution, 25,* 653–659.

Bishnoi, I. R., Ossenkopp, K. P., & Kavaliers, M. (2021). Sex and age differences in locomotor and anxiety-like behaviors in rats: From adolescence to adulthood. *Developmental Psychobiology, 63,* 496–511.

Blumstein, D. T. (2016). Habituation and sensitization: New thoughts about old ideas. *Animal Behaviour, 120,* 255–262.

Bojarska, K., Kwiatkowska, M., Skórka, P., Gula, R., Theuerkauf, J., & Okarma, H. (2017). Anthropogenic environmental traps: Where do wolves kill their prey in a commercial forest? *Forest Ecology and Management, 397,* 117–125.

Bonito-Oliva, A., Masini, D., & Fisone, G. (2014). A mouse model of non-motor symptoms in Parkinson's disease: Focus on pharmacological interventions targeting affective dysfunctions. *Frontiers in Behavioral Neuroscience, 8,* 290.

Borba, J. V., Biasuz, E., Sabadin, G. R., Savicki, A. C., Canzian, J., Luchiari, A. C., & Rosemberg, D. B. (2022). Influence of acute and unpredictable chronic stress on spatiotemporal dynamics of exploratory activity in zebrafish with emphasis on homebase-related behaviors. *Behavioural Brain Research, 435,* 114034.

Bose, A. P., Brodin, T., Cerveny, D., & McCallum, E. S. (2022). Uptake, depuration, and behavioural effects of oxazepam on activity and foraging in a tropical snail (*Melanoides tuberculata*). *Environmental Advances, 8,* 100187.

Boulay, J., Devigne, C., Gosset, D., & Charabidze, D. (2013). Evidence of active aggregation behaviour in Lucilia sericata larvae and possible implication of a conspecific mark. *Animal Behaviour, 85,* 1191–1197.

Bouskila, A. (1995). Interactions between predation risk and competition: A field study of kangaroo rats and snakes. *Ecology, 76,* 165–178.

Bouskila, A. (2001). A habitat selection game of interactions between rodents and their predators. *Annales Zoologici Fennici, 38,* 55–70.

Branchi, I., D'Andrea, I., Sietzema, J., Fiore, M., Di Fausto, V., Aloe, L., & Alleva, E. (2006). Early social enrichment augments adult hippocampal BDNF levels and survival of BrdU-positive cells while increasing anxiety-and "depression"-like behavior. *Journal of Neuroscience Research, 83*, 965–973.

Brand, J. A., Henry, J., Melo, G. C., Wlodkowic, D., Wong, B. B., & Martin, J. M. (2023). Sex differences in the predictability of risk-taking behavior. *Behavioral Ecology, 34*, 108–116.

Bravo, I. M., Luster, B. R., Flanigan, M. E., Perez, P. J., Cogan, E. S., Schmidt, K. T., & McElligott, Z. A. (2020). Divergent behavioral responses in protracted opioid withdrawal in male and female C57BL/6J mice. *European Journal of Neuroscience, 51*, 742–754.

Breit, K. R., Zamudio, B., & Thomas, J. D. (2019). The effects of alcohol and cannabinoid exposure during the brain growth spurt on behavioral development in rats. Birth Defects Research. *111*, 760–774.

Broly, P., Mullier, R., Deneubourg, J. L., & Devigne, C. (2012). Aggregation in woodlice: Social interaction and density effects. *ZooKeys, 176*, 133–144.

Burger, R. M., Boylan, J., & Aucone, B. M. (2007). The effects of phototaxis and thigmotaxis on microhabitat selection by a caecilian amphibian (genus *Ichthyophis*). *The Herpetological Journal, 17*, 19–23.

Büsse, S., Büscher, T. H., Heepe, L., Gorb, S. N., & Stutz, H. H. (2021). Sand-throwing behaviour in pit-building antlion larvae: Insights from finite-element modelling. *Journal of the Royal Society Interface, 18*, 20210539.

Byrnes, J. P., Miller, D. C., & Schafer, W. D. (1999). Gender differences in risk taking: A meta-analysis. *Psychological Bulletin, 125*, 367–383.

Camhi, J. M., & Johnson, E. N. (1999). High-frequency steering maneuvers mediated by tactile cues: Antennal wall-following in the cockroach. *Journal of Experimental Biology, 202*, 631–643.

Cao, S., Song, W., Lv, W., & Fang, Z. (2015). A multi-grid model for pedestrian evacuation in a room without visibility. *Physica A, 436*, 45–61.

Carlson, B. E., & Langkilde, T. (2013). Personality traits are expressed in bullfrog tadpoles during open-field trials. *Journal of Herpetology, 47*, 378–383.

Carter, A. J., Marshall, H. H., Heinsohn, R., & Cowlishaw, G. (2012). How not to measure boldness: Novel object and antipredator responses are not the same in wild baboons. *Animal Behaviour, 84*, 603–609.

Carty, D. R., Miller, Z. S., Thornton, C., Pandelides, Z., Kutchma, M. L., & Willett, K. L. (2019). Multigenerational consequences of early-life cannabinoid exposure in zebrafish. *Toxicology and Applied Pharmacology, 364*, 133–143.

Champagne, D. L., Hoefnagels, C. C., De Kloet, R. E., & Richardson, M. K. (2010). Translating rodent behavioral repertoire to zebrafish (*Danio rerio*): Relevance for stress research. *Behavioural Brain Research, 214*, 332–342.

Chen, A. Y., Wilburn, P., Hao, X., & Tully, T. (2014). Walking deficits and centrophobism in an α-synuclein fly model of Parkinson's disease. *Genes, Brain, and Behavior, 13*, 812–820.

Chen, Y. R., Li, D. W., Wang, H. P., Lin, S. S., & Yang, E. C. (2022). The impact of thigmotaxis deprivation on the development of the German cockroach (*Blattella germanica*). *iScience, 25*, 104802.

Cheng, R. K., Tan, J. X. M., Chua, K. X., Tan, C. J. X., & Wee, C. L. (2022). Osmotic stress uncovers correlations and dissociations between larval zebrafish anxiety endophenotypes. *Frontiers in Molecular Neuroscience, 15*, 900223.

Chiquet, C., Dover, J. W., & Mitchell, P. (2013). Birds and the urban environment: The value of green walls. *Urban Ecosystems, 16*, 453–462.

Choi, D. C., Nguyen, M. M., Tamashiro, K. L., Ma, L. Y., Sakai, R. R., & Herman, J. P. (2006). Chronic social stress in the visible burrow system modulates stress-related gene expression in the bed nucleus of the stria terminalis. *Physiology & Behavior, 89*, 301–310.

Choleris, E., Thomas, A. W., Kavaliers, M., & Prato, F. S. (2001). A detailed ethological analysis of the mouse open field test: Effects of diazepam, chlordiazepoxide and an extremely low frequency pulsed magnetic field. *Neuroscience & Biobehavioral Reviews, 25*, 235–260.

Clift, D., Richendrfer, H., Thorn, R. J., Colwill, R. M., & Creton, R. (2014). High-throughput analysis of behavior in zebrafish larvae: Effects of feeding. *Zebrafish, 11*, 455–461.

Collier, A. D., Min, S. S., Campbell, S. D., Roberts, M. Y., Camidge, K., & Leibowitz, S. F. (2020). Maternal ethanol consumption before paternal fertilization: Stimulation of hypocretin neurogenesis and ethanol intake in zebrafish offspring. *Progress in Neuro-Psychopharmacology and Biological Psychiatry, 96*, 109728.

Costanzo, J. P. (1989). Conspecific scent trailing by garter snakes (*Thamnophis sirtalis*) during autumn: Further evidence for use of pheromones in den location. *Journal of Chemical Ecology, 15*, 2531–2538.

Creed, R. P., & Miller, J. R. (1990). Interpreting animal wall-following behavior. *Experientia, 46*, 758–761.

Czaczkes, T. J. (2018). Using T-and Y-mazes in myrmecology and elsewhere: A practical guide. *Insectes Sociaux, 65*, 213–224.

d'Isa, R., Brambilla, R., & Fasano, S. (2014). Behavioral methods for the study of the ras–ERK pathway in memory formation and consolidation: Passive avoidance and novel object recognition tests. In L. Trabalzini, & S. F. Retta (Eds.). *Ras signaling: Methods and protocols* (pp. 131–156). Humana Press.

Dalesman, S. (2018). Habitat and social context affect memory phenotype, exploration and covariance among these traits. *Philosophical Transactions of the Royal Society B, 373*, 20170291.

Daniel, D. K., & Bhat, A. (2022). Alone but not always lonely: Social cues alleviate isolation induced behavioural stress in wild zebrafish. *Applied Animal Behaviour Science, 251*, 105623.

de Belle, J. S., & Sokolowski, M. B. (1987). Heredity of rover/sitter: Alternative foraging strategies of *Drosophila melanogaster* larvae. *Heredity, 59*, 73–83.

de Carvalho, T. S., Cardoso, P. B., Santos-Silva, M., Lima-Bastos, S., Luz, W. L., Assad, N., & Herculano, A. M. (2019). Oxidative stress mediates anxiety-like behavior induced by high caffeine intake in zebrafish: Protective effect of alpha-tocopherol. *Oxidative Medicine and Cellular Longevity, 2019*, 8419810.

Dean, R., Duperreault, E., Newton, D., Krook, J., Ingraham, E., Gallup, J., & Hamilton, T. J. (2020). Opposing effects of acute and repeated nicotine exposure on boldness in zebrafish. *Scientific Reports, 10*, 8570.

Dean, R., Radke, N. H., Velupillai, N., Franczak, B. C., & Hamilton, T. J. (2021). Vision of conspecifics decreases the effectiveness of ethanol on zebrafish behaviour. *PeerJ, 9*, e10566.

Deng, S., Zhang, E., Tao, J., Zhao, Y., Huo, W., Guo, H., & Bian, W. (2023). Graphene quantum dots (GQDs) induce thigmotactic effect in zebrafish larvae via modulating key genes and metabolites related to synaptic plasticity. *Toxicology, 487*, 153462.

Depickère, S., Fresneau, D., Deneubourg, J. L., & Detrain, C. (2008). Spatial organization in ants' nests: Does starvation modify the aggregative behaviour of *Lasius niger* species? *Insectes Sociaux, 55*, 163–170.

Detrain, C., Pereira, H., & Fourcassié, V. (2019). Differential responses to chemical cues correlate with task performance in ant foragers. *Behavioral Ecology and Sociobiology, 73*, 107.

Devan, B. D., McDonald, R. J., & White, N. M. (1999). Effects of medial and lateral caudate-putamen lesions on place-and cue-guided behaviors in the water maze: Relation to thigmotaxis. *Behavioural Brain Research, 100*, 5–14.

Devigne, C., Broly, P., & Deneubourg, J. L. (2011). Individual preferences and social interactions determine the aggregation of woodlice. *PLoS One, 6*, e17389.

Dhabhar, F. S. (2000). Acute stress enhances while chronic stress suppresses skin immunity: Ted behaviors in the water mazehe role of stress hormones and leukocyte trafficking. *Annals of the New York Academy of Sciences, 917*, 876–893.

Domingue, M. J., Scheff, D. S., Arthur, F. H., & Myers, S. W. (2021). Sublethal exposure of *Trogoderma granarium* everts (Coleoptera: Dermestidae) to insecticide-treated netting alters thigmotactic arrestment and olfactory-mediated anemotaxis. *Pesticide Biochemistry and Physiology, 171*, 104742.

Doolittle, J. H. (1971). The effect of thigmotaxis on negative phototaxis in the earthworm. *Psychonomic Science, 22*, 311–312.

Doria, M. D., Morand-Ferron, J., & Bertram, S. M. (2019). Spatial cognitive performance is linked to thigmotaxis in field crickets. *Animal Behaviour, 150*, 15–25.

Dos Santos, C. P., de Oliveira, M. N., Silva, P. F., & Luchiari, A. C. (2023). Relationship between boldness and exploratory behavior in adult zebrafish. *Behavioural Processes*, 104885.

Douglass, N. J., & Reinert, H. K. (1982). The utilization of fallen logs as runways by small mammals. *Proceedings of the Pennsylvania Academy of Science, 56*, 162–164.

Durier, V., & Rivault, C. (2003). Exploitation of home range and spatial distribution of resources in German cockroaches (Dictyoptera: Blattellidae). *Journal of Economic Entomology, 96*, 1832–1837.

Dussutour, A., Deneubourg, J. L., & Fourcassié, V. (2005). Amplification of individual preferences in a social context: The case of wall-following in ants. *Proceedings of the Royal Society B, 272*, 705–714.

Eilam, D. (2003). Open-field behavior withstands drastic changes in arena size. *Behavioural Brain Research, 142*, 53–62.

Eilam, D. (2014). Of mice and men: Building blocks in cognitive mapping. *Neuroscience & Biobehavioral Reviews, 47*, 393–409.

Endlein, T., & Sitti, M. (2018). Innate turning preference of leaf-cutting ants in the absence of external orientation cues. *Journal of Experimental Biology, 221*, jeb177006.

Facciol, A., Marawi, T., Syed, E., & Gerlai, R. (2022). Age-dependent effects of embryonic ethanol exposure on anxiety-like behaviours in young zebrafish: A genotype comparison study. *Pharmacology, Biochemistry, and Behavior, 214*, 173342.

Faraday, M. M., Scheufele, P. M., Rahman, M. A., & Grunberg, N. E. (1999). Effects of chronic nicotine administration on locomotion depend on rat sex and housing condition. *Nicotine & Tobacco Research, 1*, 143–151.

Faria, M., Ziv, T., Gómez-Canela, C., Ben-Lulu, S., Prats, E., Novoa-Luna, K. A., & Raldúa, D. (2018). Acrylamide acute neurotoxicity in adult zebrafish. *Scientific Reports, 8*, 7918.

Farine, J. P., & Lobreau, J. P. (1984). Aggregation in *Dysdercus cingulatus* Fabr. (Heteroptera, Pyrrhocoridae): A new statistical method of interpretation. *Insectes Sociaux, 31*, 277–290.

Farji-Brener, A. G., & Amador-Vargas, S. (2020). Plasticity in extended phenotypes: How the antlion *Myrmeleon crudelis* adjusts the pit traps depending on biotic and abiotic conditions. *Israel Journal of Ecology & Evolution, 66*, 41–47.

Farji-Brener, A. G., Barrantes, G., Laverde, O., Fierro-Calderón, K., Bascopé, F., & López, A. (2007). Fallen branches as part of leaf-cutting ant trails: Their role in resource discovery and leaf transport rates in *Atta cephalotes*. *Biotropica, 39*, 211–215.

Filgueiras, G. B., Carvalho-Netto, E. F., & Estanislau, C. (2014). Aversion in the elevated plus-maze: Role of visual and tactile cues. *Behavioural Processes, 107*, 106–111.

Fišer, Ž., Prevorčnik, S., Lozej, N., & Trontelj, P. (2019). No need to hide in caves: Shelter-seeking behavior of surface and cave ecomorphs of *Asellus aquaticus* (Isopoda: Crustacea). *Zoology, 134*, 58–65.

Forbes, S. J., & Northfield, T. D. (2017). *Oecophylla smaragdina* ants provide pest control in Australian cacao. *Biotropica, 49*, 328–336.

Francia, N., Cirulli, F., Chiarotti, F., Antonelli, A., Aloe, L., & Alleva, E. (2006). Spatial memory deficits in middle-aged mice correlate with lower exploratory activity and a subordinate status: Role of hippocampal neurotrophins. *European Journal of Neuroscience*, *23*, 711–728.

Francis, R. A. (2011). Wall ecology: A frontier for urban biodiversity and ecological engineering. *Progress in Physical Geography*, *35*, 43–63.

Frank, K. D. (2009). Exploitation of artificial light at night by a diurnal jumping spider. *Peckhamia*, *78*, 1–3.

Franks, N. R., Worley, A., Falkenberg, M., Sendova-Franks, A. B., & Christensen, K. (2019). Digging the optimum pit: Antlions, spirals and spontaneous stratification. *Proceedings of the Royal Society B*, *286*, 20190365.

Freeman, B. M., & Chaves-Campos, J. (2016). Branch width and height influence the incorporation of branches into foraging trails and travel speed in leafcutter ants *Atta cephalotes* (L.) (Hymenoptera: Formicidae). *Neotropical Entomology*, *45*, 258–264.

Fridolf, K., Ronchi, E., Nilsson, D., & Frantzich, H. (2013). Movement speed and exit choice in smoke-filled rail tunnels. *Fire Safety Journal*, *59*, 8–21.

Furukawa, M., Izumo, N., Manabe, T., Kurono, H., Hayamizu, K., Nakano, M., & Watanabe, Y. (2021). Therapeutic effects of sertraline on improvement of Ovariectomy-induced decreased spontaneous activity in mice. *Drug Discoveries & Therapeutics*, *15*, 28–34.

Garcia, A. M. B., Cardenas, F. P., & Morato, S. (2005). Effect of different illumination levels on rat behavior in the elevated plus-maze. *Physiology & Behavior*, *85*, 265–270.

George, S., van den Buuse, M., San Mok, S., Masters, C. L., Li, Q. X., & Culvenor, J. G. (2008). α-Synuclein transgenic mice exhibit reduced anxiety-like behaviour. *Experimental Neurology*, *210*, 788–792.

Gonzalez, P. V., Alvarez Costa, A., & Masuh, H. M. (2017). A video-tracking analysis-based behavioral assay for larvae of *Anopheles pseudopunctipennis* and *Aedes aegypti* (Diptera: Culicidae). *Journal of Medical Entomology*, *54*, 793–797.

Gotelli, N. J. (1993). Ant lion zones: Causes of high-density predator aggregations. *Ecology*, *74*, 226–237.

Götz, K. G., & Biesinger, R. (1985a). Centrophobism in *Drosophila melanogaster*. I. Behavioral modification induced by ether. *Journal of Comparative Physiology A*, *156*, 319–327.

Götz, K. G., & Biesinger, R. (1985b). Centrophobism in *Drosophila melanogaster*. II. Physiological approach to search and search control. *Journal of Comparative Physiology A*, *156*, 329–337.

Grabovskaya, S. V., & Salyha, Y. T. (2014). Do results of the open field test depend on the arena shape? *Neurophysiology*, *46*, 376–380.

Graham, P., & Collett, T. S. (2002). View-based navigation in insects: How wood ants (*Formica rufa* L.) look at and are guided by extended landmarks. *Journal of Experimental Biology*, *205*, 2499–2509.

Grillon, C., & Ernst, M. (2016). Gain in translation: Is it time for thigmotaxis studies in humans? *Biological Psychiatry*, *80*, 343.

Grippo, A. J., Wu, K. D., Hassan, I., & Carter, C. S. (2008). Social isolation in prairie voles induces behaviors relevant to negative affect: Toward the development of a rodent model focused on co-occurring depression and anxiety. *Depression & Anxiety*, *25*, E17–E26.

Grossen, N. E., & Kelley, M. J. (1972). Species-specific behavior and acquisition of avoidance behavior in rats. *Journal of Comparative and Physiological Psychology*, *81*, 307–310.

Grosslight, J. H., & Harrison, P. C. (1961). Variability of response in a determined turning sequence in the meal worm (*Tenebrio molitor*): An experimental test of alternative hypotheses. *Animal Behaviour*, *9*, 100–103.

Gruszka, J., Krystkowiak-Kowalska, M., Frątczak-Łagiewska, K., Mądra-Bielewicz, A., Charabidze, D., & Matuszewski, S. (2020). Patterns and mechanisms for larval aggregation in carrion beetle *Necrodes littoralis* (Coleoptera: Silphidae). *Animal Behaviour*, *162*, 1–10.

Guo, R. Y., Huang, H. J., & Wong, S. C. (2012). Route choice in pedestrian evacuation under conditions of good and zero visibility: Experimental and simulation results. *Transportation Research Part B, 46*, 669–686.

Hamilton, K. R., Berger, S. S., Perry, M. E., & Grunberg, N. E. (2009). Behavioral effects of nicotine withdrawal in adult male and female rats. *Pharmacology, Biochemistry, and Behavior, 92*, 51–59.

Hamilton, T. J., Radke, N. H., Bajwa, J., Chaput, S., & Tresguerres, M. (2021). The dose makes the poison: Non-linear behavioural response to CO_2-induced aquatic acidification in zebrafish (*Danio rerio*). *Science of The Total Environment, 778*, 146320.

Hamilton, T. J., Szaszkiewicz, J., Krook, J., Richards, J. G., Stiller, K., & Brauner, C. J. (2022). Continuous light (relative to a 12: 12 photoperiod) has no effect on anxiety-like behaviour, boldness, and locomotion in coho salmon (*Oncorhynchus kisutch*) post-smolts in recirculating aquaculture systems at a salinity of either 2.5 or 10 ppt. *Comparative Biochemistry and Physiology Part A, 263*, 111070.

Hamilton, T. J., Tresguerres, M., Kwan, G. T., Szaskiewicz, J., Franczak, B., Cyronak, T., & Kline, D. I. (2023). Effects of ocean acidification on dopamine-mediated behavioral responses of a coral reef damselfish. *Science of the Total Environment, 877*, 162860.

Hansen, M. J., Schaerf, T. M., & Ward, A. J. (2015). The effect of hunger on the exploratory behaviour of shoals of mosquitofish *Gambusia holbrooki*. *Behaviour, 152*, 1659–1677.

Hänzi, S., & Straka, H. (2018). Wall following in *Xenopus laevis* is barrier-driven. *Journal of Comparative Physiology A, 204*, 183–195.

Harati, H., Majchrzak, M., Cosquer, B., Galani, R., Kelche, C., Cassel, J. C., & Barbelivien, A. (2011). Attention and memory in aged rats: Impact of lifelong environmental enrichment. *Neurobiology of Aging, 32*, 718–736.

Harris, A. C. (2021). Magnitude of open-field thigmotaxis during mecamylamine-precipitated nicotine withdrawal in rats is influenced by mecamylamine dose, duration of nicotine infusion, number of withdrawal episodes, and age. *Pharmacology, Biochemistry, and Behavior, 205*, 173185.

Harris, A. P., D'eath, R. B., & Healy, S. D. (2008). Sex differences, or not, in spatial cognition in albino rats: Acute stress is the key. *Animal Behaviour, 76*, 1579–1589.

Harris, A. P., D'Eath, R. B., & Healy, S. D. (2009). Environmental enrichment enhances spatial cognition in rats by reducing thigmotaxis (wall hugging) during testing. *Animal Behaviour, 77*, 1459–1464.

Hassan, A., Huang, Q., Xu, H., Wu, J., & Mehmood, N. (2021). Silencing of the phosphofructokinase gene impairs glycolysis and causes abnormal locomotion in the subterranean termite *Reticulitermes chinensis* Snyder. *Insect Molecular Biology, 30*, 57–70.

Hawkley, L. C., & Capitanio, J. P. (2015). Perceived social isolation, evolutionary fitness and health outcomes: A lifespan approach. *Philosophical Transactions of the Royal Society B, 370*, 20140114.

Hayashi, T., Hayashi, K., Hayashi, N., & Hayashi, F. (2023). Optimal pit site selection in antlion larvae: The relationship between prey availability and pit maintenance costs. *Journal of Ethology, 41*, 59–72.

Henry, J., Bai, Y., Williams, D., Logozzo, A., Ford, A., & Wlodkowic, D. (2022). Impact of test chamber design on spontaneous behavioral responses of model crustacean zooplankton *Artemia franciscana*. *Lab Animal, 51*, 81–88.

Herrero, A. I., Sandi, C., & Venero, C. (2006). Individual differences in anxiety trait are related to spatial learning abilities and hippocampal expression of mineralocorticoid receptors. *Neurobiology of Learning and Memory, 86*, 150–159.

Hess, S., Allan, B. J., Hoey, A. S., Jarrold, M. D., Wenger, A. S., & Rummer, J. L. (2019). Enhanced fast-start performance and anti-predator behaviour in a coral reef fish in response to suspended sediment exposure. *Coral Reefs, 38*, 103–108.

Hewlett, S. E., Wareham, D. M., & Barron, A. B. (2018). Honey bee (*Apis mellifera*) sociability and nestmate affiliation are dependent on the social environment experienced post-eclosion. *Journal of Experimental Biology, 221*, jeb173054.

Holzer, A., Avner, U., Porat, N., & Horwitz, L. K. (2010). Desert kites in the Negev desert and northeast Sinai: Their function, chronology and ecology. *Journal of Arid Environments, 74*, 806–817.

Horev, G., Benjamini, Y., Sakov, A., & Golani, I. (2007). Estimating wall guidance and attraction in mouse free locomotor behavior. *Genes, Brain, and Behavior, 6*, 30–41.

Huang, Y., Zhou, W., & Zhang, Y. (2012). Bright lighting conditions during testing increase thigmotaxis and impair water maze performance in BALB/c mice. *Behavioural Brain Research, 226*, 26–31.

Hughson, B. N., Anreiter, I., Chornenki, N. L. J., Murphy, K. R., William, W. J., Huber, R., & Sokolowski, M. B. (2018). The adult foraging assay (AFA) detects strain and food-deprivation effects in feeding-related traits of *Drosophila melanogaster*. *Journal of Insect Physiology, 106*, 20–29.

Hunt, E. R., O'Shea-Wheller, T., Albery, G. F., Bridger, T. H., Gumn, M., & Franks, N. R. (2014). Ants show a leftward turning bias when exploring unknown nest sites. *Biology Letters, 10*, 20140945.

Hutton, S. J., Siddiqui, S., Pedersen, E. I., Markgraf, C. Y., Segarra, A., Hladik, M. L., & Brander, S. M. (2023). Comparative behavioral ecotoxicology of Inland Silverside larvae exposed to pyrethroids across a salinity gradient. *Science of the Total Environment, 857*, 159398.

Ichikawa, N., & Sasaki, M. (2003). Importance of social stimuli for the development of learning capability in honeybees. *Applied Entomology and Zoology, 38*, 203–209.

Islam, M., Deeti, S., Mahmudah, Z., Kamhi, J. F., & Cheng, K. (2023). Detouring while foraging up a tree: What bull ants (*Myrmecia midas*) learn and their reactions to novel sensory cues. *Journal of Comparative Psychology, 137*, 4–15.

Ismail, M. Z. B. H., Hodges, M. D., Boylan, M., Achall, R., Shirras, A., & Broughton, S. J. (2015). The *Drosophila* insulin receptor independently modulates lifespan and locomotor senescence. *PLoS One, 10*, e0125312.

Isobe, M., Helbing, D., & Nagatani, T. (2004). Experiment, theory, and simulation of the evacuation of a room without visibility. *Physical Review E, 69*, 066132.

Iwatsuki, K., & Hirano, T. (1995). Induction of the thigmotaxis in *Paramecium caudatum*. *Comparative Biochemistry and Physiology A, 110*, 167–170.

Iwatsuki, K., & Hirano, T. (1996). An increase in the influx of calcium ions into cilia induces thigmotaxis in *Paramecium caudatum*. *Experientia, 52*, 831–833.

Iwatsuki, K., Hirano, T., Kawase, M., Chiba, H., Michibayashi, N., Yamada, C., & Mizoguchi, T. (1996). Thigmotaxis in *Paramecium caudatum* is induced by hydrophobic or polyaniline-coated glass surface to which liver cells from rat adhere with forming multicellular spheroids. *European Journal of Protistology, 32*, 58–61.

Jékely, G. (2009). Evolution of phototaxis. *Philosophical Transactions of the Royal Society B, 364*, 2795–2808.

Jethva, S., Liversage, K., & Kundu, R. (2022). Does topography of rocky intertidal habitat affect aggregation of cerithiid gastropods and co-occurring macroinvertebrates? *Oceanologia, 64*, 387–395.

Ji, Y., Lin, J., Peng, X., Liu, X., Li, F., Zhang, Y., & Li, Q. (2017). Behavioural responses of zebrafish larvae to acute ethosuximide exposure. *Behavioural Pharmacology, 28*, 428–440.

Jingu, A., & Hayashi, F. (2018). Pitfall vs fence traps in feeding efficiency of antlion larvae. *Journal of Ethology, 36*, 265–275.

Jolles, J. W., Boogert, N. J., & van den Bos, R. (2015). Sex differences in risk-taking and associative learning in rats. *Royal Society Open Science. 2*, 150485.

Kallai, J., Karadi, K., & Feldmann, A. (2009). Anxiety-dependent spatial navigation strategies in virtual and real spaces. *Cognitive Processing, 10*, 229–232.

Kallai, J., Makany, T., Csatho, A., Karadi, K., Horvath, D., Kovacs-Labadi, B., & Jacobs, J. W. (2007). Cognitive and affective aspects of thigmotaxis strategy in humans. *Behavioral Neuroscience, 121*, 21–30.

Kapoor, A., & Matthews, S. G. (2005). Short periods of prenatal stress affect growth, behaviour and hypothalamo-pituitary-adrenal axis activity in male guinea pig offspring. *Journal of Physiology, 566*, 967–977.

Kastberger, G. (1982). Evasive behaviour in the cave-cricket, *Troglophilus cavicola. Physiological Entomology, 7*, 175–181.

Kells, S. A., & Hymel, S. N. (2017). The influence of time and distance traveled by bed bugs, *Cimex lectularius*, on permethrin uptake from treated mattress liners. *Pest Management Science, 73*, 113–117.

Kerr, G. D., Bull, C. M., & Burzacott, D. (2003). Refuge sites used by the scincid lizard *Tiliqua rugosa. Austral Ecology, 28*, 152–160.

Kitamura, A. (1986). Attachment of mating reactive Paramecium to polystyrene surfaces: IV. Comparison of the adhesiveness among six species of the genus *Paramecium. The Biological Bulletin, 171*, 350–359.

Kjær, K., Jørgensen, M. B., Hageman, I., Miskowiak, K. W., & Wörtwein, G. (2020). The effect of erythropoietin on electroconvulsive stimulation induced cognitive impairment in rats. *Behavioural Brain Research, 382*, 112484.

Kohler, S. A., Parker, M. O., & Ford, A. T. (2018a). Shape and size of the arenas affect amphipod behaviours: Implications for ecotoxicology. *PeerJ, 6*, e5271.

Kohler, S. A., Parker, M. O., & Ford, A. T. (2018b). Species-specific behaviours in amphipods highlight the need for understanding baseline behaviours in ecotoxicology. *Aquatic Toxicology, 202*, 173–180.

Korhonen, H. T., Niemelä, P., & Jauhiainen, L. (2001). Effect of space and floor material on the behaviour of farmed blue foxes. *Canadian Journal of Animal Science, 81*, 189–197.

Koto, A., Mersch, D., Hollis, B., & Keller, L. (2015). Social isolation causes mortality by disrupting energy homeostasis in ants. *Behavioral Ecology and Sociobiology, 69*, 583–591.

Kotrschal, A., Lievens, E. J., Dahlbom, J., Bundsen, A., Semenova, S., Sundvik, M., & Kolm, N. (2014). Artificial selection on relative brain size reveals a positive genetic correlation between brain size and proactive personality in the guppy. *Evolution: International Journal of Organic Evolution, 68*, 1139–1149.

Kozlovsky, D. Y., Poirier, M. A., Hermer, E., Bertram, S. M., & Morand-Ferron, J. (2022). Texas field crickets (*Gryllus texensis*) use visual cues to place learn but perform poorly when intra-and extra-maze cues conflict. *Learning & Behavior, 50*, 306–316.

Krook, J. T., Duperreault, E., Newton, D., Ross, M. S., & Hamilton, T. J. (2019). Repeated ethanol exposure increases anxiety-like behaviour in zebrafish during withdrawal. *PeerJ, 7*, e6551.

Kvist, S. B. M., & Selander, R. K. (1994). Open-field thigmotaxis during various phases of the reproductive cycle. *Scandinavian Journal of Psychology, 35*, 220–229.

Kvist, S. B. M., Selander, R. K., & Viemerö, V. (1995). The impact of newborn on adult mice: Open-field behavior along with pullus index. *Psychobiology, 23*, 214–223.

Labaude, S., O'Donnell, N., & Griffin, C. T. (2018). Description of a personality syndrome in a common and invasive ground beetle (Coleoptera: Carabidae). *Scientific Reports, 8*, 17479.

Lai, L. C., & Chao, T. Z. (2021). Random choice of the tropical fire ant in the enclosed space. *Taiwania, 66*, 73–78.

Lamprea, M. R., Cardenas, F. P., Setem, J., & Morato, S. (2008). Thigmotactic responses in an open-field. *Brazilian Journal of Medical and Biological Research, 41*, 135–140.

Laurent Salazar, M. O., Planas-Sitjà, I., Sempo, G., & Deneubourg, J. L. (2018). Individual thigmotactic preference affects the fleeing behavior of the American cockroach (Blattodea: Blattidae). *Journal of Insect Science, 18*, 9.

Le Bourg, E. (1983). Patterns of movement and ageing in *Drosophila melanogaster*. *Archives of Gerontology and Geriatrics, 2*, 299–306.

Lebreton, S., & Martin, J. R. (2009). Mutations affecting the cAMP transduction pathway disrupt the centrophobism behavior. *Journal of Neurogenetics, 23*, 225–234.

Lei, F., Xu, M., Ji, Z., Rose, K. A., Zakirov, V., & Bisset, M. (2022). Swimming behavior and hydrodynamics of the Chinese cavefish *Sinocyclocheilus rhinocerous* and a possible role of its head horn structure. *PLoS One, 17*, e0270967.

Leppänen, P. K., Ravaja, N., & Ewalds-Kvist, S. B. M. (2006). Twenty-three generations of mice bidirectionally selected for open-field thigmotaxis: Selection response and repeated exposure to the open field. *Behavioural Processes, 72*, 23–31.

Leppänen, P. K., Ravaja, N., & Ewalds-Kvist, S. B. M. (2008). Prepartum and postpartum open-field behavior and maternal responsiveness in mice bidirectionally selected for open-field thigmotaxis. *Journal of General Psychology, 135*, 37–53.

Li, Q., Lin, J., Zhang, Y., Liu, X., Chen, X. Q., Xu, M. Q., & Guo, N. (2015). Differential behavioral responses of zebrafish larvae to yohimbine treatment. *Psychopharmacology, 232*, 197–208.

Lima, S. L. (2002). Putting predators back into behavioral predator-prey interactions. *Trends in Ecology & Evolution, 17*, 70–75.

Lin, Y. E., Lin, C. H., Ho, E. P., Ke, Y. C., Petridi, S., Elliott, C. J., & Chien, C. T. (2021). Glial Nrf2 signaling mediates the neuroprotection exerted by *Gastrodia elata* Blume in Lrrk2-G2019S Parkinson's disease. *Elife, 10*, e73753.

Linton, M. C., Crowley, P. H., Williams, J. T., Dillon, P. M., Aral, H., Strohmeier, K. L., & Wood, C. (1991). Pit relocation by antlion larvae: A simple model and laboratory test. *Evolutionary Ecology, 5*, 93–104.

Liu, L., Davis, R. L., & Roman, G. (2007). Exploratory activity in *Drosophila* requires the kurtz nonvisual arrestin. *Genetics, 175*, 1197–1212.

Liu, X., Lin, J., Zhang, Y., Peng, X., Guo, N., & Li, Q. (2016). Effects of diphenylhydantoin on locomotion and thigmotaxis of larval zebrafish. *Neurotoxicology and Teratology, 53*, 41–47.

Liu, Y., Day, L. B., Summers, K., & Burmeister, S. S. (2019). A cognitive map in a poison frog. *Journal of Experimental Biology, 222*, jeb197467.

Löfgren, M., Johansson, I. M., Meyerson, B., Lundgren, P., & Bäckström, T. (2006). Progesterone withdrawal effects in the open field test can be predicted by elevated plus maze performance. *Hormones and Behavior, 50*, 208–215.

Lorenzo, M. G., & Lazzari, C. R. (1999). Temperature and relative humidity affect the selection of shelters by *Triatoma infestans*, vector of Chagas disease. *Acta Tropica, 72*, 241–249.

Lucas, J. R. (1985). Metabolic rates and pit-construction costs of two antlion species. *Journal of Animal Ecology, 54*, 295–309.

Lucon-Xiccato, T., Conti, F., Loosli, F., Foulkes, N. S., & Bertolucci, C. (2020). Development of open-field behaviour in the medaka, *Oryzias latipes. Biology, 9*, 389.

Lundholm, J. T., & Richardson, P. J. (2010). Habitat analogues for reconciliation ecology in urban and industrial environments. *Journal of Applied Ecology, 47*, 966–975.

Maciąg, M., Michalak, A., Skalicka-Woźniak, K., Zykubek, M., Ciszewski, A., & Budzyńska, B. (2020). Zebrafish and mouse models for anxiety evaluation–A comparative study with xanthotoxin as a model compound. *Brain Research Bulletin, 165*, 139–145.

Magnhagen, C. (1990). Reproduction under predation risk in the sand goby, *Pomatoschistus minutes*, and the black goby, *Gobius niger*: The effect of age and longevity. *Behavioral Ecology and Sociobiology, 26*, 331–335.

Magnhagen, C., & Borcherding, J. (2008). Risk-taking behaviour in foraging perch: Does predation pressure influence age-specific boldness? *Animal Behaviour, 75*, 509–517.

Magura, T., Mizser, S., Horváth, R., Nagy, D. D., Tóth, M., Csicsek, R., & Lövei, G. L. (2021). Are there personality differences between rural vs. urban-living individuals of a specialist ground beetle, *Carabus convexus*? *Insects, 12*, 646.

Mammola, S., Isaia, M., Demonte, D., Triolo, P., & Nervo, M. (2018). Artificial lighting triggers the presence of urban spiders and their webs on historical buildings. *Landscape and Urban Planning, 180*, 187–194.

Martin, J. R. (2004). A portrait of locomotor behaviour in *Drosophila* determined by a video-tracking paradigm. *Behavioural Processes, 67*, 207–219.

Martín, J., & López, P. (1999). An experimental test of the costs of antipredatory refuge use in the wall lizard, *Podarcis muralis*. *Oikos, 84*, 499–505.

Martínez, J. C., Cardenas, F., Lamprea, M., & Morato, S. (2002). The role of vision and proprioception in the aversion of rats to the open arms of an elevated plus-maze. *Behavioural Processes, 60*, 15–26.

Martinez, R., & Morato, S. (2004). Thigmotaxis and exploration in adult and pup rats. *Revista de Etologia, 6*, 49–54.

Masarovič, R., Zvaríková, M., Fedorová, J., & Fedor, P. (2017). Thigmotactic behavior of *Limothrips cerealium* (Thysanoptera: Thripidae) leads to laboratory equipment damage in the Czech Republic. *Journal of Entomological Science, 52*, 308–310.

Mathiron, A. G., Gallego, G., & Silvestre, F. (2023). Early-life exposure to permethrin affects phenotypic traits in both larval and adult mangrove rivulus *Kryptolebias marmoratus*. *Aquatic Toxicology*106543.

Maximino, C., Carvalho, C. M., & Morato, S. (2014). Discrimination of anxiety-versus panic-like behavior in the wall lizard *Tropidurus oreadicus*. *Psychology & Neuroscience, 7*, 227–231.

Maximino, C., de Brito, T. M., Colmanetti, R., Pontes, A. A. A., de Castro, H. M., de Lacerda, ... Gouveia Jr, A. (2010). Parametric analyses of anxiety in zebrafish scototaxis. *Behavioural Brain Research, 210*, 1–7.

Mayagoitia, K., Tolan, A. J., Shammi, S., Shin, S. D., Menchaca, J. A., Figueroa, J. D., & Soriano, S. (2021). Loss of APP in mice increases thigmotaxis and is associated with elevated brain expression of IL-13 and IP-10/CXCL10. *Physiology & Behavior, 240*, 113533.

McCreery, H. F., Dix, Z. A., Breed, M. D., & Nagpal, R. (2016). Collective strategy for obstacle navigation during cooperative transport by ants. *Journal of Experimental Biology, 219*, 3366–3375.

McGaw, I. J. (2001). Impacts of habitat complexity on physiology: Purple shore crabs tolerate osmotic stress for shelter. *Estuarine, Coastal and Shelf Science, 53*, 865–876.

McMahon, A., Patullo, B. W., & Macmillan, D. L. (2005). Exploration in a T-maze by the crayfish *Cherax destructor* suggests bilateral comparison of antennal tactile information. *The Biological Bulletin, 208*, 183–188.

Merola, C., Lucon-Xiccato, T., Bertolucci, C., & Perugini, M. (2021). Behavioural effects of early-life exposure to parabens in zebrafish larvae. *Journal of Applied Toxicology, 41*, 1852–1862.

Mishra, S., & Bande, P. (2008). *Maze solving algorithms for micro mouse. 2008 IEEE international conference on signal image technology and internet based systems.* IEEE86–93.

Mohammad, F., Aryal, S., Ho, J., Stewart, J. C., Norman, N. A., Tan, T. L., & Claridge-Chang, A. (2016). Ancient anxiety pathways influence *Drosophila* defense behaviors. *Current Biology, 26*, 981–986.

Mongeau, J. M., Demir, A., Lee, J., Cowan, N. J., & Full, R. J. (2013). Locomotion-and mechanics-mediated tactile sensing: Antenna reconfiguration simplifies control during high-speed navigation in cockroaches. *Journal of Experimental Biology, 216*, 4530–4541.

Morland, R. H., Novejarque, A., Huang, W., Wodarski, R., Denk, F., Dawes, J. D., & Rice, A. S. (2015). Short-term effect of acute and repeated urinary bladder inflammation on thigmotactic behaviour in the laboratory rat. *F1000Research, 4*, 109.

Morland, R. H., Novejarque, A., Spicer, C., Pheby, T., & Rice, A. S. C. (2016). Enhanced c-Fos expression in the central amygdala correlates with increased thigmotaxis in rats with peripheral nerve injury. *European Journal of Pain, 20*, 1140–1154.

Mosquera, K. D., & Lorenzo, M. G. (2020). Species-specific patterns of shelter exploitation in Chagas disease vectors of the genus *Rhodnius. Acta Tropica, 205*, 105433.

Mundy, P. C., Hartz, K. E. H., Fulton, C. A., Lydy, M. J., Brander, S. M., Hung, T. C., & Connon, R. E. (2021). Exposure to permethrin or chlorpyrifos causes differential dose- and time-dependent behavioral effects at early larval stages of an endangered teleost species. *Endangered Species Research, 44*, 89–103.

Muniandy, Y. (2018). The use of larval zebrafish (*Danio rerio*) model for identifying new anxiolytic drugs from herbal medicine. *Zebrafish, 15*, 321–339.

Nagle, K. J., & Bell, W. J. (1987). Genetic control of the search tactic of *Drosophila melanogaster:* An ethometric analysis of rover/sitter traits in adult flies. *Behavior Genetics, 17*, 385–408.

Newton, B. J. (1982). Early stress effects on growth and adult behavior in *Poecilia reticulata. Developmental Psychobiology, 15*, 211–220.

Nielsen, S. V., Kellner, M., Henriksen, P. G., Olsén, H., Hansen, S. H., & Baatrup, E. (2018). The psychoactive drug Escitalopram affects swimming behaviour and increases boldness in zebrafish (*Danio rerio*). *Ecotoxicology (London, England), 27*, 485–497.

O'Connor, C. M., Norris, D. R., Crossin, G. T., & Cooke, S. J. (2014). Biological carryover effects: Linking common concepts and mechanisms in ecology and evolution. *Ecosphere, 5*, 1–11.

Ou, M., Hamilton, T. J., Eom, J., Lyall, E. M., Gallup, J., Jiang, A., & Brauner, C. J. (2015). Responses of pink salmon to CO_2-induced aquatic acidification. *Nature Climate Change, 5*, 950–955.

Ovadia, O., Ziv, Y., Abramsky, Z., Pinshow, B., & Kotler, B. P. (2001). Harvest rates and foraging strategies in Negev Desert gerbils. *Behavioral Ecology, 12*, 219–226.

Pan, Y., Liu, Y., Young, K. A., Zhang, Z., & Wang, Z. (2009). Post-weaning social isolation alters anxiety-related behavior and neurochemical gene expression in the brain of male prairie voles. *Neuroscience Letters, 454*, 67–71.

Patton, P., Windsor, S., & Coombs, S. (2010). Active wall following by Mexican blind cavefish (*Astyanax mexicanus*). *Journal of Comparative Physiology A, 196*, 853–867.

Patullo, B. W., & Macmillan, D. L. (2006). Corners and bubble wrap: The structure and texture of surfaces influence crayfish exploratory behaviour. *Journal of Experimental Biology, 209*, 567–575.

Pellow, S., & File, S. E. (1986). Anxiolytic and anxiogenic drug effects on exploratory activity in an elevated plus-maze: A novel test of anxiety in the rat. *Pharmacology, Biochemistry, and Behavior, 24*, 525–529.

Peng, X., Lin, J., Zhu, Y., Liu, X., Zhang, Y., Ji, Y., & Li, Q. (2016). Anxiety-related behavioral responses of pentylenetetrazole-treated zebrafish larvae to light-dark transitions. *Pharmacology, Biochemistry, and Behavior, 145*, 55–65.

Perrot-Sinal, T. S., Heale, V. R., Ossenkopp, K. P., & Kavaliers, M. (1996). Sexually dimorphic aspects of spontaneous activity in meadow voles (*Microtus pennsylvanicus*): Effects of exposure to fox odor. *Behavioral Neuroscience, 110*, 1126.

Pinheiro-da-Silva, J., Agues-Barbosa, T., & Luchiari, A. C. (2020). Embryonic exposure to ethanol increases anxiety-like behavior in fry zebrafish. *Alcohol and Alcoholism, 55*, 581–590.

Polverino, G., Karakaya, M., Spinello, C., Soman, V. R., & Porfiri, M. (2019). Behavioural and life-history responses of mosquitofish to biologically inspired and interactive robotic predators. *Journal of the Royal Society Interface, 16*, 20190359.

Pratt, S. C., Brooks, S. E., & Franks, N. R. (2001). The use of edges in visual navigation by the ant *Leptothorax albipennis*. *Ethology: Formerly Zeitschrift fur Tierpsychologie, 107*, 1125–1136.

Prut, L., & Belzung, C. (2003). The open field as a paradigm to measure the effects of drugs on anxiety-like behaviors: A review. *European Journal of Pharmacology, 463*, 3–33.

Qin, W., Lin, S., Chen, X., Chen, J., Wang, L., Xiong, H., & Wang, C. (2019). Food transport of red imported fire ants (Hymenoptera: Formicidae) on vertical surfaces. *Scientific Reports, 9*, 3283.

Rajput, N., Parikh, K., & Kenney, J. W. (2022). Beyond bold versus shy: Zebrafish exploratory behavior falls into several behavioral clusters and is influenced by strain and sex. *Biology Open, 11*, bio059443.

Ramlan, N. F., Sata, N. S. A. M., Hassan, S. N., Bakar, N. A., Ahmad, S., Zulkifli, S. Z., & Ibrahim, W. N. W. (2017). Time dependent effect of chronic embryonic exposure to ethanol on zebrafish: Morphology, biochemical and anxiety alterations. *Behavioural Brain Research, 332*, 40–49.

Ramos, A., Correia, E. C., Izídio, G. S., & Brüske, G. R. (2003). Genetic selection of two new rat lines displaying different levels of anxiety-related behaviors. *Behavior Genetics, 33*, 657–668.

Redfern, J. C., Cooke, S. J., Lennox, R. J., Nannini, M. A., Wahl, D. H., & Gilmour, K. M. (2017). Effects of maternal cortisol treatment on offspring size, responses to stress, and anxiety-related behavior in wild largemouth bass (*Micropterus salmoides*). *Physiology & Behavior, 180*, 15–24.

Reinert, H. K., Cundall, D., & Bushar, L. M. (1984). Foraging behavior of the timber rattlesnake, *Crotalus horridus*. *Copeia, 1984*, 976–981.

Richendrfer, H., Pelkowski, S. D., Colwill, R. M., & Creton, R. (2012). On the edge: Pharmacological evidence for anxiety-related behavior in zebrafish larvae. *Behavioural Brain Research, 228*, 99–106.

Roberts, A. C., Alzagatiti, J. B., Ly, D. T., Chornak, J. M., Ma, Y., Razee, A., & Glanzman, D. L. (2020). Induction of short-term sensitization by an aversive chemical stimulus in zebrafish larvae. *Eneuro, 7*, ENEURO.0336-19.2020.

Rodgers, R. J., & Shepherd, J. K. (1993). Influence of prior maze experience on behaviour and response to diazepam in the elevated plus-maze and light/dark tests of anxiety in mice. *Psychopharmacology, 113*, 237–242.

Rose, M. R. (1991). *Evolutionary biology of aging*. New York: Oxford University Press,.

Rowsey, L. E., Johansen, J. L., Khursigara, A. J., & Esbaugh, A. J. (2019). Oil exposure impairs predator–prey dynamics in larval red drum (*Sciaenops ocellatus*). *Marine and Freshwater Research, 71*, 99–106.

Rozen-Rechels, D., Dupoué, A., Meylan, S., Decencière, B., Guingand, S., & Le Galliard, J. F. (2018). Water restriction in viviparous lizards causes transgenerational effects on behavioral anxiety and immediate effects on exploration behavior. *Behavioral Ecology and Sociobiology, 72*, 1–14.

Salehi, B., Cordero, M. I., & Sandi, C. (2010). Learning under stress: The inverted-U-shape function revisited. *Learning & Memory (Hove, England), 17*, 522–530.

Saman, A. B. S., & Abdramane, I. (2013). Solving a reconfigurable maze using hybrid wall follower algorithm. *International Journal of Computer Applications, 82*, 22–26.

Santucci, A. C., Cortes, C., Bettica, A., & Cortes, F. (2008). Chronic ethanol consumption in rats produces residual increases in anxiety 4 months after withdrawal. *Behavioural Brain Research, 188*, 24–31.

Sato, N., & Sato, A. (2022). How to turn the corner: Discrimination of path shapes in rats. *Learning & Behavior, 50*, 254–262.

Scharf, I. (2016). The multifaceted effects of starvation on arthropod behaviour. *Animal Behaviour, 119*, 37–48.

Scharf, I. (2021). The interaction between ambush predators, search patterns of herbivores, and aggregations of plants. *Behavioral Ecology, 32*, 1246–1255.

Scharf, I., Hanna, K., & Gottlieb, D. (2024). Experimental arena settings might lead to misinterpretation of movement properties. *Insect Science, 31*, 271–284.

Scharf, I., & Ruxton, G. D. (2023). Shadow competition: Its definition, prevalence, causes and measurement. *Oikose09774.*

Scharf, I., Gilad, T., Bar-Ziv, M. A., Katz, N., Gregorian, E., Pruitt, J. N., & Subach, A. (2018). The contribution of shelter from rain to the success of pit-building predators in urban habitats. *Animal Behaviour, 142*, 139–145.

Scharf, I., Silberklang, A., Avidov, B., & Subach, A. (2020). Do pit-building predators prefer or avoid barriers? Wormlions' preference for walls depends on light conditions. *Scientific Reports, 10*, 10928.

Scharf, I., Stoldt, M., Libbrecht, R., Höpfner, A. L., Jongepier, E., Kever, M., & Foitzik, S. (2021). Social isolation causes downregulation of immune and stress response genes and behavioural changes in a social insect. *Molecular Ecology, 30*, 2378–2389.

Scharf, I., Gilad, T., Taichman, Y., & Subach, A. (2021). Urban pit-building insects are attracted to walls for multiple reasons. *Biology, 10*, 635.

Schnörr, S. J., Steenbergen, P. J., Richardson, M. K., & Champagne, D. (2012). Measuring thigmotaxis in larval zebrafish. *Behavioural Brain Research, 228*, 367–374.

Schulz, D., Topic, B., Silva, M. A. D. S., & Huston, J. P. (2004). Extinction-induced immobility in the water maze and its neurochemical concomitants in aged and adult rats: A possible model for depression? *Neurobiology of Learning & Memory (Hove, England), 82*, 128–141.

Seaver, C. M. S., & Hurd, P. L. (2017). Are there consistent behavioral differences between sexes and male color morphs in *Pelvicachromis pulcher*? *Zoology, 122*, 115–125.

Segarra, A., Mauduit, F., Amer, N. R., Biefel, F., Hladik, M. L., Connon, R. E., & Brander, S. M. (2021). Salinity changes the dynamics of pyrethroid toxicity in terms of behavioral effects on newly hatched delta smelt larvae. *Toxics, 9*, 40.

Sempo, G., Depickere, S., & Detrain, C. (2006). Spatial organization in a dimorphic ant: Caste specificity of clustering patterns and area marking. *Behavioral Ecology, 17*, 642–650.

Sendova-Franks, A. B., & Franks, N. R. (1994). Social resilience in individual worker ants and its role in division of labour. *Proceedings of the Royal Society of London B, 256*, 305–309.

Shams, S., Amlani, S., Buske, C., Chatterjee, D., & Gerlai, R. (2018). Developmental social isolation affects adult behavior, social interaction, and dopamine metabolite levels in zebrafish. *Developmental Psychobiology, 60*, 43–56.

Shams, S., Chatterjee, D., & Gerlai, R. (2015). Chronic social isolation affects thigmotaxis and whole-brain serotonin levels in adult zebrafish. *Behavioural Brain Research, 292*, 283–287.

Sharma, S., Coombs, S., Patton, P., & De Perera, T. B. (2009). The function of wall-following behaviors in the Mexican blind cavefish and a sighted relative, the Mexican tetra (*Astyanax*). *Journal of Comparative Physiology A, 195*, 225–240.

Shukitt-Hale, B., Casadesus, G., Cantuti-Castelvetri, I., & Joseph, J. A. (2001). Effect of age on object exploration, habituation, and response to spatial and nonspatial change. *Behavioral Neuroscience, 115*, 1059–1064.

Sikora, J., Baranowski, Z., & Zajaczkowska, M. (1992). Two-state model of *Paramecium bursaria* thigmotaxis. *Experientia, 48*, 789–792.

Simon, P., Dupuis, R., & Costentin, J. (1994). Thigmotaxis as an index of anxiety in mice influence of dopaminergic transmissions. . *Behavioural Brain Research, 61*, 59–64.

Snihur, A. W., Hampson, E., & Cain, D. P. (2008). Estradiol and corticosterone independently impair spatial navigation in the Morris water maze in adult female rats. *Behavioural Brain Research, 187*, 56–66.

Soibam, B., Mann, M., Liu, L., Tran, J., Lobaina, M., Kang, Y. Y., & Roman, G. (2012). Open-field arena boundary is a primary object of exploration for *Drosophila*. *Brain and Behavior, 2*, 97–108.

Sparling, J. E., Baker, S. L., & Bielajew, C. (2018). Effects of combined pre-and post-natal enrichment on anxiety-like, social, and cognitive behaviours in juvenile and adult rat offspring. *Behavioural Brain Research, 353*, 40–50.

Stephen, J. M., & Ledger, R. A. (2005). An audit of behavioral indicators of poor welfare in kenneled dogs in the United Kingdom. *Journal of Applied Animal Welfare Science, 8*, 79–95.

Stewart, A., Cachat, J., Wong, K., Gaikwad, S., Gilder, T., DiLeo, J., & Kalueff, A. V. (2010). Homebase behavior of zebrafish in novelty-based paradigms. *Behavioural Processes, 85*, 198–203.

Stewart, S., Jeewajee, A., Wills, T. J., Burgess, N., & Lever, C. (2014). Boundary coding in the rat subiculum. *Philosophical Transactions of the Royal Society B, 369*, 20120514.

Street, W. R. (1968). Thigmotaxis in mealworms: Effects of barrier height and illumination. *Psychonomic Science, 11*, 37 –37.

Stryjek, R., & Modlińska, K. (2013). A thigmotaxis-based method of recapturing and transporting small mammals in the laboratory. *Lab Animal, 42*, 321–324.

Suresh, S., Abozaid, A., Tsang, B., & Gerlai, R. (2021). Exposure of parents to alcohol alters behavior of offspring in zebrafish. *Progress in Neuro-Psychopharmacology and Biological Psychiatry, 111*, 110143.

Suzuki, K., Takagi, T., & Hiraishi, T. (2003). Video analysis of fish schooling behavior in finite space using a mathematical model. *Fisheries Research, 60*, 3–10.

Svoboda, J., Telenský, P., Blahna, K., Bures, J., & Stuchlik, A. (2012). Comparison of male and female rats in avoidance of a moving object: More thigmotaxis, hypolocomotion and fear-like reactions in females. *Physiological Research, 61*, 659–663.

Swartzwelder, H. S., Hogan, A., Risher, M. L., Swartzwelder, R. A., Wilson, W. A., & Acheson, S. K. (2014). Effect of sub-chronic intermittent ethanol exposure on spatial learning and ethanol sensitivity in adolescent and adult rats. *Alcohol (Fayetteville, N. Y.), 48*, 353–360.

Szaszkiewicz, J., Leigh, S., & Hamilton, T. J. (2021). Robust behavioural effects in response to acute, but not repeated, terpene administration in Zebrafish (*Danio rerio*). *Scientific Reports, 11*, 19214.

Tallamy, D. W. (1982). Age specific maternal defense in *Gargaphia solani* (Hemiptera: Tingidae). *Behavioral Ecology and Sociobiology, 11*, 7–11.

Tamilselvan, P., & Sloman, K. A. (2017). Developmental social experience of parents affects behaviour of offspring in zebrafish. *Animal Behaviour, 133*, 153–160.

Tan, D., Patton, P., & Coombs, S. (2011). Do blind cavefish have behavioral specializations for active flow-sensing? *Journal of Comparative Physiology A, 197*, 743–754.

Tan, S., Xue, S., Behnood-Rod, A., Chellian, R., Wilson, R., Knight, P., & Bruijnzeel, A. W. (2019). Sex differences in the reward deficit and somatic signs associated with precipitated nicotine withdrawal in rats. *Neuropharmacology, 160*, 107756.

Tanaka, K. (1989). Energetic cost of web construction and its effect on web relocation in the web building spider *Agelena limbata*. *Oecologia, 81*, 459–461.

Telonis, A. G., & Margarity, M. (2015). Phobos: A novel software for recording rodents' behavior during the thigmotaxis and the elevated plus-maze test. *Neuroscience Letters, 599*, 81–85.

Teyke, T. (1985). Collision with and avoidance of obstacles by blind cave fish *Anoptichthys jordani* (Characidae). *Journal of Comparative Physiology A, 157*, 837–843.

Thiel, C. M., Müller, C. P., Huston, J. P., & Schwarting, R. K. W. (1999). High versus low reactivity to a novel environment: Behavioural, pharmacological and neurochemical assessments. *Neuroscience, 93*, 243–251.

Thompson, W. A., & Vijayan, M. M. (2020). Environmental levels of venlafaxine impact larval behavioural performance in fathead minnows. *Chemosphere, 259,* 127437.

Tinbergen, N. (1963). On aims and methods of ethology. *Zeitschrift für tierpsychologie, 20,* 410–433.

Tomczak, V. V., Schweiger, R., & Müller, C. (2016). Effects of arbuscular mycorrhiza on plant chemistry and the development and behavior of a generalist herbivore. *Journal of Chemical Ecology, 42,* 1247–1258.

Topic, B., Dere, E., Schulz, D., de Souza Silva, M. A., Jocham, G., Kart, E., & Huston, J. P. (2005). Aged and adult rats compared in acquisition and extinction of escape from the water maze: Focus on individual differences. *Behavioral Neuroscience, 119,* 127–144.

Tower, J., Agrawal, S., Alagappan, M. P., Bell, H. S., Demeter, M., Havanoor, N., & Varma, A. (2019). Behavioral and molecular markers of death in *Drosophila melanogaster*. *Experimental Gerontology, 126,* 110707.

Treit, D., & Fundytus, M. (1988). Thigmotaxis as a test for anxiolytic activity in rats. *Pharmacology, Biochemistry, and Behavior, 31,* 959–962.

Tsang, B., Ansari, R., & Gerlai, R. (2019). Dose dependent behavioral effects of acute alcohol administration in zebrafish fry. *Pharmacology, Biochemistry, and Behavior, 179,* 124–133.

Tzavara, E. T., Monory, K., Hanoune, J., & Nomikos, G. G. (2002). Nicotine withdrawal syndrome: Behavioural distress and selective up-regulation of the cyclic AMP pathway in the amygdala. *European Journal of Neuroscience, 16,* 149–153.

Uiterwaal, S. F., Dell, A. I., & DeLong, J. P. (2019). Arena size modulates functional responses via behavioral mechanisms. *Behavioral Ecology, 30,* 483–489.

Uller, T. (2008). Developmental plasticity and the evolution of parental effects. *Trends in Ecology & Evolution, 23,* 432–438.

Valle, F. P. (1970). Effects of strain, sex, and illumination on open-field behavior of rats. *American Journal of Psychology, 83,* 103–111.

van den Berg, S. J., Rodríguez-Sánchez, P., Zhao, J., Olusoiji, O. D., Peeters, E. T., & Schuijt, L. M. (2023). Among-individual variation in the swimming behaviour of the amphipod *Gammarus pulex* under dark and light conditions. *Science of the Total Environment, 872,* 162177.

Van Dyk, G., & Slotow, R. (2003). The effects of fences and lions on the ecology of African wild dogs reintroduced to Pilanesberg National Park, South Africa. *African Zoology, 38,* 79–94.

Van Straalen, N. M. (2003). Ecotoxicology becomes stress ecology. *Environmental Science & Technology, 37,* 324A–330A.

Voss, S. C., Main, B. Y., & Dadour, I. R. (2007). Habitat preferences of the urban wall spider *Oecobius navus* (Araneae, Oecobiidae). *Australian Journal of Entomology, 46,* 261–268.

Vossen, L. E., Jutfelt, F., Cocco, A., Thörnqvist, P. O., & Winberg, S. (2016). Zebrafish (*Danio rerio*) behaviour is largely unaffected by elevated pCO2. *Conservation Physiology, 4,* cow065.

Vossen, L. E., Nilsson, E., Jansson, A., & Roman, E. (2023). Open field behavior in the house cricket (*Acheta domesticus*): Effect of illumination, sex differences and individual consistency. *Journal of Insects as Food and Feed, 9,* 317–324.

Walz, N., Mühlberger, A., & Pauli, P. (2016). A human open field test reveals thigmotaxis related to agoraphobic fear. *Biological Psychiatry, 80,* 390–397.

Wang, J., Liu, T., Liu, Z., & Chai, Y. (2023). Exploring the influencing factors of wall-following behavior in a virtual reality fire evacuation game. *Computer Animation and Virtual Worlds, 34,* e2122.

Watanabe, N. M., Stahlman, W. D., Blaisdell, A. P., Garlick, D., Fast, C. D., & Blumstein, D. T. (2012). Quantifying personality in the terrestrial hermit crab: Different measures, different inferences. *Behavioural Processes, 91,* 133–140.

Webster, M. M., & Laland, K. N. (2011). Reproductive state affects reliance on public information in sticklebacks. *Proceedings of the Royal Society B, 278,* 619–627.

Webster, M. M., & Laland, K. N. (2015). Space-use and sociability are not related to public-information use in ninespine sticklebacks. *Behavioral Ecology and Sociobiology, 69,* 895–907.

Weinrich, T. W., Hogg, C., & Jeffery, G. (2018). The temporal sequence of improved mitochondrial function on the dynamics of respiration, mobility, and cognition in aged *Drosophila. Neurobiology of Aging, 70,* 140–147.

Wexler, Y., Subach, A., Pruitt, J. N., & Scharf, I. (2016). Behavioral repeatability of flour beetles before and after metamorphosis and throughout aging. *Behavioral Ecology and Sociobiology, 70,* 745–753.

Wexler, Y., Wertheimer, K. O., Subach, A., Pruitt, J. N., & Scharf, I. (2017). Mating alters the link between movement activity and pattern in the red flour beetle. *Physiological Entomology, 42,* 299–306.

White, K. E., Humphrey, D. M., & Hirth, F. (2010). The dopaminergic system in the aging brain of *Drosophila. Frontiers in Neuroscience, 4,* 205.

Winchell, K. M., Battles, A. C., & Moore, T. Y. (2020). Terrestrial locomotor evolution in urban environments. In M. Szulkin, J. Munshi-South, & A. Charmantier (Eds.). *Urban evolutionary biology* (pp. 197–216). Oxford, UK: Oxford University Press.

Xue, S., Jiang, R., Wong, S. C., Feliciani, C., Shi, X., & Jia, B. (2020). Wall-following behaviour during evacuation under limited visibility: Experiment and modelling. *Transportmetrica A, 16,* 626–653.

Yamaguchi, M., Masuda, R., & Yamashita, Y. (2018). Phototaxis, thigmotaxis, geotaxis, and response to turbulence of sea cucumber *Apostichopus japonicus* juveniles. *Fisheries Science, 84,* 33–39.

Yamana, Y., Hamano, T., & Goshima, S. (2009). Laboratory observations of habitat selection in aestivating and active adult sea cucumber *Apostichopus japonicus. Fisheries Science, 75,* 1097–1102.

Yang, X., Lin, J., Peng, X., Zhang, Q., Zhang, Y., Guo, N., & Li, Q. (2017). Effects of picrotoxin on zebrafish larvae behaviors: A comparison study with PTZ. *Epilepsy & Behavior, 70,* 224–231.

Yaski, O., Portugali, J., & Eilam, D. (2011). Arena geometry and path shape: When rats travel in straight or in circuitous paths? *Behavioural Brain Research, 225,* 449–454.

Zadicario, P., Avni, R., Zadicario, E., & Eilam, D. (2005). 'Looping'—an exploration mechanism in a dark open field. *Behavioural Brain Research, 159,* 27–36.

Zhang, X. Y., Vollert, J., Sena, E. S., Rice, A. S., & Soliman, N. (2021). A protocol for the systematic review and meta-analysis of thigmotactic behaviour in the open field test in rodent models associated with persistent pain. *BMJ Open Science, 5,* e100135.

Zuharah, W. F., Fadzly, N., Yusof, N. A., & Dieng, H. (2015). Risky behaviors: Effects of *Toxorhynchites splendens* (Diptera: Culicidae) predator on the behavior of three mosquito species. *Journal of Insect Science, 15,* 128.

CHAPTER TWO

Quiet but not forgotten: Insights into adaptive evolution and behavior from 20 years of (mostly) silent Hawaiian crickets

Nathan W. Bailey[a,*], Marlene Zuk[b,*], and Robin M. Tinghitella[c,*]
[a]School of Biology, University of St Andrews, St Andrews, United Kingdom
[b]Department of Ecology, Evolution and Behavior, University of Minnesota, St. Paul, MN, United States
[c]Department of Biological Sciences, University of Denver, Denver, CO, United States
*Corresponding authors. e-mail address: nwb3@st-andrews.ac.uk; mzuk@umn.edu; robin.tinghitella@du.edu

Contents

1. Introduction	52
1.1 Hawaiian crickets as a microcosm of behavioral and evolutionary biology	53
1.2 Eavesdropping parasitoid flies impose strong selection on crickets	58
1.3 Adaptive breakage: An understudied mode of adaptation and diversification	59
2. Behavior's role in adaptive evolution	62
2.1 Current evidence: Support (or not) for general principles	63
2.2 Insights from Hawaiian crickets	64
3. Behavior links signal, form, and function	66
3.1 State of the field	67
3.2 Insights from anti-parasitoid cricket adaptations	68
4. Rapid convergent adaptation: Causes and consequences	71
4.1 Convergent evolution of behavior	72
4.2 Parallel evolution and adaptive breakage in Hawaiian crickets	74
4.3 Consequences of rapid cricket morph evolution	76
5. Synthesis: The value of long-term insect studies in nature	78
Acknowledgements	79
References	79
Further readings	87

Abstract

Over 20 years ago, an adaptive, silent male morph called 'flatwing' was discovered in a population of Hawaiian crickets (*Teleogryllus oceanicus*). Silence protects males against lethal, eavesdropping parasitoid flies (*Ormia ochracea*). Since then, numerous independent, protective morphs have been discovered, including parallel 'flatwing' mutations, 'small-wing', 'curly-wing', 'rattling-wing', and 'defiled-wing', all of which disrupt structures that generate sound when males rub their wings together. Some crickets also produce a protective, attenuated signal called 'purring'. This cricket-fly arms race is a microcosm of behavioral and evolutionary biology. Here we provide a user's guide to the system. Our research efforts have revealed an important role for behavioral flexibility (i.e., plasticity) in accommodating and accelerating genetic adaptation by enabling both sexes to cope with a changing social environment caused by adaptive signal loss. We describe a unique mode by which behavioral flexibility and novel adaptations are bound together in this system: as each one affects the fitness of the other in a way that facilitates rapid responses to selection, the two co-evolve over time. We advocate for viewing behavior's role in evolution as dynamic rather than static. Our research supports the idea that behavior can change dynamically depending on genetic architecture, demography, and other factors. In addition, the widespread reduction of singing through morphological rather than behavioral change in *T. oceanicus* pinpoints wing morphology as a hotspot of evolution, and we describe ongoing behavioral and genomic research characterizing this underappreciated mode of adaptation—*adaptive breakage*—which disrupts previously canalized form-function relationships.

1. Introduction

Rapidly-evolving silent male crickets were discovered in Hawaiian populations of *Teleogryllus oceanicus* over 20 years ago (Zuk, Rotenberry, & Tinghitella, 2006). In Hawaii, the songs that male crickets sing to attract female mates also attract the acoustically-orienting eavesdropper, *Ormia ochracea*. This parasitoid fly eavesdrops on male advertisement songs and then deposits larvae on host crickets that will eventually eat them alive from the inside out. The result is a clear conflict between sexual and natural selection. In the early 2000s a genetic mutation, *flatwing*, that eliminates the structures on the crickets' wings that produce song emerged and spread rapidly, because silent crickets are protected from the parasitoid (Zuk et al., 2006) (Fig. 1). The silent 'flatwing' morph swept through one population to >95% of males in fewer than 20 generations. Since this initial discovery in a single population, multiple independently-evolved male-silencing mutations and other protective male morphs have been discovered across the Hawaiian archipelago. This diversity has served as a rich natural laboratory for studying signal evolution and the interaction between behavioral plasticity and evolutionary change.

1.1 Hawaiian crickets as a microcosm of behavioral and evolutionary biology

In field crickets in the family Gryllidae, males generate sexual advertisement songs by drawing a toothed file on the underside of their top forewing (tegmen) across the scraper—a thickened vein on the edge of the opposing forewing (Fig. 1A). This causes the surface of both wings to vibrate, and modified wing veins form structures which together produce calls at a characteristic frequency—c. 5 kHz in *T. oceanicus* (Bennet-Clark, 2003). All of the male-protecting variants discovered so far involve morphological modification of male forewings that either eliminates or disrupts sound production. An updated nomenclature of male morphs and known modes of inheritance is provided in a Periodic Table of Quiet Hawaiian Crickets (Table 1). Fig. 2 provides a detailed overview of each protective

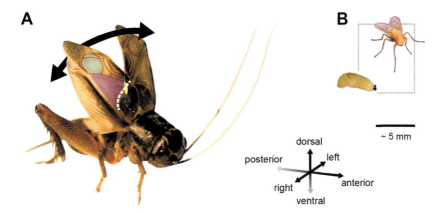

Fig. 1 Rapidly evolving Hawaiian crickets and their parasitoid fly enemies. (A) A normal-wing *Teleogryllus oceanicus* male, illustrating typical forewing sound production. Males sing by rubbing their right forewing across the top of the left forewing, an action called stridulation. A stridulatory file on the underside of the top wing (thick white dashed line) contacts a scraper (yellow) on the proximal edge of the wing beneath. As the wings move across one another, regularly-spaced ridges along the length of the file strike the scraper and cause the forewings to vibrate. Specialised structures on the wing surface including the mirror (blue) and harp (magenta), resonate and produce the characteristic, pure-tone frequency of male song. (B) An adult female and late larval endoparasitoid *Ormia ochracea*. Gravid female flies locate singing hosts using a specialised thoracic ear; they then eject nearly-microscopic planidia onto hosts. These larvae then burrow into the host's body where they develop through several instars before emerging and pupating, which is always deadly for the host and causes a clear conflict between natural and sexual selection on male song. Photo credits: NW Bailey. Figure adapted from Bailey, Pascoal, & Montealegre-Z (2019); Zhang, Rayner, Blaxter, & Bailey (2021).

Table 1 A periodic table of quiet Hawaiian crickets. Nomenclature and descriptions of adaptive, song-disrupting male forewing phenotypes in Hawaiian *Teleogryllus oceanicus*. Phenotype names are given in bold, genotype abbreviations in bold italics, and where known, modes of inheritance in plain italics. Plain-text phenotype descriptions correspond to Fig. 1, and audible sounds associated with each morph are coded with colored symbols; see key. The genetic basis of variation between purring vs. silent vs. shifted song (i.e. frequency change) within forms is unclear. Male forewings vary on two dimensions: 3-dimensional shape versus surface venation comprising the stridulum and sound resonators in wild-type males. Venation categories include multiple independently-evolved flatwing forms (solid call-out box). Wild-type shape is mutually exclusive with curly-wing and small-wing shape, but curly-wing and small-wing shapes can co-occur in more complex forms shown in the dashed call-out box. Grey cells indicate as-yet unobserved morph combinations.

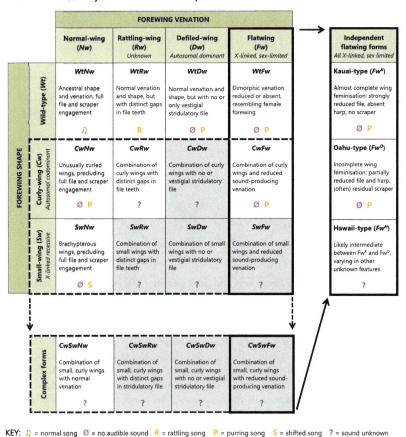

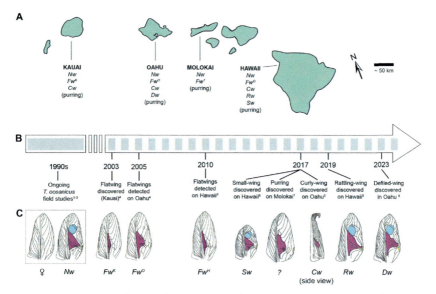

Fig. 2 Geography, timeline, and description of quiet Hawaiian cricket evolution. (A) Hawaiian archipelago, showing known occurrence of different male morphs. Morph descriptors correspond to Table 1 and panel (C) below. Purring has been observed on all studied islands. (B) Timeline of cricket morph discoveries. Ongoing studies during the 1990s and early 2000s investigated conflicting natural and sexual selection in normal-wing cricket populations subject to selection by *Ormia ochracea*. Numbers correspond to key references: [1] Zuk, Simmons, and Rotenberry (1995); [2] Zuk, Rotenberry, and Simmons (1998); [3] Simmons, Zuk, and Rotenberry (2001); [4] Zuk et al. (2006); [5] Pascoal et al. (2014); [6] Rayner et al. (2018); [7] Tinghitella, Broder, Gurule-Small, Hallagan, and Wilson (2018); [8] Gallagher, Zonana, Broder, Herner, and Tinghitella (2022); [9] Bailey et al. *pers obs*. (C) Diagrams of representative forewings for each morph, with colors corresponding to Fig. 1. Wild-type cricket wings are indicated in the grey box and correspond to normal-wing crickets in study populations during the 1990s and early 2000s; a female forewing is provided as a comparator. Where known, genotype abbreviations corresponding to Table 1 are provided. Wing drawings based on photographs by NW Bailey and RM Tinghitella. Figure adapted from Bailey, Pascoal, & Montealegre-Z (2019); Rayner et al. (2018); Tinghitella et al. (2018, 2021); Zhang et al. (2021).

variant: the timeline of its initial discovery, geographic location, and physical properties. Fig. 3 explores in detail the structural features of wings and their consequences for acoustic signals, and gives examples of the potential for co-expression of different male-protective mutations.

Research on the Hawaiian cricket-fly study system over the preceding two decades has delivered insights across a broad set of subfields within animal behavior and evolutionary biology. In addition, integrative approaches

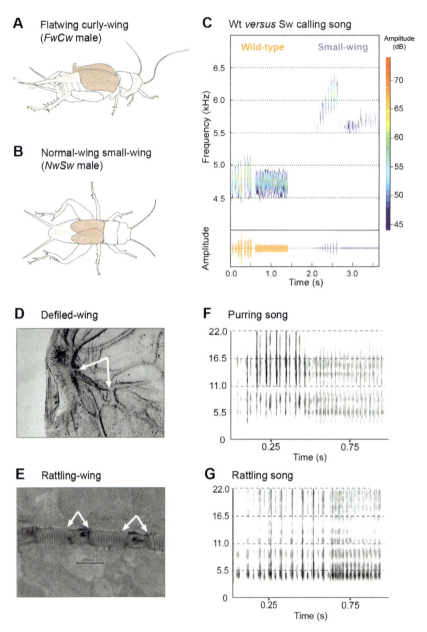

Fig. 3 Wing morph details and consequences for acoustic sound production. (A) Flatwing venation co-expressed with curly-wing structure. (B) Small-wing male. (C) Comparison of courtship song between wild-type versus sound-producing small-wing males. Amplitude is indicated by the heatmap colors and is plotted in the lower panel. (D) Reduced stridulatory file (between arrows) on the underside of a defiled-wing stridulum.

(Caption continued on next page)

spanning these disciplines have contributed to wider understanding of behavior's influence (or lack thereof) on evolutionary pattern and process. Such large-scale, long-term and collaborative efforts mirror approaches in other prominent study systems, confirming the value of research that combines observation and testing of natural population dynamics with innovative laboratory-based approaches. This tradition in behavioral and evolutionary biology includes work that has tested the evolutionary origins and maintenance of mimicry in *Heliconius* butterflies (Jiggins, Naisbit, Coe, & Mallet, 2001); reproductive isolation in European house mice (Smadja & Ganem, 2005), sticklebacks (Boughman, 2001), cichlids (Terai, Seehausen, Sasaki, Takahashi, & Mizoiri, 2006), and stick insects (Nosil, 2004); quantitative evolution of behavior in red deer (Wilson, Morrissey, Adams, Walling, & Guinness, 2011), Soay sheep (Wilson, Pilkington, Pemberton, Coltman, & Overall, 2005), zebra finches (Fehér, Wang, Saar, Mitra, & Tchernichovski, 2009), and collared flycatchers (Qvarnström, Pärt, & Sheldon, 2000), and of course seminal work on radiations in Galapagos finches (Grant & Grant, 2006) and Hawaiian picture-wing fruit flies (Magnacca & Price, 2015), spiders (Gillespie, Croom, & Palumbi, 1994), and crickets in the genus *Laupala* (Mendelson & Shaw, 2005).

Rapidly evolving Hawaiian *T. oceanicus* have some unusual characteristics that are particularly useful to researchers. Chief among these is that bouts of adaptation can be investigated in their earliest stages due to the geographic mosaic of cricket and fly populations that exist with different distributions of polymorphic host adaptations (Fig. 2A). This allows an investigation of the behavioral, genomic, and ecological dynamics of host-parasite adaptation in space and time, where all populations are parasitized by the fly, but male-protecting wing variants have invaded only a subset of these and spread over contemporary timeframes to different frequencies. Thus, comparatively un-adapted populations serve as proxies for earlier stages of adaptive evolution, whereas populations fixed for song-reduction variants such as *flatwing* serve as exemplars for "completed" adaptation. In addition, the contemporary timeframe of adaptive bouts has been directly recorded owing to the long-term nature of field studies that were initiated more than a decade before silent males were observed to have invaded the

---

(E) Recurrent tooth gaps (between arrows) on a ratting-wing stridulatory file. (F) Sonogram of a purring call, showing broad-band frequency spectrum. (G) Sonogram of a rattling call, showing broad-band spectrum with a dominant ~4.8 kHz component. Photographs: NW Bailey, JH Gallagher, and RM Tinghitella. Figure modified from Rayner & Zhang (2021); Gallagher et al. (2022); Zhang, Rayner, & Bailey (2024).

first population (e.g., Simmons et al., 2001; Zuk et al., 2006; Tinghitella et al., 2018; Rayner, Aldridge, Montealegre-Z, & Bailey, 2019). This makes real-time study of adaptive evolution more feasible. It is exceedingly uncommon to be able to study the initial invasion of an adaptive variant into a population under pressure—either by *de novo* mutation or via introgression. The majority of wild study systems used to study behavior and adaptive evolution exist in a state of comparatively advanced adaptive response to pressure, and it is necessary to infer historical selection using techniques such as comparative or population genomics. However, the initial generations during which populations transitioned from no evolutionary response to a response to selection are essential to study, if some of the foundational questions established during the early Modern Synthesis regarding adaptive evolution and behavior's role in it are to be answered.

1.2 Eavesdropping parasitoid flies impose strong selection on crickets

Nothing makes sense about the evolution of silent crickets except in the light of their lethal natural enemy, *O. ochracea* (Fig. 1B). This endoparasitoid, a tachinid fly, is endemic to the southern United States and Mexico where it is a generalist parasitoid of many species of field crickets (Cade, 1975). Host detection and attack proceeds as follows. First, a gravid female fly hears and approaches a singing male. Then, free-living parasitoid larvae (planidia) are ejected from the female's reproductive opening (Feener & Brown, 1997). The planidia invade the host's body cavity, most likely through the soft exoskeletal junction between the thorax and abdomen, and consume host body tissues. Then, larvae pass through several instars inside the cricket. Their rapid growth soon makes their surface area-to-volume ratio unfavorable for absorbing oxygen from the host's open circulatory system, and larvae gnaw a hole in the abdominal wall and attach to the outside oxygen source using a respiratory funnel that grows with them (Vinson, 1990; Bailey & Zuk, 2008a). Invasion by *O. ochracea* larvae has considerable consequences for gene regulation and immunological responses in the host (Sikkink, Bailey, Zuk, & Balenger, 2020), yet hosts remain alive until mature larvae chew a hole and crawl out of them. At that point, larvae pupate and then emerge as adults approximately two weeks later to continue the life cycle.

O. ochracea females have highly acute, highly directional hearing. Only gravid females respond to male cricket songs, and when doing so the precision of their response enables rapid disgorgement of planidia directly onto hosts and possibly onto the surrounding substrate. Such efficacious attacks are made possible by a highly specialized thoracic ear (Miles, Robert, & Hoy, 1995). Ordinarily, crickets achieve directional, long-range hearing through the spatial separation of left and right tympanal organs on the fore-tibia connected via acoustic trachea, which allows an adequate distance for sound waves to create directional acoustic pressure differentials that can be detected and neurally integrated (Montealegre-Z & Robert, 2015). However, the wavelength in air of a typical 4.8 kHz *T. oceanicus* song is 7.1 cm, far longer than any such mechanism could achieve in a ca. 0.5 cm fly. *O. ochracea* has evolved a solution to this problem which mechanically delays sound impulses entering from right versus left sides of the ear, enabling sensitive directional hearing (Mason, Oshinsky, & Hoy, 2001).

In Hawaii, the fly appears to primarily parasitize singing *T. oceanicus* males, although it is capable of parasitizing several alternative hosts that have been observed in field sites, albeit at lower densities (Broder, Gallagher, Wikle, Welsh, & Zonana, 2023). In the semi-tropical climate of Hawaii, both *T. oceanicus* and *O. ochracea* breed continuously, but in North American populations the flies appear to be seasonal, mainly parasitizing hosts in early autumn (Paur & Gray, 2011b). In the latter range, the flies show evidence of local adaptation to prevailing host songs (Gray, Banuelos, Walker, Cade, & Zuk, 2007), and gravid females learn about host song based on prior experience (Paur & Gray 2011a). The fly's co-occurrence with *T. oceanicus* on Hawaii predated the discovery of flatwing crickets, and it exerts natural selection on male song in a way that has shaped the evolution of song characteristics and singing behavior under countervailing sexual selection pressure. The rate of parasitism is notably high, with ca. 30% of males in Kauai populations harboring parasitoid larvae prior to the emergence and spread of flatwing males (Zuk et al., 1993). Silent crickets have a major advantage: the original study of flatwing crickets on Kauai found *O. ochracea* larvae in only one of 121 flatwing crickets dissected (Zuk et al., 2006). In Hawaii, while silent male morphs of *T. oceanicus* are protected from parasitism by the fly (Zuk et al., 2006; Rayner et al., 2018), there is evidence to suggest that the attenuated sounds made by purring crickets are detectable by the flies, albeit less so (Broder, Gallagher, Wikle, Venable, & Zonana, 2022).

1.3 Adaptive breakage: An understudied mode of adaptation and diversification

A characteristic that makes the study of silent Hawaiian crickets so fruitful is that adaptation has occurred through trait loss. *Loss* of sexually-selected traits is a central prediction of Fisherian models for the evolution of ornaments, weapons, and mating preferences, due to the expectations that natural selection should eventually check their elaboration and that they may experience unstable evolutionary dynamics (Fisher, 1958; Lande, 1981; Kirkpatrick, 1982). However, research scrutiny has primarily focused on identifying conditions that favor rapid elaboration of sexual traits and preferences, possibly because of the interest that such extreme and seemingly maladaptive phenotypes stimulate. In contrast, sexual trait loss has remained understudied despite being commonly observed (Weins, 2001).

Among the few well-studied examples of sexual trait loss are phrynosomatid lizards that have repeatedly lost sexually-dimorphic color patterns, apparently due to countervailing natural selection pressure (Weins, 1999), and a species of swordtail fish, *Xiphophorus continens*, in which males have lost their swords (Morris, Moretz, Farley, & Nicoletto, 2005). Adaptive evolution via trait loss where the lost trait is not a sexual ornament or preference is a broadly-observed phenomenon, with well-known examples occurring in cave-dwelling organisms that have lost sight due to under-expression of eye pigment or wholesale loss of eye structures (Lavoie, Helf, & Poulson, 2007; Jeffery, 2009). The recurrent and variable evolutionary loss of an acoustic mate recognition signal in Hawaiian crickets is a similar example of "breaking things to make them better".

It is worth probing the nuances of what, exactly, evolved loss of behavior constitutes: must all constitutive components of a behavior such as morphology, neurophysiological responses, hormonal state, and movement patters be lost for the behavior to be considered lost, or is the evolutionary loss of just one of these integrated components of a behavioral phenotype sufficient to consider the behavior "lost"? As an example, secondary loss of morphology in cave-dwelling organisms discussed above is relatively easy to define and therefore encode in comparative evolutionary studies. Similarly, coloration, or lack thereof, in phrynosomatid lizards can be readily quantified. At a more basic biological level, entire genes are commonly lost (Albalat & Cañestro, 2016; Sharma, Hecker, Roscito, Foerster, & Langer, 2018), and even if gene sequence is preserved, gene function may be lost due to disrupted expression (Monroe, McKay, Weigel, & Flood, 2021). However, defining what constitutes the evolved loss of behavior is likely to be as difficult as defining what behavior is in the first place—something even behavioral ecologists do not agree upon (Levitis, Lidicker, & Freund, 2011) and which is particularly salient in the case of silent crickets. Acoustic signals are an emergent property of coordinated physiological states, morphological structures, and movements in an individual animal. As such, it is ambiguous whether evolved signal loss by definition represents a loss of behavior; the answer depends on whether animal communication is considered to be a behavior in and of itself. In this review, we treat cricket acoustic signals as behaviors but also explore the advantages and disadvantages of partitioning behaviors into constitutive morphological, physiological, or movement-based components to better understand their evolution. Such definitional problems might contribute to the relative lack of literature on evolved loss of behavior, but they are unlikely to be the entire explanation (Rayner, Sturiale, & Bailey, 2022). Nor is a genuine scarcity of evolved behavioral trait loss likely to be the explanation. As complex, multifactorial, context-dependent traits, behaviors likely represent large mutational targets for loss-of-function changes at the genomic level.

Determining when a behavior has been evolutionarily lost may be uniquely difficult due to the inherent reversibility of behavior's expression. For example, a species in which no individual expresses a particular behavioral phenotype may be incapable of expressing it under any circumstances, or it may simply not encounter the circumstance required to release its expression during a researcher's investigation. This makes negative evidence more difficult to correctly interpret. A tantalizing hint that behaviors can remain 'hidden', encoded in the genome of a species but not expressed, comes from a North American field cricket, *Gryllus ovisopis*, in which vestigial male advertisement song that it does not normally produce can be provoked by administering the neurotransmitter acetylcholine (Gray, Hormozi, Libby, & Cohen, 2018).

Another issue arises when considering mechanisms of behavioral trait loss. In Hawaiian *T. oceanicus*, male acoustic sexual advertisement behavior has technically been lost: some males no longer produce a normal song or any song at all. However, it is arguable whether the signal constitutes the behavior that has been lost, or whether signaling behavior in this system should be strictly defined as the movement of structures by which form—here, the stridulatory and resonating structures on the forewing—is transformed into function—the signal. The difference is not purely semantic. Although they produce no audible song (Zuk et al., 2006), flatwing males retain the ability to stridulate and do so as often and in the same temporal pattern as males who produce the typical, ancestral song, despite the energetic costs involved (Schneider, Rutz, Hedwig, & Bailey,

2018; Rayner, Schneider, & Bailey, 2020). The mechanisms by which behaviors are evolutionary lost may influence the likelihood of certain downstream evolutionary consequences, such as re-emergence of the behavior at a later time, release of cryptic variation that facilitates diversification, or evolutionary transformation into a novel signal. The complex, integrated properties of male song in Hawaiian *T. oceanicus* create conceptual challenges for researchers, but also opportunities to clarify fundamental questions in behavior and evolutionary biology.

We focus on three major themes that have been informed by the study of what we refer to as *adaptive breakage*. These are: (1) behavior's role in adaptive evolution; (2) how behavior connects form and function to create animal signals; and (3) factors that promote massively parallel adaptive evolution. For each theme, we describe the state of the field and provide context for the work, then highlight insights gleaned from the Hawaiian cricket-fly system. This now textbook example (Dugatkin, 2020) of sexual signal loss has sparked a broad body of work in fields from genomics to animal behavior and serves as an example of the value of interdisciplinary, diverse, long-term collaborations for modern behavioral research. We conclude with a synthesis of the biggest insights and surprises arising from research on (mostly) silent Hawaiian crickets and advocate for the value of long-term studies in wild insects.

2. Behavior's role in adaptive evolution

The question of whether behavior has evolutionary consequences that are different from those of morphological or physiological traits has intrigued biologists for centuries. Wcislo (2021) points out that the idea that behavior is important in the pace of evolution was sidelined for over a century after Baldwin (1896) and others suggested it, and only in the last decade or two is experiencing a resurgence. It is not clear why the problem has been so difficult to tackle, or why it was ignored. Perhaps it is easier to slip into anthropomorphic language about behavior, so that even Darwin's (1871) ordinarily careful language about adaptation is peppered with phrases about beauty and females admiring males when he proposed sexual selection. Such a difference in the way that behavior and morphology are discussed may also have contributed to the notion that behavior is different from other traits. Because behavior is ephemeral, it can also be difficult to study, or to envision as the target of selection.

2.1 Current evidence: Support (or not) for general principles

Behavior is like other traits: subject to the interaction between genes and the environment (Zuk & Spencer, 2020). This means that behavior evolves like those other traits, and both behavior and plasticity in general can be both a cause and a consequence of evolutionary change (Wcislo, 2021). Behavior does nevertheless have some interesting characteristics that are important for considering how it influences the rate of evolution or the establishment of novel traits. For example, the time delay between the expression of causative genes and the execution of a downstream behavior can mean that behavior regulates the rate at which traits are subject to selection. This "behavior-first" scenario means that in some cases behavior precedes the evolution of other characteristics (West-Eberhard, 2003).

Behavior and morphology are, of course, closely connected, with physical attributes needing to be able to accommodate the evolution of behavior; as West-Eberhard (2003, p. 180) notes, "You cannot move an arm until you have one." Novel traits may also require pre-existing behavior, such as tail vibration in snakes serving as a prerequisite for the evolution of rattles (Carscadden, Batstone, & Hauser, 2023). Wcislo (2021) points out that the analogy of behavior merely as a "pacemaker" is incomplete, because it contains only the notion that behavior regulates the rate, rather than the direction, of evolution.

Behavior can thus be considered a component of phenotypic plasticity, although that connection has not always been made in the literature (Wund & Stevens, 2023). Echoing the notion of behavior as leading the way, several authors have proposed that such plasticity in general paves the way for evolution, so that animals respond to a change in selection pressure via plasticity, enabling a path toward eventual genetic evolution (references in Wund & Stevens, 2023). Under this scenario, the plasticity buys time, so to speak, until genetic change can occur. Alternatively, one can imagine that because plasticity can accommodate environmental changes without more permanent genetic changes, further adaptation never occurs (Wund & Stevens, 2023).

Either way, behavior acts as the meeting point between an individual's physiological state and outside stimuli, or as Wund and Stevens (2023, p. 357) note, "Behavior is the interface between internal and external conditions and is therefore responsive to all environmental changes, no matter the source." This means that behavioral responses to anthropogenic change may be particularly important in determining whether native populations persist or invasive ones succeed (Ruland & Jeschke, 2020). Invasive species have prompted behavioral changes in taxa including mammals, birds and insects (Ruland & Jeschke, 2020). Understanding behavior's role in the rate and direction of evolution of a broad variety of traits thus has practical implications for conservation of biodiversity.

How can behavior favor the establishment of a novel trait? Following Zuk, Bastiaans, Langkilde, and Swanger (2014), we suggest that, perhaps obviously, the behavior and the trait need to occur in the same generation. The trait then needs to be favored by selection, so that individuals with the novel trait also exhibit behavior that supports it. Finally, the selection favoring the novel trait needs to persist over a sufficient number of generations to allow the novel trait to spread.

Note that we do not necessarily think novel traits must be rare; as long as a heritable change in a trait allows its bearer to thrive under a new set of environmental circumstances, it can be considered novel (Zuk et al., 2014; Moczek, Cruickshank, & Shelby, 2006; Prum, 2005). Carscadden et al. (2023) emphasize the non-homologous nature of novel traits, such that the novelty arises because of the absence of similar structures in an ancestral lineage. Novel traits in sympatric populations can also play a role in hybridization, particularly if the trait is important in mate recognition (Carscadden et al., 2023).

Other examples of behavior facilitating the establishment of evolutionary change include escape behavior in fence lizards following exposure to a novel predator and several alterations in locomotion and reproduction in cane toads introduced to Australia, where toads at the leading edge of the dispersal wave are large with longer legs and can move faster under controlled conditions (Shine & Baeckens, 2023). Dung beetles reared at high temperatures changed their brood ball characteristics, which then influenced offspring fitness, potentially buffering the species from the effects of climate change (Kirkpatrick & Sheldon, 2022). Life history related behaviors, such as those concerned with dispersal, predator avoidance, thermoregulation, and of course reproduction, appear to be most likely to facilitate lasting evolutionary change (Zuk et al., 2014). In our case, the Hawaiian populations of *T. oceanicus* offer a compelling system for the study of the effects of behavior on the evolution of novel traits, because a behavior (calling) is obligately linked to an aspect of morphology (the structure of the wings).

2.2 Insights from Hawaiian crickets

How do these principles about the role of behavior in evolution and the establishment of novel traits manifest in our system? From the outset, it was puzzling that flatwing males could persist, given their obvious disadvantage in both attracting females and courting them. Our initial work (Zuk et al., 2006) showed that they were differentially phonotactic, approaching a playback more readily than normal-wing males, which should facilitate finding females—but why? It seemed unlikely, to say the least, that another concomitant genetic change that altered ability of males to respond to other males happened to appear. We suggested instead that pre-existing behavioral plasticity enabled flatwings to become established (Bailey & Zuk, 2008b; Bailey, McNabb, & Zuk, 2008; Bailey, Gray, & Zuk, 2010; Tinghitella, Wang, & Zuk, 2009; Zuk et al., 2014). If crickets in general respond to differences in the acoustic environment by altering the degree to which they are able to find one another by alternative means, that behavior could help crickets in a silent world where flatwing males predominate.

The basic premise is simple: say the crickets have internal algorithms about how to respond to different environmental conditions, the way that developmental phenotypic plasticity enables toads to develop into different morphs depending on the available water. For the crickets, if the world is silent, imagine that males perceive a low population density and hence lower mate availability. In that case, it is advantageous to be more responsive to calls that do occur and to behave as a satellite, the males adopting the latter strategy staying nearer signaling individuals as a way to increase encounter rates with females (Brockmann, Oliviera, & Taborsky, 2008; Kasumovic & Brooks, 2011). Such an alternative reproductive tactic is common among animals, including crickets (Cade, 1981; Hissmann, 1990; Bent & Hedwig, 2023). For the females, a similar rule of thumb could apply, with increased responsiveness and decreased discrimination among potential mates arising as a consequence of hearing few callers. In both situations, the result is a greater clumping of flatwings around the few remaining callers, which facilitates encounters between females and the silent males. This plasticity might be pre-existing because the acoustic environment of crickets is expected to be variable—a catastrophic event such as a storm or habitat degradation could temporarily result in a relatively silent environment, as well as more ordinary processes causing variation in the operational sex ratio could such as differences in eclosion or maturation rates. Crickets that responded to such changes in their surroundings would have higher reproductive success than those that had a more fixed threshold for phonotaxis. This in turn means that behavioral flexibility can provide the scaffolding for new mutations to take hold.

We and others have tested the idea that the acoustic environment in which crickets became adults helped determine their later behavior. Males reared in silence move toward a playback of calling song faster than those reared with sound (Bailey et al., 2010). This difference was amplified in older males, providing further support for the idea that responsiveness is malleable during an individual's lifetime (Bailey et al., 2010). Females reared in silence similarly respond more quickly to playback and move closer to the speaker than those reared in incubators playing conspecific song (Bailey & Zuk, 2008a). In addition, females reared in silence are less choosy about the quality of the song to which they respond (Bailey & Zuk, 2008b).

How rearing environment interacts with genetic changes in the crickets other than the *flatwing* mutation itself is still an open question. Flatwing males show different gene expression patterns than normal-wing male crickets, and although both flatwings and normal-wings are sensitive to their acoustic environment, crickets carrying the *flatwing* genotype appear to be more sensitive (Pascoal et al., 2018; Zhang et al. revision in review) and differences remain. For example, flatwing males discriminate among different songs in much the same way as females, moving closer to a speaker playing the same combination of song characteristics preferred by females (Olzer & Zuk, 2018). Normal-wing males showed no such preference, despite being reared in the same environment as the flatwing males in the experiment (Olzer & Zuk, 2018).

3. Behavior links signal, form, and function

Many traits with significant fitness consequences involve the coordinated expression of underlying morphological components (*forms*) with physiology, neurological sensory systems, and behavior to produce phenotypes with a specific consequence to the organism upon which selection acts (trait 'functions', sensu Bock, 1980; Arnold, 1983; Losos, 2011; e.g. Alfaro, Bolnick, & Wainwright, 2005; Grether, Kolluru, & Nersissian, 2004). Though selection ultimately acts on total fitness, the nature of form-function relationships has long been argued to have important evolutionary consequences (Thompson, 1917). For example, phenotypic integration, or the manner in which different traits covary, can be influenced by genetic architecture and developmental constraints, and impact evolutionary trajectories (Wagner & Altenberg, 1996; Wagner, Pavlicev, & Cheverud, 2007).

Consider a simple hypothetical scenario, in which we imagine two separate cell layers in a butterfly wing containing different pigments that additively dictate function, in this case color (or signal value; described in Gallagher et al., 2022 and inspired by Rutowski, Macedonia, Morehouse, & Taylor-Taft, 2005). Of course, things can be much more complex. What if many pigments and cell types were to interact to determine wing coloration, and thus there were several pigment combinations that could produce similar signal values (many-to-one-mapping)? Or if signal components were produced through shared genetic architecture, and thus their effects were not simply additive? Finally, what if the perceived color of the wing display depended upon the behavior of the signaler (Stuart-Fox, Ospina-Rozo, Ng, & Franklin, 2021)? Sexual signals offer fertile ground for examining the consequences of such variation in form-function relationships, as they often include multiple sensory components (Elias, Hebets, Hoy, & Mason, 2005; Hebets & Papaj, 2005; Mullen et al., 2007), each of which is produced by underlying morphology (Hebets et al., 2016). Thus, signal evolution might proceed through modifications of the relationships between form and function.

3.1 State of the field

Investigating the emergence of new cricket morphs in Hawaiian *T. oceanicus* populations from morphological (form), acoustic (function), and fitness (mate and predator attraction) perspectives has yielded important insights into how form-function relationships contribute to sexual signal divergence. The wholescale rewiring of such form-function relationships (for instance through the gain, loss or alteration of underlying forms) can even facilitate the evolution of phenotypes that exist in new ecological space (Heard & Hauser, 1995; Mayr, 1960; Simpson, 1984; Wainwright, 2007; Gallagher et al., 2022). Across African starling species, for instance, three distinct modifications to ancestral solid rod-shaped melanosomes (pigment-bearing organelles responsible for the colorful iridescence of starling feathers) have led to the evolution of brighter and more saturated plumage, and lineages with derived forms show faster rates of signal evolution (Maia, Rubenstein, & Shawkey, 2013). Yet how form-function relationships contribute to the diversification of sexual signals (the emergent sensory characteristics that receivers experience) remains poorly understood (Eliason, 2018).

Animal behavior provides a critical link that connects form and function. To generate cricket song, males repeatedly open and close the wings (stridulate), dragging a guitar pick of sorts (the scraper) on one wing across the teeth of the file on the upper wing. That resonates important veins and structures like the harp and mirror, generating loud pulses of sound at ~5 kHz (Fig. 1A). Wing form thereby generates the emergent signal subject to selection by intended and unintended receivers, like the female crickets and parasitoid flies. The ears of both of these receivers are closely attuned to the auditory frequency of the songs of their cricket mates and hosts, respectively (Robert, Amoroso, & Hoy, 1992). Males who produce no song or attenuated songs when they stridulate have altered signal function.

3.2 Insights from anti-parasitoid cricket adaptations

As described above, silent flatwing males are missing many of the conspicuous wing structures that produce song. They have a vestigial file that is reduced to about 10% of its typical size and relocated on the wing, a dramatically reduced harp, and are often missing the scraper and mirror altogether (Zuk et al., 2006; Fig. 2C). These changes in wing form appear to stem from relatively simple X-linked mutations (Tinghitella, 2008; Pascoal et al., 2014) that feminize the wings. Twenty years ago, when one population on the island of Kauai went quiet, we might never have imagined the evolutionary opportunity generated by the maintenance of stridulation in flatwing males; if some sound-generating structures were to re-emerge or wing components to change such that they contact one another in a different way, those changes in form might restore signaling ability (Bailey et al., 2019).

The collective repeated sampling of Hawaiian *T. oceanicus* populations by our labs before and after the evolution of flatwing males has allowed us to capture the evolution of at least half a dozen male cricket morphs in real time, each of which produces variable, attenuated, or no song as a result of modified wing structures (Fig. 2). The morphological diversity in these populations is now large— known modifications to form include changes in wing size, overall wing shape, and discrete changes to multiple wing structures that generate song. But when they are audible, what do these males' songs sound like? And are they attractive to intended and/or unintended receivers?

For two of the new morphs, purring and rattling, we have a fairly well-developed understanding of how form-function relationships have been reconfigured during this burst of increased signal variation. In 2017, 14 years after the discovery of flatwing, one new morph was discovered on the neighboring island of Molokai (Tinghitella et al., 2018; Fig. 2B). These purring male *T. oceanicus* have wing structures strikingly similar to those of flatwing males from Oahu (Tinghitella et al., 2018; Gallagher et al., 2022; Fig. 2C), but when they stridulate they produce an audible, attenuated song (Tinghitella et al., 2018; Gallagher et al. in press, Fig. 3F). Purring songs have higher dominant frequency and are much quieter and more broadband than the typical ancestral *T. oceanicus* song generated by normal-wing males, giving them a noisy, rather than tonal quality (Tinghitella et al., 2018; Fig. 3). Gallagher et al. (2022) compared the wings of males collected in Wailua, Kauai between 2015 and 2019 when purring was observed to increase in frequency in Wailua. They found one striking morphological change—in 2015 none of the Wailua males had a scraper, whereas 60% had a scraper in 2019, suggesting that purring males may be flatwing males who regained the scraper. If so, a simple loss of structure eliminated the signaling function of the crickets' wing and a seemingly simple gain of structure reinstated signaling, but with changed function (given the dramatically different properties of purring and the typical ancestral song).

At nearly the same time, rattling males were discovered on the Big Island of Hawaii in Hilo (Gallagher et al., 2022; Fig. 2B), which has historically contained an overwhelming majority of typical normal-wing males (Zuk, Bailey, Gray, & Rotenberry, 2018). Like purring, rattling males produce an attenuated song that is higher in frequency, quieter and more broadband than the typical song (but less so than purring; Gallagher et al., 2022). However, morphometric landmarking approaches revealed no differences in wing morphology between rattling and typical ancestral males, despite clearly different signal properties. More detailed three-dimensional microscopy of the underside of the wing revealed that, instead, a key component of the cricket stridulatory apparatus had been modified; rattling males possess distinct gaps in the teeth of the file (Gallagher et al., 2022, Fig. 3E,G).

Gallagher et al. (2022) combined the detailed morphometric wing analyses described above with bioacoustic investigation of calling and courtship songs across six Hawaiian populations to understand whether and how male signal diversification proceeds through changes to form–function relationships. They tested two hypotheses. The first hypothesis, 'form–function continuity', was that diversification of sexual signals occurs without disruption to form–function relationships; it predicted that wing morphology and song characteristics covary similarly across morphs. The second hypothesis, 'form–function decoupling', was that adaptive evolution might rewire form–function relationships; it predicted different relationships between wing morphology and song characteristics among different morphs. Results supported the latter. Form–function relationships were nonlinear across male types, indicating that males produce different sexual signals through different relationships between wing and song (Gallagher et al., 2022).

Simultaneous with the discovery of purring and rattling, several other morphs have arisen throughout Hawaii. Rayner et al. (2019) discovered and described two of these, curly-wing and small-wing (Fig. 2B,C; Fig. 3A–C). Curly-wing males have wings that peel up, preventing the structures on the wings that produce song from engaging with one another in the typical manner (Rayner et al., 2019) (Fig. 3A). The degree of curliness varies, and can range from minor flaring at the wing margins to tightly scrolled, crozier-like structures involving most of the wing (Rayner et al., in review). Curly-wing male songs are lower in amplitude than typical *T. oceanicus* song (Rayner et al., 2019). Small-wing males have small forewings approximately two-thirds the size of wild-type males, and sing courtship songs with varied song properties; some below the level of atmospheric noise, some on par with typical courtship song amplitudes, but most with reduced song amplitude (Rayner et al., 2019; Zhang et al., 2024) (Fig. 3B,C). That small-wing males can retain normal-wing venation but on a much smaller scale suggests this may be an example of innovation via form–function continuity. In the latest development, we discovered males whose wings show normal venation save for the complete or near-complete loss of the stridulatory file (Figs. 2B, 3D). Many of these 'defiled-wing' males cannot produce any sound, and those that do generate a highly attenuated, broadband scratching noise (Bailey & Dukas, *pers obs.*) They were first characterized in laboratory stock derived from Oahu, and the phenotype has been detected in the corresponding wild population. Relationships between morphology and emergent sexual signals thus have been rewired in different ways for each new *T. oceanicus* morph: flatwing males lost sound-producing structures, purring males may have regained the scraper restoring sound where there once was none, small-wing males have reduced overall wing size, curly-wing males have a change in curvature of the wing, and the modification of an existing structure (the file) has allowed rattling males to produce attenuated song.

Intriguingly these new morphs are also either spreading across the Hawaiian archipelago or have evolved repeatedly (as with flatwing; Pascoal et al., 2014; Rayner et al., in review; see below). Purring is now found in five populations across three islands (Tinghitella et al., 2021) (Fig. 2A) and the morphological and acoustic characteristics of purring songs already differ across island populations, suggesting either rapid divergence, repeated emergence of the morph (as with flatwing, see below), or environmental/developmental influences (Gallagher, Zonana, Broder, Syammach, & Tinghitella, 2023). Similarly, curly-wing occurs on at least three islands and in a multitude of populations (Rayner et al., in review) (Fig. 2A). There is notable variation in the proportion of males within each morph that cannot produce any audible signal, versus those that can produce an altered signal of decreased amplitude. All purring males purr, by definition. However, not all curly-wing or small-wing males can produce sound (Rayner et al., 2019, in review). Whether the ability to generate any audible sound at all from modified wings is influenced by genes, developmental instability, the environment, or all of the above remains to be determined.

Questions about the performance of novel morphs (how they fare in the contexts of mate location and eavesdropping parasitoids) are also being addressed, including in field-based experiments conducted across the Hawaiian archipelago. Intriguingly, like the silencing flatwing mutation (Zuk et al., 2006), the songs produced by each of the recently discovered morphs—when they can produce any acoustic signal at all—provide signaling males protection from the primary eavesdropper, *O. ochracea* (Rayner et al., 2019; Gallagher et al., 2022; Gallagher et al., revision in review). The novel sound producing morphs, however, may have an advantage over silent flatwing males because their attenuated songs can be used as signals in mating contexts and are attractive to females (to varying degrees; Tinghitella et al., 2018; Tinghitella et al., 2021; Gallagher et al., 2022; Gallagher et al., revision in review). Recently evolved *T. oceanicus* morphs thus appear to be alternative evolutionary solutions to a shared set of natural and sexual selection pressures. Our repeated sampling in key island populations has also revealed that the presence of different morphs and relative morph abundance within populations is highly dynamic. We are beginning to learn not only how each morph individually balances the natural and sexual selection pressures, but how they fare in direct competition with one another when multiple morphs are present in one location and at varying frequencies. For instance, in one population on the Big Island of Hawaii, rattling, small-wing, curly-wing, and typical normal-wing crickets are found on the same lawns. This population has experienced recent fluctuations in morph composition that seem to reflect our understanding of each morph's relative performance in mate location and parasitism contexts (Gallagher et al., revision in review). Long term mesocosm studies and continued regular field sampling will add to our growing understanding of how selection on novel male songs (and thus their underlying form-function relationships) varies across realistic socio-sexual contexts.

4. Rapid convergent adaptation: Causes and consequences

Biologists increasingly appreciate that convergent evolution is a general rule, rather than exception, to explaining the origins of similar adaptations across the tree of life (Orgogozo, 2015). In Hawaiian *T. oceanicus*, the proliferation of male–silencing solutions that have evolved in response to the selective problem of eavesdropping parasitoids confirms this view—implying that if one were to 'replay life's tape' à la Gould (1991), one might expect a predictable series of events to unfold during the process of adaptation to lethal eavesdropping parasitoids. Indeed, the system represents an optimal natural laboratory for experimentally replaying that tape, because different populations are currently experiencing different stages of adaptive evolution due to the variable timing of protective morph emergence (Zuk et al., 2006; Zuk et al., 2018; Tinghitella et al., 2018; Rayner et al., 2019; Zhang et al., 2021; Gallagher et al., 2023).

The detection of rapid, widespread, multifarious, parallel evolution in *T. oceanicus* prompts some questions that we explore in the following sections. What conditions permit this seemingly extraordinary outcome in Hawaiian *T. oceanicus* that do not exist, and therefore do not permit it, in other parasitised populations of crickets in the fly's non-Hawaiian range? How has it happened so (apparently) quickly, and why are there not one, or two, but at least six unique male-protective phenotypes? What is the role of standing variation versus *de novo* mutation? Do the patterns we see of recurrent adaptive trait loss violate the received wisdom that gene flow inhibits convergent evolution? And what if the detection of so many instances of sexual signal loss is a case of finding something simply because you are looking for it, not because it is particularly extraordinary or rare? Prompted by these questions, ongoing investigations into the functional and genetic bases of convergent song loss in *T. oceanicus* have shed light on wider issues about evolvability and evolutionary potential (Wagner & Altenberg, 1996; McGhee, 2011), and new findings are coalescing around the idea that *adaptive breakage* of behavior is not only a potent mechanism of adaptation, but also a driver of diversification.

4.1 Convergent evolution of behavior

Convergent evolution, which we define as evolution of the same functional adaptation in two different lineages with divergent ancestral states, is arguably most readily (and therefore commonly) studied in the context of physiological or morphological traits as opposed to behavior, for example venom in cobras (Kazandjian, Petras, Robinson, van Thiel, & Greene, 2021), limb length in lizards (Sanger, Revell, Gibson-Brown, & Losos, 2012), and coloration in rodents and other vertebrates (Hoekstra, 2006). This apparent research bias might arise for many of the same reasons that make behavior itself challenging to quantify; the latter is highly reversible, context-dependent, and by definition ephemeral. A behavioral trait's absence in a particular lineage might be because it has been evolutionarily lost from the gene pool, but a more prosaic explanation is that the behavior is retained but not measured in conditions that release its expression (Gray et al., 2018; Rayner et al., 2022).

Convergent evolution contrasts with a situation in which ancestral adaptation is shared by divergent lineages because it has been retained by each through the process of evolutionary divergence (Stern, 2013). It also contrasts with the slightly different, but equally important, process of parallel evolution (Stern, 2013). Parallelism occurs when lineages with a shared genetic background due to common ancestry acquire adaptations with the same function, not as a result of retained ancestral variation but as a result of independent mutations with similar functional outcomes. The key difference is whether trait evolution in isolated lineages converges on the same functional solution to selection from *different* genetic starting points, or converges to a new state under selection despite *similar* genetic starting points. The latter process might also occur through recurrent reversals, that is, mutations that cause traits in different lineages to converge in function due to independent back-mutations to an original shared ancestral state, which appears to have occurred for many sexually-selected traits (Weins, 2001).

To explore the implications of adaptive breakage of cricket song, it is necessary to consider how convergence of behavior does or does not differ from other forms of convergence. Much of the apparent complexity of behavior arises from the fact that it generally involves movement of at least part of an animal's body, requiring coordination of form, physiology, and neural processes sensitive to environmental context, and in many cases modification via learning. The interaction of these subcomponents has been argued to make behavioral traits particularly susceptible to evolutionary dynamics arising from socio-environmental feedback, which may alter their evolutionary trajectories in a different manner compared to other traits (see Bailey et al., 2017 and references therein). However, behavior's complexity is not inscrutable, and the fields of ethology and related disciplines have long examined behavioral traits as discrete, measurable, and evolvable; arguably this was the field of ethology's greatest insight of the 20th century (Lorenz, 1954; Zuk & Spencer, 2020). And yet, behavior's notorious complexity provides opportunities to understand how different levels of biological organization interact to produce convergent phenotypic outcomes (Gallant & O'Connell, 2020). Convergent flight loss in paleognathous birds, which include ostriches, rheas, and moas, has occurred numerous times due to different patterns of regulatory evolution (Sackton, Grayson, Cloutier, Hu, & Liu, 2019). In other cases, behavioral convergence has been detected at physiological levels. Consider parental egg provisioning in toxic dendrobatid and mantellid frogs. These lineages are separated by approximately 140 million years, yet egg provisioning behavior shows distinctive neurotransmitter profiles in shared brain regions (Fischer, Roland, Moskowitz, Vidoudez, & Ranaivorazo, 2019).

4.2 Parallel evolution and adaptive breakage in Hawaiian crickets

Convergence of behavior can be studied at many levels, from phenotypic to genetic, but genetic information is ultimately required to differentiate independent mutational origins of adaptations from shared common ancestry, and to tease apart the roles of standing variation, *de novo* mutation, and gene flow (Stern, 2013). Genomic resources have been developed for *T. oceanicus* that permit such investigations, including the first published, annotated reference genome for a cricket scaffolded to chromosome-level linkage groups (Pascoal, Risse, Zhang, Blaxter, & Cezard, 2020). Improvements thereafter have tracked technical developments in next-generation sequencing technologies (e.g. Zhang et al., revision in review). One of the features of this way of working—of developing resources from scratch in non-model organisms—is that technical limitations often necessitate conceptual discipline in experimental design and inference. For example, although gene editing and transcription interference technologies such as transcription activator-like effector nucleases (Watanabe, Noji, & Mito, 2014) and RNAi (Takekata, Matsuura, Goto, Satoh, & Numata, 2012) have been available in field crickets for some time now, reliable CRISPR/Cas9 genome-editing procedures in crickets has blossomed relatively recently, and principally among groups addressing questions in evolutionary developmental genetics (Barry, Nakamura, Matsuoka, Straub, & Horch, 2019; Ohde, Mito, & Niimi, 2022).

The quest is underway to identify causal genetic variants underlying altered wing morphology in *T. oceanicus*. From the first investigations using the basic technique of bulked segregant analysis with restriction site associated DNA markers (RAD tags), it became apparent that flatwing morphology has evolved via more than one independent mutational event (Pascoal et al., 2014). This finding has since been confirmed and expanded, and the development of flatwing morphology is strongly associated with downregulated expression of the gene *doublesex* (Zhang et al., 2021). *Doublesex* has widely-studied and well-known roles in the development of sexually dimorphic traits in insects, from neural patterning that establishes sex-specific behavior in *Drosophila* (Rideout, Dornan, Neville, Eadie, & Goodwin, 2010) to sexually dimorphic wing pattern mimicry in *Papilio* butterflies (Kunte, Zhang, Tenger-Trolander, Palmer, & Martin, 2015). This critical gene has received negligible research attention in orthopteran insects (Price, Egizi, & Fonseca, 2015). While the involvement of *doublesex* in establishing male-specific wing patterning is unsurprising given its similar mode of action in other insects, what is surprising is the variability of mutational inputs affecting this locus that have resulted in three flatwing phenotypes in populations on three different Hawaiian islands (Zhang et al., 2021). Our findings point to a genomic hotspot of adaptation underlying the recurrent emergence of protective flatwing morphs, which is important because it explains why parallel adaptation to the fly is rife despite extensive and ongoing gene flow among islands.

If gene flow routinely introduces adaptive variants to populations under shared fly pressure, then evolutionary novelties would be expected to be out-competed by established adaptive variants (Sackton & Clark, 2019). This has been the explanation for widespread parallel loss of the pelvic girdle in freshwater sticklebacks (*Gasterosteus aculeatus*) through repeated deletions in an enhancer of the *pitx1* gene: fish that invaded separate freshwater lakes subsequently become genetically isolated due to restricted gene flow, and structural fragility of the *pitx1* enhancer sequence has promoted independent mutational reversals under relaxed predator selection (Chan, Marks, Jones, Villarreal, & Shapiro, 2010; Xie, Wang, Thompson, Wucherpfennig, & Reimchen, 2019). Introgression has been similarly invoked to explain widespread parallel evolution during diversification in sticklebacks (Wang, Wang, Cheng, Ding, & Wang, 2023).

The parallelism is not limited to flatwing morphology, however, and additional genetic variants underlying small-wing morphology have been mapped to the X chromosome, and curly-wing morphology appears to have arisen multiple times independently in association with distinct autosomal loci related to copies from the same *serpin* gene family, which are known to cause altered physical wing development in *Drosophila* (Rayner et al., in review). To find such extensive parallel adaptation despite extensive gene flow in Hawaiian crickets would superficially appear to challenge the orthodox view of introgression's role in convergent evolution. And yet, our findings may be explainable by two plausible, non-mutually exclusive situations. The first is that acoustic signaling represents an enormous mutational target, and the second is the possibility that mutational hotspots affect forewing development.

Cricket forewing venation is a key determinant of spectral qualities of male advertisement song across ensiferan taxa (Desutter-Grandcolas & Robillard, 2004), so it stands to reason that the genomic architecture of forewing venation is particularly evolvable given its highly varied and evolutionarily significant role in speciation and diversification across this group (Bailey et al., 2019). This contention is also supported by the observation that acoustic communication is highly evolvable in crickets, which stands to reason given the outsized role of male acoustic signals in mate recognition (Blankers, Lubke, & Hannig, 2015). We should therefore expect to find similar instances of rapid, repeated, and co-occurring parallel adaptation affecting organisms and traits for which loss, rather than gain, is adaptive, and which have played a particularly prominent role in diversification and speciation. Put another way, sexually-selected traits involved in mate recognition systems might be particularly susceptible to parallel evolutionary reversals, a prediction that can be readily tested if and when sufficient empirical data exist across a diversity of study systems.

4.3 Consequences of rapid cricket morph evolution

Callers (normal-wing males) and flatwings coexist because of the persistence and effectiveness of satellite behavior; non-callers, regardless of their wing morphology, can benefit by approaching callers and intercepting phonotactic females. What keeps the system from collapsing as selection favors one or the other tactic? Understanding how the different reproductive tactics of calling vs. acting as a satellite contribute to male reproductive success is difficult to do empirically, whether in the lab or the field, because so many variables contribute to male behavior. Instead, we have used spatially explicit agent-based modeling to explore the relative roles of sex ratio, overall mortality rate, parasitism and other characteristics on the evolution and maintenance of the satellite strategy. A mix of signaling and acting as a satellite for individual males prevailed even with high parasitism risk under conditions of higher background mortality rate, decreasing density, increasing female-biased sex ratio, and increasing female choosiness (Rotenberry, Swanger, & Zuk, 2015). These results suggest that high parasitoid pressure alone would not cause the fixation of satellite behavior. Interestingly, another set of models showed that while satellite behavior counteracted the negative effects of parasitism, it was less important than factors such as female choosiness and the density of females in the population (Rotenberry & Zuk, 2016). Whether and how these factors influence satellite mating strategies when more than one adaptive, sound-reduction morph segregate within a population remain to be seen; the level of complexity is potentially significant given the co-occurrence of numerous morphs at multiple field sites (Fig. 2A), and the co-expression of some morphs, for example in curly-wing flatwing males (Fig. 3A).

Findings arising from two decades of research on (mostly) silent Hawaiian field crickets have in many cases supported longstanding ideas in animal behavior and evolutionary biology. For example, behavioral flexibility clearly facilitated rapid adaptive evolution in this system. Lability of form-function relationships enhances the potential for signal evolution, and sexual signal loss is widespread and has occurred many times independently, likely driven by genomic hotspots of adaptation. But there have also been surprises. Behavioral flexibility turns out to be inseparable from genetic evolution – a property that we suggest is of widespread significance across multiple systems where plasticity is thought to influence evolution. While pre-existing behavioral flexibility helps prevent the extinction of novel adaptations due to drift or counter-selection, behavioral flexibility itself can and does evolve alongside those adaptations (Bailey et al., 2008; Tinghitella et al. 2009; Tinghitella & Zuk, 2009; Bailey & Zuk, 2012; Balenger et al., 2015; Pascoal et al., 2018; Sturiale & Bailey, 2022). Behavior and plasticity are thus not static properties of populations, but evolvable, dynamic traits in and of themselves, so it stands to reason that the behavioral dynamics facilitating or impeding the evolution of new adaptations will not be temporally stable. Testing whether and how variation in behavioral flexibility is genetically coupled with causal variants underlying male-silencing phenotypes will improve our understanding of behavior's role in evolution, for such dynamics can generate evolutionary feedback loops that drive extremely rapid, in some cases almost instantaneous, genetic adaptation (Bailey, Desjonquères, Drago, Rayner, & Sturiale, 2022; Zhang et al., revision in review).

How, exactly, cricket genotypes map to forewing morphology, and how that morphology maps to signal values via behavior, turns out to be a far more complex relationship than might first have been presumed (Gallagher et al., 2022; Gallagher et al., revision in review). The linkages among levels of biological organization in this rapidly-evolving system will depend critically on the nuances of what form, intensity and source of selection each signaling phenotype experiences (Richardson, Heinen-Kay, & Zuk, 2021; Tinghitella et al. 2021; Zhang et al., 2021). Associated or indirect fitness consequences—that is negative pleiotropy—are a large factor in dictating such dynamics, as R. A. Fisher (1950) predicted nearly a century ago and subsequent generations of evolutionary biologists have confirmed (Orr, 2005). Pleiotropy is difficult to demonstrate without the precision afforded by genetic knock-out and knock-in mutants, but it is now well-established that some combination of pleiotropy and genomic hitchiking have genetically associated *flatwing* variants on the X chromosome with traits not directly related to wing morphology, including cuticular hydrocarbon pheromone profiles (Simmons, Thomas, Gray, & Zuk, 2014; Pascoal et al., 2020), reproductive tissue morphology (Bailey et al., 2010; Rayner, Hitchcock, & Bailey, 2021; Richardson et al., 2021); locomotion (Balenger & Zuk, 2015; Sturiale & Bailey, 2022); phenotypic plasticity (Balenger & Zuk, 2015; Pascoal et al., 2018; Zhang et al. revision in review); transcriptome and proteome profiles (Pascoal, Liu, Ly, Fang, & Rockliffe, 2016), dosage compensation (Rayner et al. 2021), and mating behavior (Heinen-Kay, Nichols, & Zuk, 2020). It seems almost certain that additional traits will be found to be indirectly affected by the causal variants underlying flatwing, small-wing, curly-wing morphology and purring and rattling signaling types. It remains to be seen whether these covary in a manner similar to the discrete behavioral and morphological profiles associated with other intrasexual dimorphisms, for example in side-blotch lizards (Sinervo & Lively, 1996), ruff (Küpper, Stocks, Risse, dos Remedios, & Farrell, 2016), and damselflies (Bybee, Córdoba-Aguilar, Duryea, Futahashi, & Hansson, 2016).

5. Synthesis: The value of long-term insect studies in nature

Research integration across groups, fields and subfields has been an important factor driving new conceptual insights from Hawaiian crickets and flies that would not have been gained in the absence of such an approach. Innovative approaches bridging genetics, bioacoustics, morphometrics, and machine learning have been brought to bear on questions about the retained expression of non-functional behavioral motor patterns (Schneider et al., 2018; Rayner et al., 2020); measuring behavior in heterogeneous field settings (Tinghitella et al., 2021), the role of genomic approaches to behavioral feedback during adaptive evolution (Zhang et al., revision in review), and circadian control of signaling behavior (Westwood, Geissmann, O'Donnell, Rayner, & Schneider, in press).

We advocate for more long-term study systems in insects, in nature. Compatively few wild long-term insect study systems exist compared with vertebrates. These include a field cricket (*Gryllus campestris*) population in Spain that has been under constant surveillance via marking and video monitoring for over a decade (Rodríguez-Muñoz, Bretman, Slate, Walling, & Tregenza, 2010), *Heliconius* species, *Papilio* species, and other Central and South American lepidopterans that form a cornerstone of modern speciation and adaptation genomics (Jiggins et al., 2001; Joron, Papa, Beltran, Chamberlain, & Mavarez, 2006), and of course the iconic peppered moth, *Biston betularia* (Cook, 2003). The chief advantage of using insects in long-term studies in the wild is their short generation time compared to most vertebrates, and the spatial scale over which work can be done to address interesting hypotheses. Small, relatively isolated island populations permit consideration of fine-grained landscape-scale investigation where varying connectivity, environmental conditions, and ecological dynamics can be readily addressed. Ongoing work examining the coevolutionary dynamics of *T. oceanicus* and *O. ochracea* is poised to determine the conditions favoring surprising potential for rapid, parallel evolution of adaptations against natural enemies, and test constraints on this evolution in both host and parasitoid. Hawaii might have become a little bit quieter over the last two decades, but its cricket populations are no less crowded with adaptive forms—perhaps not endless—but surprisingly diverse and abundant.

Acknowledgements

The authors gratefully acknowledge funding from the UK Natural Environment Research Council to NWB (Ref. NE/I027800/1, NE/L011255/1, NE/T000619/1, NE/W001616/1), from grants from the US National Science Foundation, the Carper Foundation, the National Geographic Society and the Orthopterists' Society to MZ, and from the US National Science Foundation to RT (Ref. IOS 1846520, IOS 2240950, DEB 2012041). The editors and reviewers provided constructive comments that helped us improve the manuscript. We thank Leigh W Simmons for his longstanding encouragement, as well as the many collaborators, students, postdocs, technical and administrative staff, landowners, and local communities in Hawaii who have generously contributed insight and supported our research over the years. There are too many to enumerate individually, but this collective research effort has been a source of great scientific insight and enriching collaborative connections. Long may they continue.

References

Albalat, R., & Cañestro, C. (2016). Evolution by gene loss. *Nature Reviews: Genetics, 17*, 379–391.

Alfaro, M. E., Bolnick, D. I., & Wainwright, P. C. (2005). Evolutionary consequences of many-to-one mapping of jaw morphology to mechanics in labrid fishes. *American Naturalist, 165*, E140–E154.

Arnold, S. J. (1983). Morphology, performance and fitness. *American Zoologist, 23*, 347–361.

Bailey, N. W., Desjonquères, C., Drago, A., Rayner, J. G., Sturiale, S. L., et al. (2022). A neglected conceptual problem regarding phenotypic plasticity's role in adaptive evolution: The importance of genetic covariance and social drive. *Evolution Letters, 5*, 444–457.

Bailey, N. W., Gray, B., & Zuk, M. (2010). Acoustic experience shapes alternative mating tactics and reproductive investment in male field crickets. *Current Biology, 20,* 845–849.

Bailey, N. W., McNabb, J. R., & Zuk, M. (2008). Preexisting behavior facilitated the loss of a sexual signal in the field cricket *Teleogryllus oceanicus. Behavioral Ecology, 19,* 202–207.

Bailey, N. W., Pascoal, S., & Montealegre-Z, F. (2019). Testing the role of trait reversal in evolutionary diversification using song loss in wild crickets. *Proceedings of the National Academy of Sciences, USA, 116,* 8941–8949.

Bailey, N. W., & Zuk, M. (2008a). Acoustic experience shapes female mate choice in field crickets. *Proceedings of the Royal Society of London, B, 275,* 2645–2650.

Bailey, N. W., & Zuk, M. (2008b). Changes in immune effort of male field crickets infested with mobile parasitoid larvae. *Journal of Insect Physiology, 54,* 96–104.

Bailey, N. W., & Zuk, M. (2012). Socially flexible female choice differs among populations of the Pacific field cricket: geographical variation in the interaction coefficient psi (Ψ). *Proceedings of the Royal Society B: Biological Sciences, 279,* 3589–3596.

Baldwin, J. M. (1896). A new factor in evolution. *American Naturalist, 30*(441–451), 536–553.

Balenger, S. L., & Zuk, M. (2015). Roaming Romeos: Male crickets evolving in silence show increased motor behaviours. *Animal Behaviour, 101,* 213–219.

Barry, S. K., Nakamura, T., Matsuoka, Y., Straub, C., Horch, H. W., et al. (2019). Injecting *Gryllus bimaculatus* eggs. *JOVE—Journal of Visualised Experiments, 150,* e59726.

Bennet-Clark, H. C. (2003). Wing resonances in the Australian field cricket *Teleogryllus oceanicus. Journal of Experimental Biology, 206,* 1479–1496.

Bent, A., & Hedwig, B. (2023). Phonotaxis of male field crickets, *Gryllus bimaculatus,* to conspecific calling song. *Animal Behaviour, 205,* 173–181.

Blankers, T., Lubke, A. K., & Hannig, R. M. (2015). Phenotypic variation and covariation indicate high evolvability of acoustic communication in crickets. *Journal of Evolutionary Biology, 28,* 1656–1669.

Bock, W. J. (1980). The definition and recognition of biological adaptation. *American Zoologist, 20,* 217–227.

Boughman, J. W. (2001). Divergent sexual selection enhances reproductive isolation in sticklebacks. *Nature, 411,* 944–948.

Brockmann, H. J., Oliviera, R. F., & Taborsky, M. (2008). *Integrating mechanisms and function: Prospects for future research. Alternative Reproductive Tactics: An Integrative Approach.* Cambridge, UK: Cambridge University Press.

Broder, E. D., Gallagher, J. H., Wikle, A. W., Venable, C. P., Zonana, D. M., et al. (2022). Behavioral responses of a parasitoid fly to rapidly evolving host signals. *Ecology and Evolution, 12,* e9193.

Broder, E. D., Gallagher, J. H., Wikle, A. W., Welsh, G. T., Zonana, D. M., et al. (2023). A well-studied parasitoid fly of field crickets uses multiple alternative hosts in its introduced range. *Evolutionary Ecology, 37,* 477–492.

Bybee, S., Córdoba-Aguilar, A., Duryea, M. C., Futahashi, R., Hansson, B., et al. (2016). Odonata (dragonflies and damselflies) as a bridge between ecology and evolutionary genomics. *Frontiers in Zoology, 13,* 46.

Cade, W. (1975). Acoustically orienting parasitoids: Fly phonotaxis to cricket song. *Science (New York), 190,* 1312–1313.

Cade, W. (1981). Alternative male strategies: Genetic differences in crickets. *Science (New York), 212,* 536–564.

Carscadden, K. A., Batstone, R. T., & Hauser, F. E. (2023). Origins and evolution of biological novelty. *Biological Reviews, 98,* 1472–1491.

Chan, Y. F., Marks, M. E., Jones, F. C., Villarreal, G., Shapiro, M. D., et al. (2010). Adaptive evolution of pelvic reduction in sticklebacks by recurrent deletion of a *Pitx1* enhancer. *Science (New York), 327,* 302–305.

Cook, L. M. (2003). The rise and fall of the Carbonaria form of the peppered moth. *Quarterly Review of Biology, 78,* 399–417.

Darwin, C. R. (1871). *The descent of man, and selection in relation to sex, 2 vols.* London: John Murray.

Desutter-Grandcolas, L., & Robillard, T. (2004). Acoustic evolution in crickets: Need for phylogenetic study and a reappraisal of signal effectiveness. *Anais de Academia Brasileira Ciências, 76,* 301–315.

Dugatkin, L. A. (2020). *Principles of animal behavior* (4th ed.). Chicago, USA: Chicago University Press.

Elias, D. O., Hebets, E. A., Hoy, R. R., & Mason, A. C. (2005). Seismic signals are crucial for male mating success in a visual specialist jumping spider (Araneae: salticidae). *Animal Behaviour, 69,* 931–938.

Eliason, C. M. (2018). How do complex animal signals evolve? *PLoS Biology, 16,* e3000093.

Feener, D. H., & Brown, B. V. (1997). Diptera as parasitoids. *Annual Review of Entomology, 42,* 73–97.

Fehér, O., Wang, H., Saar, S., Mitra, P. P., & Tchernichovski, O. (2009). *De novo* establishment of wild-type song culture in the zebra finch. *Nature, 459,* 564–568.

Fischer, E. K., Roland, A. B., Moskowitz, N. A., Vidoudez, C., Ranaivorazo, N., et al. (2019). Mechanisms of convergent egg provisioning in poison frogs. *Current Biology, 29,* 4145–4151.

Gallagher, J. H., Zonana, D. M., Broder, E. D., Herner, B. K., & Tinghitella, R. M. (2022). Decoupling of sexual signals and their underlying morphology facilitates rapid phenotypic diversification. *Evolution Letters, 6,* 474–489.

Gallagher, J. H., Zonana, D. M., Broder, E. D., Syammach, A., & Tinghitella, R. M. (2023). A novel cricket morph has diverged in song and wing morphology across island populations. *Journal of Evolutionary Biology, 36,* 1609–1617. https://doi.org/10.1111/jeb.14235.

Gallagher, J. H., Wikle, A. W., Broder, E. D., Durso, C., O'Toole H., & Tinghitella, R. M. *Revision in review.* Surviving the serenade: How conflicting selection pressures shape the early stages of sexual signal diversification. *Evolution; International Journal of Organic Evolution.*

Gallant, J. R., & O'Connell, L. A. (2020). Studying convergent evolution to relate genotype to phenotype. *Journal of Experimental Biology, 223,* jeb213447.

Gillespie, R. G., Croom, H. B., & Palumbi, S. R. (1994). Multiple origins of a spider radiation in Hawaii. *Proceedings of the National Academy of Sciences, USA, 91,* 2290–2294.

Gould, S. J. (1991). *Wonderful life-th10.1073/pnas.91.6.2290e Burgess shale and the nature of history.* New York: WW. Norton & Company,.

Grant, P. R., & Grant, R. B. (2006). Evolution of character displacement in Darwin's finches. *Science (New York), 313,* 224–226.

Gray, D. A., Banuelos, C., Walker, S. E., Cade, W. H., & Zuk, M. (2007). Behavioural specialization among populations of the acoustically orienting parasitoid fly *Ormia ochracea* utilizing different cricket species as hosts. *Animal Behaviour, 73,* 99–107.

Gray, D. A., Hormozi, S., Libby, F. R., & Cohen, R. W. (2018). Induced expression of a vestigial sexual signal. *Biology Letters, 14,* 20180095.

Grether, G. F., Kolluru, G. R., & Nersissian, K. (2004). Individual colour patches as multicomponent signals. *Biological Reviews of the Cambridge Philosophical Society, 79,* 583–610.

Heard, S. B., & Hauser, D. L. (1995). Key evolutionary innovations and their ecological mechanisms. *Historical Biology, 10,* 151–173.

Hebets, E. A., Barron, A. B., Balakrishnan, C. N., Hauber, M. E., Mason, P. H., & Hoke, K. L. (2016). A systems approach to animal communication. *Proceedings of the Royal Society of London, B, 283,* 20152889.

Hebets, E. A., & Papaj, D. R. (2005). Complex signal function: Developing a framework of testable hypotheses. *Behavioral Ecology and Sociobiology, 57*, 197–214.

Heinen-Kay, J. L., Nichols, R. E., & Zuk, M. (2020). Sexual signal loss, pleiotropy, and maintenance of a male reproductive polymorphism in crickets. *Evolution; International Journal of Organic Evolution, 74*, 1002–1009.

Hissmann, K. (1990). Strategies of mate finding in the European field cricket (*Gryllus campestris*) at different population densities: A field study. *Ecological Entomology, 15*, 281291.

Hoekstra, H. E. (2006). Genetics, development and evolution of adaptive pigmentation in vertebrates. *Heredity, 97*, 222–234.

Jeffery, W. R. (2009). Regressive evolution in *Astyanax* cave fish. *Annual Review of Genetics, 43*, 25–47.

Jiggins, C., Naisbit, R., Coe, R., & Mallet, J. (2001). Reproductive isolation caused by colour pattern mimicry. *Nature, 411*, 302–305.

Joron, M., Papa, R., Beltran, M., Chamberlain, N., Mavarez, J., et al. (2006). A conserved supergene locus controls colour patterns diversity in Heliconius butterflies. *PLoS Biology, 4*, 1831–1840.

Kasumovic, M. M., & Brooks, R. C. (2011). It's all who you know: The evolution of socially cued anticipatory plasticity as a mating strategy. *The Quarterly Review of Biology, 86*, 181–197.

Kazandjian, T. D., Petras, D., Robinson, S. D., van Thiel, J., Greene, H. W., et al. (2021). Convergent evolution of pain-inducing defensive venom components in spitting cobras. *Science (New York), 371*, 386–390.

Kirkpatrick, W. H., & Sheldon, K. S. (2022). Experimental increases in temperature mean and variance alter reproductive behaviours in the dung beetle *Phanaeus vindex*. *Biology Letters, 18*, 20220109.

Kunte, K., Zhang, W., Tenger-Trolander, A., Palmer, D. H., Martin, A., et al. (2015). *Doublesex* is a mimicry supergene. *Nature, 507*, 229–232.

Küpper, C., Stocks, M., Risse, J. E., dos Remedios, N., Farrell, L. L., et al. (2016). A supergene determines highly divergent male reproductive morphs in the ruff. *Nature Genetics, 48*, 79–83.

Lavoie, K. H., Helf, K. L., & Poulson, T. L. (2007). The biology and ecology of North American cave crickets. *Journal of Cave and Karst Studies, 69*, 114–134.

Levitis, D. A., Lidicker, Jr, W. Z., & Freund, G. (2011). Behavioural biologists do not agree on what constitutes behaviour. *Animal Behaviour, 78*, 103–110.

Losos, J. B. (2011). Convergence, adaptation, and constraint. *Evolution; International Journal of Organic Evolution, 65*, 1827–1840.

Magnacca, K. N., & Price, D. K. (2015). Rapid adaptive radiation and host plant conservation in the Hawaiian picture wing *Drosophila* (Diptera: Drosophilidae). *Molecular Phylogenetics and Evolution, 92*, 226–242.

Maia, R., Rubenstein, D. R., & Shawkey, M. D. (2013). Key ornamental innovations facilitate diversification in an avian radiation. *Proceedings of the National Academy of Sciences, USA, 110*, 10687–10692.

Mason, A. C., Oshinsky, M. L., & Hoy, R. R. (2001). Hyperacute directional hearing in a microscale auditory system. *Nature, 410*, 686–690.

Mayr, E. (1960). The emergence of evolutionary novelties. *Evolution After Darwin, 349–380.*

McGhee, G. R. (2011). *Convergent evolution: Limited forms most beautiful. Vienna Series in Theoretical Biology.* Cambridge, MA: The MIT Press.

Mendelson, T. C., & Shaw, K. L. (2005). Rapid speciation in an arthropod. *Nature, 433*, 375–376.

Miles, R. N., Robert, D., & Hoy, R. R. (1995). Mechanically coupled ears for directional hearing in the parasitoid fly *Ormia ochracea*. *Journal of the Acoustical Society of America, 98*, 3059–3070.

Moczek, A. P., Cruickshank, T. E., & Shelby, A. (2006). When ontogeny reveals what phylogeny hides: Gain and loss of horns during development and evolution of horned beetles. *Evolution; International Journal of Organic Evolution, 60*, 2329–2341.

Monroe, J. G., McKay, J. K., Weigel, D., & Flood, P. D. (2021). The population genomics of adaptive loss of function. *Heredity, 126*, 383–395.

Montealegre-Z, F., & Robert, D. (2015). Biomechanics of hearing in katydids. *Journal of Comparative Physiology A, 201*, 5–18.

Morris, M. R., Moretz, J. A., Farley, K., & Nicoletto, P. (2005). The role of sexual selection in the loss of sexually selected traits in the swordtail fish *Xiphophorus continens*. *Animal Behaviour, 69*, 1415–1424.

Nosil, P. (2004). Reproductive isolation caused by visual predation on migrants between divergent environments. *Proceedings of the Royal Society of London, B, 271*, 1521–1528.

Ohde, T., Mito, T., & Niimi, T. (2022). A hemimetabolous wing development suggests the wing origin from lateral tergum of a wingless ancestor. *Nature Communications, 13*, 979.

Olzer, R., & Zuk, M. (2018). Obligate, but not facultative, satellite males prefer the same male sexual signal characteristics as females. *Animal Behaviour, 144*, 37–43.

Orgogozo, V. (2015). Replaying the tape of life in the twenty-first century. *Interface Focus, 5*, 20150057.

Orr, H. A. (2005). The genetic theory of adaptation: A brief history. *Nature Reviews: Genetics, 6*, 119–127.

Pascoal, S., Cezard, T., Eik-Nes, A., Gharbi, K., Majewska, J., Payne, E., et al. (2014). Rapid convergent evolution in wild crickets. *Current Biology, 24*, 1369–1374.

Pascoal, S., Liu, X., Ly, T., Fang, Y., Rockliffe, N., et al. (2016). Rapid evolution and gene expression: A rapidly evolving Mendelian trait that silences field crickets has widespread effects on m RNA and protein expression. *Journal of Evolutionary Biology, 29*, 1234–1246.

Pascoal, S., Liu, X., Fang, Y., Paterson, S., Ritchie, M. G., Rockliffe, N., Zuk, M., & Bailey, N. W. (2018). Increased socially mediated plasticity in gene expression accompanies rapid adaptive evolution. *Ecology Letters, 21*, 546–556.

Pascoal, S., Risse, S., Zhang, X., Blaxter, M., Cezard, T., et al. (2020). Field cricket genome reveals the footprint of recent, abrupt adaptation in the wild. *Evolution Letters, 4*, 19–33.

Paur, J., & Gray, D. (2011a). Individual consistency, learning and memory in a parasitoid fly, *Ormia ochracea*. *Animal Behaviour, 82*, 825–830.

Paur, J., & Gray, D. (2011b). Seasonal dynamics and overwintering strategy of the tachinid fly (Diptera: Tachinidae), *Ormia ochracea* (Bigot) in southern California. *Terrestrial Arthropod Reviews, 4*, 145–156.

Price, D. C., Egizi, A., & Fonseca, D. M. (2015). The ubiquity and ancestry of insect doublesex. *Scientific Reports, 5*, 13068.

Prum, R. O. (2005). Evolution of the morphological innovations of feathers. *Journal of Experimental Zoology, 304B*, 570–579.

Qvarnström, A., Pärt, T., & Sheldon, B. C. (2000). Adaptive plasticity in mate preference linked to differences in reproductive effort. *Nature, 18*, 344–347.

Rayner, J. G., Aldridge, S., Montealegre-Z, F., & Bailey, N. W. (2019). A silent orchestra: Convergent song loss in Hawaiian crickets is repeated, morphologically varied, and widespread. *Ecology, 100*, e02694.

Rayner, J. G., Eichenberger, F., Bainbridge, J. V. A., Zhang, S., Zhang, X., Yusuf, L., & Bailey, N. W. (in review). Competing adaptations maintain non-adaptive variation in a wild cricket population. Preprint https://doi.org/10.1101/2023.10.14.562337.

Rayner, J. G., Hitchcock, T. J., & Bailey, N. W. (2021). Variable dosage compensation is associated with female consequences of an X-linked, male-beneficial mutation. *Proceedings of the Royal Society B, 288*, 20210355.

Rayner, J. G., Schneider, W. T., & Bailey, N. W. (2020). Can behaviour impede evolution? Persistence of singing effort after morphological song loss in crickets. *Biology Letters, 16*, 20190931.

Rayner, J. G., Sturiale, S. L., & Bailey, N. W. (2022). The persistence and evolutionary consequences of vestigial behaviours. *Biological Reviews, 97*, 1389–1407.

Rayner, J. G., & Zhang, X. (2021). A mute-point: Genomic hotspots underlie parallel song-loss in crickets. *Nature Ecology and Evolution* Behind the Paper' blog. Jan 05, 2021.

Richardson, J., Heinen-Kay, J. L., & Zuk, M. (2021). Sex-specific associations between life-history traits and a novel reproductive polymorphism in the Pacific field cricket. *Journal of Evolutionary Biology, 34*, 549–557.

Rideout, E. J., Dornan, A. J., Neville, M. C., Eadie, S., & Goodwin, S. F. (2010). Control of sexual differentiation and behaviour by the *doublesex* gene in *Drosophila melanogaster. Nature Neuroscience, 13*, 458–466.

Robert, D., Amoroso, J., & Hoy, R. R. (1992). The evolutionary convergence of hearing in a parasitoid fly and its cricket host. *Science (New York), 258*, 1135–1137.

Rodríguez-Muñoz, R., Bretman, A., Slate, J., Walling, C. A., & Tregenza, T. (2010). Natural and sexual selection in a wild insect population. *Science (New York), 328*, 1269–1272.

Rotenberry, J. T., Swanger, E., & Zuk, M. (2015). Alternative reproductive tactics arising from a continuous behavioral trait: callers versus satellites in field crickets. *The American Naturalist, 185*, 469–490.

Rotenberry, J. T., & Zuk, M. (2016). Alternative reproductive tactics in context: How demography, ecology, and behavior affect male mating success. *The American Naturalist, 188*, 582–588.

Ruland, F., & Jeschke, J. M. (2020). How biological invasions affect animal behaviour: A global, cross-taxonomic analysis. *Journal of Animal Ecology, 89*, 2531–2541.

Rutowski, R. L., Macedonia, J. M., Morehouse, N., & Taylor-Taft, L. (2005). Pterin pigments amplify iridescent ultraviolet signal in males of the orange sulphur butterfly, *Colias eurytheme. Proceedings of the Royal Society of London, BB, 272*, 2329–2335.

Sackton, T. B., & Clark, N. (2019). Convergent evolution in the genomics era: New insights and directions. *Philosophical Transactions of the Royal Society of London, B, 374*, 20190102.

Sackton, T. B., Grayson, P., Cloutier, A., Hu, Z., Liu, J. S., et al. (2019). Convergent regulatory evolution and loss of flight in paleognathous birds. *Science (New York), 364*, 74–78.

Sanger, T. J., Revell, L. J., Gibson-Brown, J. J., & Losos, J. B. (2012). Repeated modification of early limb morphogenesis programmes underlies the convergence of relative limb length in Anolis lizards. *Proceedings of the Royal Society of London, B, 279*, 739–748.

Schneider, W. T., Rutz, C., Hedwig, B., & Bailey, N. W. (2018). Vestigial singing behaviour persists after the evolutionary loss of song in crickets. *Biology Letters, 14*, 20170654.

Sharma, V., Hecker, N., Roscito, J. G., Foerster, L., Langer, B. E., et al. (2018). A genomics approach reveals insights into the importance of gene losses for mammalian adaptations. *Nature Communications, 9*, 1215.

Shine, R., & Baeckens, S. (2023). Rapidly evolved traits enable new conservation tools: Perspectives from the cane toad invasion of Australia. *Evolution; International Journal of Organic Evolution, 77*, 1744–1755.

Sikkink, K. L., Bailey, N. W., Zuk, M., & Balenger, S. L. (2020). Immunogenetic and tolerance strategies against a novel parasitoid of wild field crickets. *Ecology and Evolution, 10*, 13312–13326.

Simmons, L. W., Thomas, M. L., Gray, B., & Zuk, M. (2014). Replicated evolutionary divergence in the cuticular hydrocarbon profile of male crickets associated with the loss of song in the Hawaiian archipelago. *Journal of Evolutionary Biology, 27*, 2249–2257.

Simmons, L. W., Zuk, M., & Rotenberry, J. T. (2001). Geographic variation in female preference functions and male songs of the field cricket *Teleogryllus oceanicus*. *Evolution; International Journal of Organic Evolution, 55*, 1386–1394.

Simpson, G. G. (1984). *Tempo and mode in evolution*. New York: Columbia University Press.

Sinervo, B., & Lively, C. M. (1996). The rock–paper–scissors game and the evolution of alternative male strategies. *Nature, 380*, 240–243.

Smadja, C., & Ganem, G. (2005). Asymmetrical reproductive character displacement in the house mouse. *Journal of Evolutionary Biology, 18*, 1485–1493.

Stern, D. L. (2013). The genetic causes of convergent evolution. *Nature Reviews. Genetics, 14*, 751–764.

Stuart-Fox, D., Ospina-Rozo, L., Ng, L., & Franklin, A. M. (2021). The paradox of iridescent signals. *Trends in Ecology and Evolution, 36*, 187–195.

Sturiale, S. L., & Bailey, N. W. (2022). Within-generation and transgenerational social plasticity interact during rapid adaptive evolution. *Evolution; International Journal of Organic Evolution, 77*, 409–421.

Takekata, H., Matsuura, Y., Goto, S. G., Satoh, A., & Numata, H. (2012). RNAi of the circadian clock gene period disrupts the circadian rhythm but not the circatidal rhythm in the mangrove cricket. *Biology Letters, 8*, 488–491.

Terai, Y., Seehausen, O., Sasaki, T., Takahashi, K., Mizoiri, S., et al. (2006). Divergent selection on opsins drives incipient speciation in Lake Victoria cichlids. *PLoS Biology, 4*, e433.

Thompson, D. W. (1917). *On growth and form*. Cambridge: Cambridge University Press.

Tinghitella, R. M. (2008). Rapid evolutionary change in a sexual signal: Genetic control of the mutation "flatwing" that renders male field crickets (*Teleogryllus oceanicus*) mute. *Heredity, 100*, 261–267.

Tinghitella, R. M., Broder, E. D., Gallagher, J. H., Wikle, A. W., & Zonana, D. M. (2021). Responses of intended and unintended receivers to a novel sexual signal suggest clandestine communication. *Nature Communications, 12*, 797.

Tinghitella, R. M., Broder, E. D., Gurule-Small, G. A., Hallagan, C. J., & Wilson, J. D. (2018). Purring crickets: The evolution of a novel sexual signal. *American Naturalist, 192*, 773–782.

Tinghitella, R. M., Wang, J. M., & Zuk, M. (2009). Preexisting behavior renders a mutation adaptive: Flexibility in male phonotaxis behavior and the loss of singing ability in the field cricket *Teleogryllus oceanicus*. *Behavioral Ecology, 20*, 722–728.

Tinghitella, R. M., & Zuk, M. (2009). Asymmetric mating preferences accommodated the rapid evolutionary loss of a sexual signal. *Evolution; International Journal of Organic Evolution, 63*, 2087–2098.

Vinson, S. B. (1990). How parasitoids deal with the immune system of their host: An overview. *Archives in Insect Biochemistry and Physiology, 13*, 3–27.

Wagner, G. P., & Altenberg, L. (1996). Complex adaptations and the evolution of evolvability. *Evolution, International Journal of Organic Evolution, 50*, 967–976.

Wagner, G. P., Pavlicev, M., & Cheverud, J. M. (2007). The road to modularity. *Nature Reviews. Genetics, 8*, 921–931.

Wainwright, P. C. (2007). Functional versus morphological diversity in macroevolution. *Annual Review of Ecology, Evolution, and Systematics, 38*, 381–401.

Wang, Y., Wang, Y., Cheng, X., Ding, Y., & Wang, C. (2023). Prevalent introgression underlies convergent evolution in the diversification of *Pungitius* sticklebacks. *Molecular Biology and Evolution, 40*, msad026.

Watanabe, T., Noji, S., & Mito, T. (2014). Gene knockout by targeted mutagenesis in a hemimetabolous insect, the two-spotted cricket *Gryllus bimaculatus*, using TALENs. *Methods (San Diego, Calif.), 69*, 17–21.

Wcislo, W. T. (2021). A dual role for behavior in evolution and shaping organismal selective environments. *Annual Review of Ecology, Evolution, and Systematics, 52*, 343–362.

Weins, J. J. (1999). Phylogenetic evidence for multiple losses of a sexually selected character in phrynosomatid lizards. *Proceedings of the Royal Society of London, B, 266*, 1529–1535.

Weins, J. J. (2001). Widespread loss of sexually selected traits: How the peacock lost its spots. *Trends in Ecology and Evolution, 16*, 517–523.

West-Eberhard, M. J. (2003). *Developmental plasticity and evolution*. Oxford: Oxford University Press.

Westwood, M., Geissmann, Q., O'Donnell, A. J., Rayner, J. G., Schneider, W. T., et al. (2023). Machine learning reveals singing rhythms of male Pacific field crickets are clock controlled. *Behavioral Ecology, 35*, arad098 (in press).

Wilson, A. J., Morrissey, M. B., Adams, M. J., Walling, C. A., Guinness, F. E., et al. (2011). Indirect genetics effects and evolutionary constraint: An analysis of social dominance in red deer, *Cervus elaphus.*. *Journal of Evolutionary Biology, 24*, 772–783.

Wilson, A. J., Pilkington, J. G., Pemberton, J. M., Coltman, D. W., Overall, A. D. J., et al. (2005). Selection on mothers and offspring: Whose phenotype is it and does it matter? *Evolution; International Journal of Organic Evolution, 59*, 451–463.

Wund, M. A., & Stevens, I. I., D. R. (2023). An introduction to the Special Issue honouring Susan A. Foster. *Animal Behaviour, 200*, 221–224.

Xie, K. T., Wang, G., Thompson, A. C., Wucherpfennig, J. I., & Reimchen, T. E. (2019). DNA fragility in the parallel evolution of pelvic reduction in stickleback fish. *Science (New York), 363*, 81–84.

Zhang, X., Blaxter, M., Wood, J., Tracey, A., McCarthy, S., Thorpe, P., & Bailey, N.W. Revision in review. Temporal genomics in Hawaiian crickets reveals compensatory intragenomic coadaptation during adaptive evolution.

Zhang, X., Rayner, J. G., & Bailey, N. W. (2024). Rapid sexual signal diversification is facilitated by permissive females. *Current Biology, 34*, 403–409.

Zhang, X., Rayner, J. G., Blaxter, M., & Bailey, N. W. (2021). Rapid parallel adaptation despite gene flow in silent crickets. *Nature Communications, 12*, 50.

Zuk, M., Bailey, N. W., Gray, B., & Rotenberry, J. T. (2018). Sexual signal loss: The link between behaviour and rapid evolutionary dynamics in a field cricket. *Journal of Animal Ecology, 87*, 623–633.

Zuk, M., Bastiaans, E., Langkilde, T., & Swanger, E. (2014). The role of behaviour in the establishment of novel traits. *Animal Behaviour, 92*, 333–344.

Zuk, M., Rotenberry, J. T., & Simmons, L. W. (1998). Calling songs of field crickets (*Teleogryllus oceanicus*) with and without phonotactic parasitoid infection. *Evolution; International Journal of Organic Evolution, 52*, 166–171.

Zuk, M., Rotenberry, J. T., & Tinghitella, R. M. (2006). Silent night: Adaptive disappearance of a sexual signal in a parasitized population of field crickets. *Biology Letters, 2*, 521–524.

Zuk, M., Simmons, L. W., & Cupp, L. (1993). Calling characteristics of parasitized and unparasitized populations of the field cricket *Teleogryllus oceanicus*. *Behavioral Ecology and Sociobiology, 33*, 339–343.

Zuk, M., Simmons, L. W., & Rotenberry, J. T. (1995). Acoustically-orienting parasitoids in calling and silent males of the field cricket *Teleogryllus oceanicus*. *Ecological Entomology, 20*, 380–383.

Zuk, M., & Spencer, H. G. (2020). Killing the behavioral zombie: Genes, evolution, and why behavior isn't special. *Bioscience, 70*, 515–520.

Further readings

Fisher, R. A. (1930). *The genetical theory of natural selection*. Oxford: Oxford University Press.

Lorenz, K. (1941). Vergleichende bewegungstudien an anatinen. *Journal für Ornithologie, 89* (Sonderheft. (Tr. by Martin, R. D. as: Comparative Studies of the Motor Patterns of Anatinae.) In).

Lorenz, K. (1971). *Studies in animal and human behaviour*. London: Methuen.

Pavlicev, M., & Wagner, G. P. (2011). A model of developmental evolution: Selection, pleiotropy and compensation. *Trends in Ecology and Evolution, 27*, 316–322.

CHAPTER THREE

Patterns of host specificity in interactions involving behavioral manipulation of spiders by Darwin wasps

Marcelo O. Gonzaga[a,*], Rafael R. Moura[b], Alexander Gaione-Costa[c], and Thiago G. Kloss[d]

[a]Instituto de Biologia, Universidade Federal de Uberlândia,Uberlândia, MG, Brazil
[b]Núcleo de Extensão e Pesquisa em Ecologia e Evolução (NEPEE), Departamento de Ciências Agrárias e Naturais, Universidade do Estado de Minas Gerais, Ituiutaba, MG, Brazil
[c]Programa de Pós-graduação em Ecologia, Universidade Federal de Viçosa, Viçosa, MG, Brazil
[d]Departamento de Biologia Geral, Universidade Federal de Viçosa, Viçosa, MG, Brazil
*Corresponding author. e-mail address: mogonzaga@yahoo.com.br

Contents

1. Introduction	90
1.1 General patterns of host specificity in parasitoid wasps	91
1.2 Host-parasitoid interactions in the *Polysphincta* group	95
1.3 A brief historical overview of spider-parasitoid interactions	98
1.4 Macroecological perspective of host specificity in polysphinctine wasps	99
2. Methods	101
2.1 Systematic review	101
2.2 Data analysis	103
3. State-of-art and trends in studies of polysphinctine-host interactions	105
4. Patterns of host specificity	107
5. Parasitoid-spider networks	115
6. Factors influencing specificity patterns	127
6.1 Phylogenetic constraints	127
6.2 Web structures, shelters, and other defenses	128
6.3 Morphological and chemical host traits	130
6.4 Variation in the attack behavior of polysphinctine wasps on spiders	132
7. Conclusions	143
Acknowledgements	145
Appendix A. Supporting information	145
References	145

Advances in the Study of Behavior, Volume 56
ISSN 0065-3454, https://doi.org/10.1016/bs.asb.2024.02.002
Copyright © 2024 Elsevier Inc. All rights are reserved, including those for text and data mining, AI training, and similar technologies.

Abstract

Several factors, such as the susceptibility of different host species to the attacks and particular nutritional requirements of the parasitoids, may influence the patterns of host specificity in host-parasitoid interactions. These patterns are relevant in determining the geographic range of parasitoid species and the impacts on their hosts' population dynamics. In this review, we systematically compile the information available on the use of spider hosts by a group of koinobiont parasitoid wasps, the polysphinctines (Ichneumonidae). These wasps are known by the capacity of their larvae to induce behavioral changes in their hosts, obtaining web structures suitable for the attachment and permanence of the cocoons. We present a host-parasitoid network including data on 173 interactions between 143 spider species and 89 wasp species, discussing the factors involved in the determination of host specificity patterns, such as phylogenetic constraints, host defenses, and the variation in the attack behaviors of wasps during host immobilization. We also investigated the longitudinal and latitudinal patterns of distribution of host-parasitoid interactions within the group. Although some polysphinctines establish associations with numerous hosts, there seems to be a high level of specialization, which becomes evident when we consider the connectivity levels in their interaction network and the limited number of spider families they target. Although traits such as the structural pattern of webs and host size do not appear to be critical factors determining specificity, the identification of stereotyped and specific behaviors adjusted for attacking particular hosts reinforces the hypothesis that specificity within this group of koinobiont manipulative parasitoids is influenced by host's defensive strategies. Our analysis demonstrated that the number of hosts and host diversity per polysphinctine species were not influenced by latitudinal variation, which suggests that these parasitoids have limited tolerance for a wide range of abiotic conditions. Finally, a broad longitudinal distribution of the preferential host species may increase the chances for some of these parasitoids to be in contact with other potential suitable hosts, favoring the use of multiple hosts.

1. Introduction

While parasitism is widely recognized as one of the most successful and diverse lifestyles in nature, parasitoidism represents a more restricted and specialized variation of this strategy (Harvey, Kadash, & Strand, 2000; Lafferty, Dobson, & Kuris, 2006). Parasitoidism can be defined as a specialized form of parasitism wherein the parasite feeds on the host's tissues and ultimately kills it to complete its life cycle (Kuris & Lafferty, 2000). While several parasites possess the necessary characteristics to be considered parasitoids, this strategy is predominantly associated with insects included in the orders Hymenoptera and Diptera. These insects often utilize other arthropods as hosts, particularly during the larval stage, for their development within the host's body.

Host specificity is one of the most relevant properties of host-parasitoid interactions, directly determining the interdependence of their population dynamics. It also significantly influences the potential for a parasitoid to expand its geographical distribution and impact populations of new hosts (Andow & Imura, 1994; Novotny et al., 2003). The success of a particular parasitoid species in attacking distinct hosts may include complex morphological, physiological, and behavioral adaptations (Harvey, 2005; Stireman & Singer, 2003). Accordingly, exploiting suboptimal hosts may induce a higher frequency of failures during the larval and pupal stages (Kruitwagen, Beukeboom, Wertheim, & van Doorn, 2021), but it may open a pathway for the evolution of novel host-parasitoid interactions. The degree of specificity may depend on several factors, including for instance: (1) availability and susceptibility of different host species to the attacks; (2) limitations in the ability of parasitoids to accurately locate new hosts in the environment; (3) specific quantitative and qualitative nutritional requirements of the parasitoids; (4) behavioral plasticity of the parasitoids, and the variability of host defenses during the attacks; and (5) presence of physiological barriers and immune responses of hosts. The restrictions to parasitoids — especially endoparasitoids with an inevitable and extended interaction with their host's immune system—for expanding the number of species used as hosts (i.e., host range) often determine strict patterns of host specificity. In turn, the expansion of the host range could be associated with a series of advantages, such as the reduction of intraspecific competition and lower dependence on temporal fluctuations of a specific host availability.

1.1 General patterns of host specificity in parasitoid wasps

All the parasitoid wasps descend from a single endophytic parasitoid ancestor that lived between 289 and 211 mya (Peters et al., 2017). The exploitation of other arthropods as a food source for their larvae has been the dominant lifestyle in Hymenoptera since the late Triassic, and parasitoidism has become a prevailing strategy among a broad range of wasps, playing a significant role in driving the remarkable diversity observed within the group (Blaimer et al., 2023). Several of them have evolved complex life cycles, involving behavioral manipulation of their hosts and symbiotic interactions with polydnaviruses, which can suppress the immune response of lepidopteran larvae (Schaack, Gilbert, & Feschotte, 2010; Webb et al., 2006).

Two distinct developmental strategies of parasitoids, namely koinobiosis and idiobiosis, are usually considered to have a major role in determining their ability to use multiple hosts (Askew & Shaw, 1986). *Koinobiont* parasitoids lay their eggs inside or on the host's body, typically at an early stage of host development. The parasitoid larvae feed on the host's hemolymph and grow with the host as it develops. The host is kept alive for extended periods and can continue to provide nutrients and resources to the developing parasitoid. *Idiobiont* parasitoids, on the other hand, lay their eggs either inside or on the host's body, swiftly incapacitating or terminating it, usually by injecting venom or other harmful substances. The host is then used as a source of nutrients and protection for the parasitoid larvae. This last strategy allows the use of a broader range of host species compared to koinobiont parasitoids, probably because idiobionts do not need to rely on a specific host developmental stage or particular host physiology to complete their development. In addition, as idiobionts do not require a prolonged period of interaction with their hosts, they may be able to rapidly evolve new strategies for finding and attacking novel hosts, or they may be more generalist in their host-searching behaviors (Cuny & Poelman, 2022; Santos & Quicke, 2011). The main limitation, in this case, usually concerns host quality (comprising the total biomass available and nutritional composition) at the oviposition, once all the resources required for the parasitoid development had to be present.

The hypothesis that koinobiont parasitoids present a narrower host range was firstly tested by Askew & Shaw (1986). They studied leaf-mining communities in Great Britain and found that, on average, idiobiont parasitoids attacked 4.2 host families, whereas koinobiont attacked only 1.5 host families (Fig. 1A). Sheehan & Hawkins (1991) compared the host-parasitoid associations involving two subfamilies of Ichneumonidae parasitoids that attack forest lepidopterans: the idiobiont subfamily Pimplinae (excluding the tribe Polysphinctini, which is composed of koinobiont parasitoid of spiders and will be considered in detail in the present study) and the koinobiont subfamily Metopiinae. They used records obtained by the Canadian Forest Insect and Disease Survey (Bradley, 1974) of 25 pimplines and 28 metopiines. The idiobiont pimplines were reared from 2.3 times more species and 2.7 times more genera than the metopiines (koinobionts). Finally, Althoff (2003) also evaluated the effect of the two parasitoid strategies on host range, comparing the number of host families attacked by 184 braconid genera. Confirming the pattern, he found that 62% of the koinobiont genera attack just one host family, whereas only 34% of the idiobiont genera have the same restriction.

However, it is important to emphasize that the terms idiobiont and koinobiont are applied to the extremes of a life strategies continnum. Hosts of koinobionts, for example, may experience a significant increase in

Fig. 1 (A) Number of host families attacked by koinobiont (green bars) and idiobiont (black bars) species of Braconidae (Data from Althoff, D. M. (2003). Does parasitoid attack strategy influence host specificity? A test with New World braconids. *Ecological Entomology, 28*, 500–502. https://doi.org/10.1046/j.1365-2311.2003.00533.x). (B) Cocoons of *Meteorus* sp. (Braconidae) hanging from the host's body.

biomass before being completely consumed by a large parasitoid larva. Alternatively, the parasitoid may consume all the tissues necessary to pupate in a few days. The association interval is influenced by a trade-off between growing larger at the cost of a longer development or developing rapidly at the cost of reaching a reduced size (Harvey et al., 2000). The advantages of each strategy depend on the exposition of the host to predators and the nutritional requirements of the parasitoid larvae (Harvey & Strand, 2002). Interestingly, the action of some parasitoid larvae on their hosts may induce changes in their feeding activities, defensive behaviors and/or microhabitat preferences, interfering with mortality risks (Adamo, 1997).

Some koinobionts groups, as well-studied members of the braconid genus *Meteorus* (and other braconids included in the subfamily Euphorinae), have successfully expanded their host range. This worldwide distributed genus comprises over 340 species, attacking Coleoptera (especially Cerambycidae, Tenebrionidae, Scolytidae, Cryptophagidae, Melandryidae, and Ciidae) and Lepidoptera larvae (15 families, such as Limacodidae, Papilionidae, Pyralidae,

Sphingidae, and Noctuidae) (Aguirre, de Almeida, Shaw, & Sarmiento, 2015; Almeida & Dias, 2015; Shaw & Huddleston, 1991). These wasps are usually recognized by their peculiar silk-spinning and cocoon-forming behaviors (Zitani & Shaw, 2002; Fig. 1B), and present a remarkable immune suppression mechanism, which is effective against the responses of a wide range of caterpillars. *Meteorus pulchricornis*, for example, is a polyphagous koinobiont endoparasitoid that attacks more than 60 species from at least 15 families within 10 lepidopteran superfamilies (Maeto, 2018). This impressive host range is possibly influenced by the following factors: (1) unlike microgastroid braconids and ophioniform ichneumonids (which regulate host-specific immunity with symbiotic polydnaviruses), *M. pulchricornis* uses a broad-spectrum immune suppression mechanism, causing massive apoptosis of host granulocytes by the co-injection of virus-like particles from its venom glands (Suzuki, Miura, & Tanaka, 2008); (2) the larvae of *M. pulchricornis* can physiologically adapt to wide interspecific variations in body size, growth rate, and growth potential of their hosts; (3) they are aggressive and morphologically well adapted to fight against competitors, presenting a pair of sharp mandibles; (4) host location is based on visual cues and not on specific kairomones emitted by the hosts; and (5) the parasitoid may evade predation during the critical phase by suspending mature larvae and cocoons until adult emergence (Maeto, 2018).

The strategy of *M. pulchricornis* of remaining suspended by a silk thread attached to the host body during the pupal stage is effective against predators (Shirai & Maeto, 2009), being less specific than alternative strategies used by other endoparasitoids. Some species, for instance, obtain protection during the fragile period of pupae by inducing their hosts to perform unusual or altered behaviors, such as aggressive reactions against potential predators. This is what happens in the interaction between the microgastroid braconid *Glyptapanteles* sp. and its host, the caterpillar *Thyrinteina leucocerae* (Grosman et al., 2008). Although the proximate mechanism of these behavioral alterations remains to be determined, it is probably involved in the determination of the narrow host range of these parasitoids (Arias-Penna et al., 2019).

Our focus in this review will be on another group of manipulative parasitoids, the *Polysphincta* group (Ichneumonidae, Pimplinae). Unlike the koinobiont braconids, these wasps are exclusive ectoparasitoids of spiders. We will present a brief overview of these wasps' biology and discuss the potential implications of some relevant traits on host specificity patterns.

1.2 Host-parasitoid interactions in the *Polysphincta* group

The *Polysphincta* group is a monophyletic lineage of wasps belonging to the tribe Ephialtini (Ichneumonidae, Pimplinae), hereafter 'polysphinctines' (Gauld & Dubois, 2006; Matsumoto, 2016; Quicke, Laurenne, Fitton, & Broad, 2009). The group is currently composed of 25 genera and more than 300 species (including seven fossil species), all of them with parasitoid habits (Eberhard & Gonzaga, 2019; Gaione-Costa, Pádua, Delazari, Santos, & Kloss, 2022; Khoramabadi, Talebi, Broad, & Zwakhals, 2022; Kloss et al., 2022). The group has a worldwide distribution (with limits between 27° S and 66°N), occupying all biogeographical regions except Antarctica. Their host range includes sub-adults and adults of at least eleven spider families: Agelenidae, Araneidae, Cheiracanthidae, Clubionidae, Dictynidae, Linyphidae, Salticidae, Tetragnathidae, Theridiidae, Thomisidae, Phonognathidae, and Titanoecidae (Bánki et al., 2023; Gadallah & El-Hennawy, 2017; Matsumoto, 2016).

One of the most remarkable features of the host-parasitoid interactions involving polysphinctine wasps is their capacity to manipulate the web-building behavior of their hosts. The cocoon webs constructed by spiders, just before being killed and consumed by the third instar larva of the parasitoid, usually lack viscid components and structures used to intercept and retain insects. In addition, structural elements are often reinforced, offering stable and long-lasting support for parasitoid development during the pupal stage (Kloss, Gonzaga, Roxinol, & Sperber, 2016a; Korenko, 2022; Matsumoto, 2009; Fig. 2).

It is known that the behavioral modification increases the survival of the parasitoid during its pupal phase. The first suggestion regarding the benefits of cocoon webs for parasitoids was made by Eberhard (2001), who observed the web-building behavior of the spider *Leucauge argyra* (Tetragnathidae) parasitized by *Hymenoepimecis argyraphaga*. He observed that, during the behavioral manipulation, the spider continued performing the initial routines of web construction continuously. This "routine imprisonment" keeps the spider constantly producing new threads on the already built radii, reinforcing the cocoon web, and increasing its resistance, which is not characteristic of the spider's normal web. Additionally, due to this behavior, structures involved in prey capture are not included on the webs, and the reinforcement of the radii results in a reduced web. Therefore, it was suggested that this web should increase the survival of the parasitoid by reducing the risk of being broken by interception of flying insects and debris that could fall and collide with the web (Eberhard, 2001).

Fig. 2 (A) Normal horizontal orb web of *Leucauge volupis* (Tetragnathidae). (B) Parasitized female of *L. volupis* carrying a second instar larvae of *Hymenoepimecis pinheirensis*. (C) Cocoon web of *L. volupis* holding a cocoon of *H. pinheirensis*. (D) Another cocoon web of *L. volupis* showing the three-dimensional structure of threads, similar to that observed in molting webs.

The first experimental confirmation of the benefits of modified webs for parasitoids was obtained by Matsumoto (2009) studying the cocoon webs constructed by the spider *Agelena silvatica* (Agelenidae), a species parasitized by the wasp *Brachyzapus nikkoensis* (Matsumoto, 2009, 2016). *A. silvatica* constructs funnel webs in vegetation and typically stays near the retreat opening, waiting for its prey. However, when parasitized by the larva of *B. nikkoensis*, the spider is manipulated to produce a kind of "veil" of threads at the retreat opening, which becomes blocked. After constructing this veil, the larva kills the spider and then builds its cocoon inside the closed retreat. In situations where the veil was experimentally removed, most of the pupae were killed by ants. In addition, Kloss et al. (2016a) conducted a study on behavioral manipulation using two species of *Cyclosa* (Araneidae) parasitized by the larvae of *Polysphincta purcelli* and *Polysphincta janzeni*. They removed parasitized spiders that had their behavior manipulated from their cocoon webs and subsequently placed them in normal webs built by non-parasitized spiders. Meanwhile, for comparison purposes, the authors used another group of parasitized spiders that, after constructing the modified web, were removed and reinserted into the same web. Ultimately, it was observed that the pupae attached to normal webs were more susceptible to death than those attached to cocoon webs. The higher mortality risk observed in this interaction was mainly associated with predation by ants and web collapsing caused by falling leaves and branches (Kloss et al., 2016a).

Several lines of evidence suggest that the increase of ecdysone levels (or a precursor of this substance) in the host spiders is the mechanism by which the parasitoid larva manipulates the behavior of its host (Eberhard & Gonzaga, 2019; Kloss, Gonzaga, Oliveira, & Sperber, 2017; Takasuka et al., 2015). Reducing molting web architecture decreases the risk of the web being broken during the spider's vulnerable molting process, when it is susceptible to environmental threats. Activating altered behavior seems to be an anachronic manifestation of the host spider's innate behavior. However, the modified webs of some spiders in the Palaearctic region resemble only the webs constructed during hibernation (Korenko & Pekar, 2011). Spiders in this region build a dome-shaped structure in the center of their webs that assists their survival during winter. Parasitoids appear to take advantage of this spider mechanism by inducing host spiders to construct a similar dome in their cocoon webs, where they undergo pupation (Korenko & Pekar, 2011). Therefore, regardless of the specific mechanism inducing modified webs, manipulating spider behavior likely relies on exploiting mechanisms associated with behavioral variations that enhance the protection and survival of the parasitoid larva in diverse environments.

This general description of host manipulation by polysphinctines hides several particularities observed in each modified web that may be important to ensure the protection and, consequently, the success of the parasitoid development during the pupal stage. For instance, including barrier threads in specific positions and densities may be relevant in reducing the susceptibility of the parasitoid pupae to attacks by hyperparasitoids (Pádua et al., 2022). Different hosts may build webs with significant differences in this structure, consequently providing distinct levels of protection. The possibility of these particular requirements regarding the architectural patterns of ideal cocoon webs adds an unusual restriction to these ectoparasitoids to expand their host ranges. In addition, other relevant aspects that may constrain the occurrence of generalist strategies in polysphinctines include specific approaching behaviors required to subdue hosts with distinct web patterns and escaping behaviors, and the availability of host species within the narrow size range required to allow an efficient immobilization of the host during the oviposition and larval nutrition. Despite that, the host range seems very variable in polysphinctines, and the reasons for this pattern remain to be investigated.

One critical limitation for understanding host specificity patterns of parasitoids is the need for more information or the uneven availability of information on natural history within most taxonomic groups. Fortunately, the increasing interest in ecological interactions involving behavioral manipulation of hosts by parasites and parasitoids allowed the rapid accumulation of information on some taxa in the last 20 years. The currently available data on interactions between polysphinctines and their spider hosts, including details of several aspects of their behavior during host selection and oviposition, host size preferences, characteristics of cocoon webs, and geographical distribution of hosts and parasitoids, represent an excellent opportunity to identify and evaluate the proximate causes of host specificity patterns in a large group of parasitoids. Thus, our main purpose in this review is to analyze the currently available information on the patterns of host specificity within this taxonomic group of parasitoids and to discuss some factors that may be involved in determining such patterns. Some of those factors are restricted to interactions between parasitoids and spiders. Others can be analyzed in a broader context involving limitations and preferences shared by distinct groups of parasitoids.

1.3 A brief historical overview of spider-parasitoid interactions

The study and recognition of interactions between parasitoid wasps and spiders have a rich history that dates back to the 18th century. The first documented observation of a parasitized spider was made by De Geer (1771), who discovered a small spider with a white larva attached to its abdomen feeding on its fluids. De Geer placed the parasitized spider in a box and meticulously documented the complete larval development period. Through this study, he provided valuable information on an orb web spun by the spider after its demise. The description and illustration of this web revealed characteristics later observed in other cases of host behavioral manipulation, such as a reduction in the number of radii and the absence of sticky spiral threads, with a cocoon positioned at the web's center.

Subsequently, there was a widespread recognition that a group of Ichneumonidae wasps develop their larvae by targeting adult spiders and their egg sacs (Blackwall, 1843; Howard, 1982; Nielsen, 1923; also see Fitch, 1882). These descriptions contributed to refining information on species interactions and taxonomic classification within the group, and expanding our knowledge of these wasps' biology and life cycles (Fitton, Shaw, & Gauld, 1988). Some authors have included illustrations and brief descriptions showing details of the webs produced by host spiders at different stages of the parasitoid's larval development. However, despite the significance of these early contributions, it was only from the 2000s onwards that investigations into the interactions between polysphinctines wasps and spiders began to focus on a comprehensive understanding of the behavioral mechanisms involved in these interactions. This change in approach came about after Eberhard (2000a) conducted a detailed examination of the normal webs built by the spider species *L. argyra* and the webs created by parasitized individuals of the same species. Since then, the last two decades have flourished with many studies describing new interactions between parasitoid and spider species, revealing a wide range of adaptations adult parasitoids use to manipulate their hosts, increasing their offspring survival. These studies have greatly expanded our understanding of this fascinating phenomenon and continue to shed light on the complex relationships between parasitoids and their hosts. The accumulation of data on these interactions may allow further investigations of other aspects, such as the general patterns of host specificity.

1.4 Macroecological perspective of host specificity in polysphinctine wasps

Optimal foraging theory considers the net balance between the costs and benefits of consuming a prey weighted by predators' searching and handling time as determining factors of predator-prey interactions (MacArthur & Pianka, 1966). Costs are the energy spent searching for and handling prey, while benefits are the energy gained from consuming the prey. Therefore, the nutritional value of prey is predicted to be one of the major drivers of foraging strategies. However, a recent mathematical model of individual specialization has shown that the nutritional value of prey does not influence the dynamics of foraging strategies, especially when considering that an *individual's niche breadth may be narrow compared to the population's niche* breadth (Araujo & Moura, 2022). When some individuals exhibit generalist (or euryphagous) and others exhibit specialist (or stenophagous) strategies, a population with mixed strategies tends to emerge. The relative predator efficiency and prey reproductive rates determine whether generalists will coexist with at least one specialist or whether specialists will lead generalists to extinction (Araujo & Moura, 2022). In any scenario, the ecological theory of individual specialization states that a mixture of foraging strategies coexists within populations.

The ecological theory of individual specialization provides new predictions that can be applied to parasitoids. The relative efficiency of individual parasitoids in consuming different host species is difficult to assess from the literature, but we can obtain proxies of host reproductive rates, such as their spatial distributions. Host species with wide distribution may exhibit higher reproductive rates than species with narrower distributions (Gaston et al., 2000; Gaston, Blackburn, & Lawton, 1997). This assumption allows us to draw macroecological predictions on the host specificity of parasitoid species. Individual parasitoids of wasp species that parasitize hosts with large ranges of distribution may have more opportunities to interact with new host species and diversify individual niches, thus increasing the population niche (Araujo & Moura, 2022). Within a community, this phenomenon can be generally considered an 'amplification effect', which assumes that parasitoids with a broader host range may have an increased host encounter rate (Keesing, Holt, & Ostfeld, 2006).

In larger spatial scales, parasitoids interacting with hosts presenting wide distributions can evolve more interactions with additional host species than parasitoids exploiting hosts with narrower ranges. Therefore, we hypothesized that parasitoids consuming hosts with large spatial distributions have lower host specificity than parasitoids interacting with spatially restricted hosts. We can measure spatial distribution using the range of the two coordinates that capture different processes: latitude and longitude. Large latitudinal range means that individuals can tolerate diverse abiotic conditions beyond spatial component (i.e., high tolerance) because it includes both a large spatial distribution and a greater variation in abiotic conditions, specially temperature and pluviosity. Large longitudinal ranges also encompass large spatial distribution, but with a lower variation in abiotic conditions. Therefore, we investigated the influence of latitudinal and longitudinal ranges on different properties of host specificity for parasitoids, such as the number of host species.

Another question that emerges from trophic interactions at the community level is how specialization (or generalization) affects parasitoid performance. Adaptations to explore one host efficiently usually evolve at the cost of reducing the efficiency of exploiting other hosts (Futuyma & Moreno, 1988). Hence, specialists may be more efficient than generalists because natural selection has favored specialized behaviors that increase the capture success of one or a few host species. This scenario favors the evolution of exclusive interactions between a parasitoid species and a host of a particular taxonomic level, such as species, genus, or family (i.e., the compensation hypothesis). Conversely, parasitoid performance may increase with the degree of generalization, thus enhancing the diversity of hosts from different genera or families (i.e., the resource breadth hypothesis) (Brown, 1984;

Krasnov, Poulin, Shenbrot, Mouillot, & Khokhlova, 2004). Depending on the environmental gradient, more complex scenarios can evolve (Felix, Pinheiro, Poulin, Krasnov, & Mello, 2022).

Finally, host-parasitoid interactions can exhibit diverse structures. When grouping all known interactions between spiders and parasitoid wasps, we can assess network properties and investigate the relationship between performance and host specificity. However, monospecific interactions can be a consequence of low sampling effort and the record of a wasp species parasitizing a spider species does not necessarily mean that this is an exclusive association. However, information on parasitoid species interacting with many hosts at species, genus, and family levels can provide valuable information on the host characteristics (behavioral, morphological, or physiological) influencing host range. In this study, we describe the topological properties of these networks and assess the degree of specialization of wasp species for different taxonomic levels of hosts to identify generalist parasitoids.

2. Methods
2.1 Systematic review

To understand the factors affecting the specificity of interactions between behavior-manipulating parasitoids and their hosts, we systematically reviewed interactions between wasps and spiders in the ISI Web of Knowledge, Scopus, and Google Scholar databases in February 2023. The search was carried out without any limitations on the year or publication type, encompassing all three databases, to retrieve publications containing the keywords "cocoon web," "Polysphinctine," and "Ephialtini." Furthermore, we used the terms "behavioral manipulation" and "spider?" in the Scopus and ISI Web of Knowledge databases.

During the searching process, we started by excluding unreadable or untranslatable articles. Hence, the articles that lacked abstracts or excerpts translatable by Google Translator or other online translation tools were omitted from the review. In addition, we analyzed websites and the reference list of selected articles in the three online databases to broaden the scope of the search for publications. In this review, we avoided using data from theses and dissertations. We reviewed these publication types, but only used information from them when the same data were not already available in articles (which only occurred in the cases of Almeida, Mendes-Pereira, & Kloss, 2020; Manuel, 1976; Messas, 2014).

After searching for publications, we examined all abstracts of the articles found in the databases. Then, we selected for the review only those publications that described the interaction between polysphinctine wasps and spiders or that referred to the distribution of wasps from the *Polysphincta* group. Initially, we obtained 584 publications from the databases and another 67 publications through the reference lists of the reviewed articles. Then, all articles were read in full, and we selected for the extraction of information only those publications that simultaneously mentioned: (1) the identity of the parasitoid wasp species down to the genus level, (2) the specific identity of the spider host; and (3) the location where the wasp was recorded on the host spider. Through these inclusion criteria, we had access to a total of 122 publications (Supplementary Fig. S1).

From the 122 publications obtained, we extracted information about the identity of the species of polysphinctine wasps and spiders involved in the interaction, as well as the number of hosts per parasitoid. In addition, we obtained data on geographic coordinates, countries, and the biogeographical realm of the sites where interactions occurred, along with information on web modifications described for host spiders. To ensure the currentness of the scientific names of the species mentioned in the articles, we checked and, when necessary, updated the scientific names of the polysphinctine wasps using the Taxapad—Catalogue of Life (https://www.catalogueoflife.org) (Bánki et al., 2023). Likewise, the scientific names of the host spider species of the parasitoids were verified and updated using the World Spider Catalog (2023) platform (https://wsc.nmbe.ch). In situations where the host spider species was only identified up to the genus level, we only considered the record if there were no other spiders from the same genus described as hosts for the parasitoid. We followed this criterion to avoid the possibility of considering the same interaction more than once in the analyses.

To obtain data on wasp locations, we considered the geographic coordinates where the studies were conducted. For this, we used the following approaches: (1) coordinates provided by the authors; (2) Google Earth search of the place described by the authors, when the coordinates were not specified, but the place of interaction was mentioned; and (3) search for the name of the city or center of the most specific region cited by the authors, also obtained from Google Earth. While there may be some variation in the exact location of each interaction due to these extraction methods (2) and (3), this variation is minimal relative to the scale of the study, which minimizes its impact on the results. In addition, in articles focused on taxonomic descriptions of species or in compilations including several species (e.g., Korenko & Giovanni, 2019; Matsumoto & Takasuka, 2010), we examined the lists of occurrences and the species types to identify the locations where other researchers recorded these species. However, we only included occurrence records in which the host spider was observed with the larva developing on its back, excluding data from occurrences in which only the cocoon web was recorded for the wasp. We followed this criterion to avoid errors in identifying the host spider in which the parasitoid developed and any potential mistakes in identifying the host spider itself.

2.2 Data analysis

First, we obtained coordinates in GBIF database for hosts of 73 wasp species using the *Rgbif* packages (Chamberlain et al., 2023) and *CoordinateCleanner* (Zizka et al., 2019). Then, we calculated distances between extremes of latitude and longitude from the distribution of hosts using the distHaversine function in the *geosphere* package (Hijmans, 2022). Finally, we calculated the z-scores of the latitude and longitude ranges to standardize their scales (hereafter, standardized latitude and standardized longitude). To test whether the number of host species (response variable) was related to the standardized latitude and longitude (predictors), we initially built a generalized linear mixed model (GLMM) with Poisson error distribution and log link function. However, we detected underdispersion in our data. Therefore, to deal with the underdispersion, we built a GLMM with Conway-Maxwell Poisson error distribution and log link function using the *glmmTMB* package (Brooks et al., 2017). Finally, we added the number of studies (to control for sampling effort biases) and wasp genera (to control for taxonomic biases) as random variables.

We also investigated whether the host diversity for each parasitoid species was related to the standardized latitude and longitude. Host diversity (response variable) was quantified using Simpsons' index of host diversity for each parasitoid species. We calculated Simpsons' index using a matrix with parasitoid species in lines and host species in columns utilizing the diversity function of R base packages. We built a GLMM with negative binomial error distribution and log link function. As in the previous analyses, we included the number of studies and the wasp genera as the random variables. We tested the assumptions of all models using the simulateResiduals function in the *DHARMa* package (Hartig, 2022). To evaluate whether the mean effect differs from zero, we report untransformed slope and Wald-type 95% confidence intervals of the GLMM (β [2.5%CI to 97.5%CI]), calculated using the confint function in the R base packages. To interpret effect sizes, we calculated the exponential values of coefficients. We also estimated the marginal and conditional pseudo-R^2, which measure variance explained by fixed factors and by both, fixed and random factors, respectively (Nakagawa & Schielzeth, 2013).

Data on host-parasitoid interactions were analyzed in a matrix with wasp species in the columns and spider species in the lines. We then calculated the metrics of the parasitoid-wasp network using the *bipartite* package (Dormann & Strauss, 2014). Our dataset included 240 species (89 wasp species and 143 spider species), and we measured connectance, cluster coefficient, specialization index, nestedness, number of shared partners, generality, and vulnerability using the networklevel function in the bipartite package (Dormann, Gruber, & Fruend, 2008). We organized two additional matrices with different taxonomic levels of spiders: genus and family. We weighted the links between hosts and parasitoids using the number of interactions and calculated weighted measures of network topology.

Connectance (C) quantifies the proportion of realized interactions from all possible interactions between species in the network. A C value of 0 indicates no interactions between species, and a value of 1 indicates that all species are connected to each other. Cluster coefficient (Cw) has a similar interpretation to C, as it is the number of realized links divided by the number of possible links. The NODF (Nestedness metric based on Overlap and Decreasing Fill) measures nestedness, that is the degree to which the interactions of parasitoids with fewer hosts correspond to a subset of the parasitoid species that attack more hosts. NODF ranges from 0 (for no nestedness) to 100 (for a perfectly nested network). The number of shared partners is a metric that quantifies the extent to which two species in the network share common interaction partners, which is calculated as the sum of links divided by the number of species. It can range from 0 (no shared partners) to the maximum number of partners both species interact with. Generality is the mean effective number of spider species per wasp species, while vulnerability is the opposite, both weighted by their marginal totals.

The specialization index (H_2') measures the extent to which a species interacts with a subset of the available partners rather than interacting with all potential partners in the network. It quantifies the partitioning or sharing of interactions between two parties in the network. The H_2' ranges from 0 to 1, with 0 indicating complete generalization, where species interact with all available partners equally, and 1 indicating complete specialization, where species interact with only one partner. We can also calculate the degree of specialization for each species in a network. It can be quantified using a standardized specialization index (d′), from the Kullback-Leibler distance, similar to Shannon's diversity index. It calculates how strongly a species deviates from a random sampling of interacting partners available. The d′ index ranges from 0 (indicating no specialization) to 1 (indicating a perfect specialist). We used this metric to find the identity of parasitoid species with the lowest specialization (i.e., that interact with a higher diversity of host species). We conducted all analyses in R, version 4.2.3 (R Development Core Team, 2023).

3. State-of-art and trends in studies of polysphinctine-host interactions

The studies describing interactions between spider hosts and polysphinctines were conducted in 25 countries, mainly Brazil (27.8%) and Japan (16.3%). Most studies were restricted to one country (89.3%), but thirteen studies provided data from two to five countries (Fig. 3). Interactions were observed in eight (Palearctic, Sino-Japanese, Neotropical, Nearctic, Australian, Panamanian, Indo-Malayan, and Afrotropical) of the ten biogeographic realms recognized by Holt et al. (2013), being especially frequent in the Palearctic (46.6%) and Neotropical realms (20.7%). Most interactions are restricted to only one biogeographic realm, and only two interactions were recorded simultaneously in two different realms.

We found 173 interactions between 143 spider hosts and 89 species (including morphotypes) of polysphinctines in the literature. Information regarding the host and location of occurrence was only available for 18 out of 25 polysphinctine genera, specifically *Acrodactyla, Acrotaphus, Brachyzapus, Eriostethus, Eruga, Flacopimpla, Hymenoepimecis, Iania, Inbioia, Megaetaira, Oxyrrhexis, Piogaster, Polysphincta, Reclinervellus, Schizopyga, Sinarachna, Zabrachypus, Zaglyptus*, and *Zatypota*. Additionally, only 79 interactions (40.9%) include details of web modification, in which parasitoid larvae induce their spider host to construct cocoon webs. In 25 of these interactions, the descriptions of cocoon webs were based solely on a single web.

Finally, 81.1% of the articles described aspects of the biology and taxonomy of parasitoid species. Among them, 9.8% provided information about the ontogeny of wasps. 10.7% of all studies described the wasp behavior of attacking spiders, 2.5% tested how cocoon webs affected wasp survival, and 5.7% contributed to understanding manipulation mechanisms.

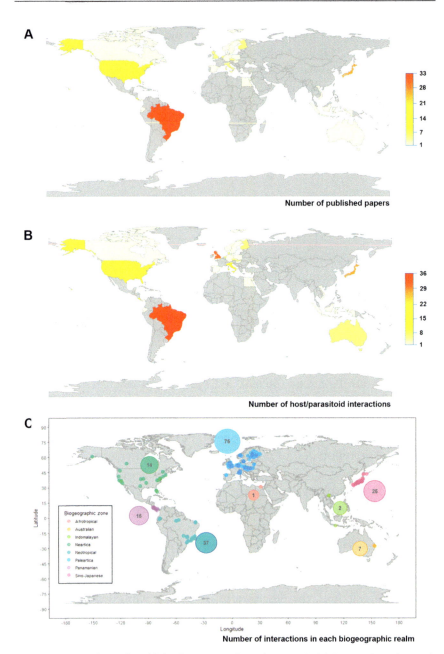

Fig. 3 (A) Number of published papers of spider-parasitoid interactions in each country. (B) Number of host-parasitoid interactions reported in each country. (C) Number of interactions with the geographic location of occurrence described in each biogeographic domain.

In general, 37.7% of the studies on manipulative interactions of spiders by wasps described multiple interactions. The studies that described the greatest number of interactions provided data on 10 wasp species and 12 spider species (Matsumoto & Takasuka, 2010) and 10 wasp species and 14 spider species (Korenko & Giovanni, 2019). The majority, however, recorded interactions between one wasp species (72.9%) and one spider species (64.8%). Nevertheless, we observed that only 16 wasp species with multiple hosts (9.6%) provided information about normal and modified web traits for at least two spider species.

4. Patterns of host specificity

Polysphinctine wasps attacked spiders of the following 11 families: Araneidae (36.4%), Theridiidae (30.6%), Tetragnathidae (11.6%), Linyphiidae (8.7%), Dictynidae (4.0%), Clubionidae (2.3%), Agelenidae (2.3%), Titanoecidae (1.7%), Salticidae (1.2%), Phonognathidae (0.6%), and Cheiracanthiidae (0.6%). Thomisidae is a family cited in the literature as a host for the genus *Oxyrrhexis*, but there are still uncertainties about the veracity and location of this interaction (Gauld & Dubois, 2006; Matsumoto, 2016).

Relying on the host morphospecies described by the authors, six parasitoid species interacted with six or more host species. *Acrodactyla quadrisculpta* is associated with seven different hosts species; *Sinarachna pallipes* and *Zatypota albicoxa* oviposited in eight spider species, with the hosts of *Z. albicoxa* belonging to the families Theridiidae and Araneidae; *Zatypota anomala* and *Zatypota percontatoria* attacked nine spider species; and *Z. percontatoria* parasitized ten host species. However, our review indicates that Polysphinctine species associated with multiple hosts rarely use species from different families. Out of the 16 known interactions with host traits descriptions (Table 1), only *Hymenoepimecis japi*, *Z. kaurus*, and *Zatypota riverai* are associated with host spiders from different families. *Z. kaurus* parasitizes spiders of the genus *Anelosimus* (Theridiidae), but it is also associated with three species from the family Araneidae: *Cyrtophora exanthematica*, *Cyrtophora hirta*, and *Trichonephila plumipes* (Korenko, Hamouzova et al., 2018). A similar pattern is observed in *Zatypota riverai*, which is associated with two species from the family Theridiidae, *Anelosimus baeza* and *Theridium* sp., and one species from the family Araneidae, *Cyclosa fililineata* (Sobczak, Messas, & Pádua, 2017; Sobczak, Pádua, Villanueva-Bonilla, Nóbrega, & Messas, 2019; Sobczak, Paiva Arruda, De Pádua, & Villanueva-Bonilla, 2019; Villanueva-Bonilla et al., 2021). On the other hand,

Table 1 Interactions between Polysphinctine wasps and spiders, including descriptions of cocoon webs in at least two host spider species. We list detailed information on several host traits, including host identity, female host size, the location of cocoon web observations, the structure of normal webs and cocoon webs, cocoon position, and types of behavioral modifications.

Wasp	Host Species[a]	Host family	Female host size[b]	Observation[c]	Normal web	Types of cocoon webs[d]	Parasitoid cocoon[e]
Acrotaphus tibialis	*Argiope trifasciata* [1]	Araneidae	15.65 (NA) [1]	LF	Orb web - 3D	D	Exposed
	Eustala perfida [2]	Araneidae	6.85 (5) [2]	F	Orb web - 2D	D	Exposed
Eriostethus minimus	*Nihonhimea mundula* [3]	Theridiidae	8.0 (1) [3]	LF	Tangled web − 3D	B	Sheltered
	Parasteatoda sp. [3]	Theridiidae	8.0 (1) [3]	LF	Tangled web − 3D	B	Exposed
Eruga unilabiana	*Dubiaranea* sp. [4]	Lyniphiidae	NA	L	Sheet web − 3D	C	Exposed
	Eurymorion sp. [5]	Lyniphiidae	NA	L	Sheet web − 3D	C	Exposed
	Sphecozone sp. [5]	Lyniphiidae	NA	L	Sheet web − 3D	C	Sheltered

Hymenoepimecis bicolor	*Cyrtophora citricola* [6]	Araneidae	8.8 (8) [4]	LF	Sheet web – 3D	D	Exposed
	Trichonephila clavipes [7]	Araneidae	24.8 (6) [5]	F	Orb web - 3D	D	Exposed
Hymenoepimecis japi	*Leucauge roseosignata* [8]	Tetragnat-hidae	10.0 (NA) [6]	F	Orb web - 3D	K	Exposed
	Mecynogea bigibba [9]	Araneidae	3.78 (38) [7]	F	Sheet web – 3D	A	Exposed
Hymenoepimecis veranii	*Araneus omnicolor* [10]	Araneidae	8.95 (NA) [8]	F	Orb web - 3D	D	Sheltered
	Araneus órgãos [11]	Araneidae	6.4 (1) [8]	F	Orb web - 3D	D	Sheltered
Polysphincta janzeni	*Cyclosa fililineata* [12,13]	Araneidae	4.3 (NA) [9]	F	Orb web - 2D	D	Sheltered
	Cyclosa morretes [12,13]	Araneidae	6.4 (NA) [9]	F	Orb web - 2D	D	Sheltered
Polysphincta tuberosa	*Araneus diadematus* [14]	Araneidae	12.0 (NA) [10]	L	Orb web - 2D	A	Exposed

(continued)

Table 1 Interactions between Polysphinctine wasps and spiders, including descriptions of cocoon webs in at least two host spider species. We list detailed information on several host traits, including host identity, female host size, the location of cocoon web observations, the structure of normal webs and cocoon webs, cocoon position, and types of behavioral modifications. (*cont'd*)

Wasp	Host Species[a]	Host family	Female host size[b]	Observation[c]	Normal web	Types of cocoon webs[d]	Parasitoid cocoon[e]
	Araneus sturmi [15]	Araneidae	4.15 (NA) [10]	L	NA	A	Exposed
	Araniella cucurbitina [14]	Araneidae	6.1 (NA) [10]	L	Orb web – 2D	A	Exposed
	Araniella opisthographa [14]	Araneidae	5.2 (NA) [10]	L	Orb web – 2D	A	Exposed
Reclinervellus nielseni	*Cyclosa argenteoalba* [16,17,18,19]	Araneidae	6.5 (NA) [11]	LF	Orb web – 2D	D	Sheltered
	Cyclosa conica [19]	Araneidae	5.49 (NA) [12]	L	Orb web – 2D	D	Sheltered
	Cyclosa laticauda [19]	Araneidae	11.0 (NA) [11]	L	Orb web – 2D	D	Sheltered
	Cyclosa omonaga [20]	Araneidae	6.47 (NA) [13]	L	Orb web – 2D	D	Sheltered

Sinarachna pallipes	Araniella cucurbitina [14]	Araneidae	5.8 (NA) [14]	L	Orb web - 2D	A	Exposed
	Araniella displicata [14]	Araneidae	6.5 (NA) [14]	L	Orb web - 2D	A	Exposed
	Araniella opisthographa [14]	Araneidae	6.2 (NA) [15]	L	Orb web - 2D	A	Exposed
Zatypota alborhombarta	Achaearanea tingo [21]	Theridiidae	2.3 (NA) [16]	F	Tangled web − 3D	K	Sheltered
	Cryptachaea migrans [22]	Theridiidae	2.7 (NA) [16]	LF	Tangled web − 3D	I	Sheltered
Zatypota kauros	Anelosimus sp. [3]	Theridiidae	NA	L	Tangled web − 3D	B	Exposed
	Cyrtophora exanthematica [3]	Araneidae	18.0 (NA) [17]	L	Sheet web − 3D	H	Exposed
	Cyrtophora hirta [3]	Araneidae	NA	L	Sheet web − 3D	H	Exposed
	Trichonephila plumipes [3]	Araneidae	20.52 (5) [06]	L	Orb web - 3D	D	Exposed

(continued)

Table 1 Interactions between Polysphinctine wasps and spiders, including descriptions of cocoon webs in at least two host spider species. We list detailed information on several host traits, including host identity, female host size, the location of cocoon web observations, the structure of normal webs and cocoon webs, cocoon position, and types of behavioral modifications. (*cont'd*)

Wasp	Host Species[a]	Host family	Female host size[b]	Observation[c]	Normal web	Types of cocoon webs[d]	Parasitoid cocoon[e]
Zatypota percontatoria	*Neottiura bimaculata* [23]	Theridiidae	3.05 (50) [10]	L	Tangled web – 3D	C	Sheltered
	Theridion varians [23]	Theridiidae	3.45 (24) [10]	L	Tangled web – 3D	C	Sheltered
Zatypota picticollis	*Cyclosa conica* [24]	Araneidae	5.49 (NA) [12]	L	Orb web - 2D	D	Sheltered
	Mangora acalypha [19]	Araneidae	4.05 (25) [10]	L	Orb web - 2D	D	Exposed
	Zilla diodia [24]	Araneidae	4.2 (1) [10]	L	Orb web - 2D	F	Exposed
Zatypota riverai	*Anelosimus baeza* [25]	Theridiidae	4.0 (1) [18]	L	Tangled web – 3D	C	Exposed
	Cyclosa fililineata [26]	Araneidae	4.3 (*) [9]	F	Orb web - 2D	D	Sheltered
	Theridium sp. [27]	Theridiidae	NA	F	NA	B	Sheltered

Zatypota solanoi	*Anelosimus octavius* [28]	Theridiidae	5.01 (1) [18]	LF	Tangled web – 3D	C	Exposed
	Anelosimus studiosus [28]	Theridiidae	4.0 (1) [18]	L	Tangled web – 3D	C	Exposed

[a]The number following the names of the host spiders indicates the corresponding references: [1] Eberhard (2013); [2] Messas (2014); [3] Korenko et al. (2018a); [4] Sobczak et al. (2017c); [5] Pereira et al. (2022); [6] Gonzaga et al. (2022); [7] Gonzaga et al. (2010); [8] Sobczak et al. (2009); [9] Messas et al. (2017); [10] Gonzaga & Sobczak (2007); [11] Sobczak et al. (2014); [12] Gonzaga et al. (2015b); [13] Kloss et al. (2016a); [14] Korenko et al. (2014); [15] Korenko et al. (2017); [16] Matsumoto & Konishi (2007); [17] Takasuka (2019a); [18] Takasuka et al. (2015); [19] Takasuka et al. (2017); [20] Takasuka et al. (2018); [21] Gonzaga et al. (2016); [22] Almeida et al. (2020); [23] Korenko & Pekar (2011); [24] Korenko et al. (2015b); [25] Sobczak et al. (2017a); [26] Villanueva-Bonilla et al. (2021); [27] Sobczak et al. (2019b); [28] Eberhard (2010b).

[b]The female size represents the average total body length (mm). Numbers in parentheses represent the number of individuals measured to obtain the size. NA indicates the absence of information regarding the measurement of the host spiders or the number of individuals measured for each measurement. Letters following the measurements indicate the reference used to obtain the corresponding measurement: [1] Levi (2004); [2] Poeta et al. (2010); [3] Korenko et al. (2018); [4] Alvares & De-Maria (2004); [5] Kuntner et al. (2019); [6] Mello Leitão (1943); [7] Messas et al. (2017); [8] Levi (1991); [9] Levi (1999); [10] Almquist (2005); [11] Bösenberg & Strand (1906); [12] Bayram & Unal (2002); [13] Tanikawa (1992); [14] Hu (2001); [15] Levy (1987); [16] Levi (1963); [17] Yin et al. (2012); [18] Agnarsson (2006).

[c]The location of cocoon web observations. L = laboratory, F = field.

[d]The classification of cocoon webs was based on the system proposed by Eberhard & Gonzaga (2019): (A) Two-dimensional orbs change to three-dimensional tangle webs, sometimes including non-sticky reinforced threads. In some cases, radial reinforced lines are present; (B) No changes observed; (C) Some areas of an original three-dimensional structure are modified, with the addition of more threads or protective structures; (D) Suppression or reduction of orb components (viscid spirals and radii). Some had web reinforcements and/or added protective structures (e.g., barrier threads). In some cases, a distinct platform supported the cocoon. (E) There was a hole through the center of the hub and a few additional threads in the central section of the orb, to which the cocoon was then attached; (F) Orb web is reduced to one highly reinforced main thread, sometimes tensioned by a side thread; (G) A platform supports the cocoon in a position away from the normal resting position occupied by the host spider; (H) A closed silk chamber; (I) Reduced three-dimensional structure without gumfoot threads, with added threads connected laterally to vegetation; (J) Possible removal of the curled leaf used as a refuge; (K) Three-dimensional structure is reduced to two reinforced threads attached to vegetation.

[e]We considered exposed pupae as those attached to the web by a single or multiple threads, where the cocoon remains visually exposed to the environment. Sheltered pupae were considered as those visually protected, either within a leaf shelter or within dome-shaped silk structures. We also consider sheltered webs that increase the density of threads around the pupa.

H. japi is associated with spiders from the families Tetragnathidae and Araneidae, parasitizing *Leucauge roseosignata* and *Mecynogea bigibba*. The rarity of transitions between host spider families demonstrates that Polysphinctine wasps maintain a strong phylogenetic association with their hosts, which may be attributed to the similarity of morphological and behavioral traits among the hosts within each family.

The standardized latitude and longitude varied 81.6% and 96.3%, respectively, in relation to the mean. Thus, there was great potential for these spatial measures to capture diverse host ranges, including the possibility of parasitoids to interact with new spider species across the host species distribution. There was no effect of standardized latitude ($\beta_{lat} = -0.02$ [-0.13 to 0.09]). However, the number of articles ($\beta_{articles} = 0.09$ [$0.05-0.13$]) and the standardized longitude influenced the number of host species ($\beta_{long} = 0.37$ [$0.23-0.50$]). The number of host species increased by 1.09 [$1.05-1.14$] and 1.44 [$1.26-1.65$] times with an increase of one article and one standard deviation of longitude, respectively (Figs. 4A,B). The fixed predictors explained 49% of variance in the number of host species, similar to the full model including random variables ($R_m^2 = 0.49$, $R_c^2 = 0.50$). For the Simpsons' index of host diversity, we did not detect effects of the standardized latitude ($\beta_{lat} = -0.02$ [-0.70 to 0.62]) and number of articles ($\beta_{article} = 0.03$ [-0.22 to 0.23]). However, the standardized longitude also affected host diversity ($\beta_{long} = 0.84$ [0.11 to 1.61]). Simpsons' index of host diversity increased by 2.32 [1.12 to 5.03] times with an increase of one standard deviation of longitude (Fig. 4C). The fixed predictor explained 28% of variance in host diversity ($R_m^2 = 0.28$, $R_c^2 = 0.28$).

The absence of a correlation between the number of hosts, host diversity per parasitoid species, and latitude suggests that parasitoids may not demonstrate tolerance towards a wide array of abiotic conditions. Consequently, climate may contribute to an increase in the specificity of interactions with hosts that co-occur within the tolerated limits of each parasitoid species. Furthermore, it is plausible that this factor may facilitate specific adaptations within each interaction, particularly in relation to the immobilization strategy of host spiders (see Section 6.4) and the induction of behavioral modifications.

However, we observed that the number and diversity of hosts per parasitoid species were associated with longitudinal range, thereby highlighting the significant influence of distribution area breadth on enhancing diversity within interactions between spiders and wasps. This

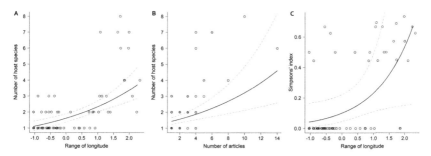

Fig. 4 Relationship between the number of host species parasitized by wasp species and: (A) the scaled range of longitude (in units of standard deviation), and (B) the number of articles that described the interactions for each wasp species. (C) Relationship between Simpsons' index of host diversity and the (scaled) range of longitude. The black lines correspond to the relationship predicted by the model, and the gray dashed lines represent the 95% confidence interval.

finding implies that host spiders face heightened parasitism pressure as their spatial distribution widens longitudinally. Furthermore, the presence of host species with extensive longitudinal distributions can enhance the stability of parasitoid populations relying on multiple hosts, thereby reducing the likelihood of local extinction resulting from a population decline in a specific host spider species. Additionally, in local scenarios where alternative potential hosts become more abundant, parasitoids may exhibit flexibility by shifting between host species or attacking multiple hosts.

5. Parasitoid-spider networks

At host species level, there were 173 interactions between 143 spider species and 89 wasp species. The network exhibited low connectance ($C = 0.01$), low clustering ($Cw = 0.01$), and low nestedness ($NODF = 0.67$; Fig. 5). The mean number of links per species was 0.75, and the mean number of shared partners was 0.01 for wasps and 0.02 for spiders, which explains the low generality of wasp species (3.33) and low vulnerability of host species (1.42). Specialization was high ($H_2' = 0.99$), probably because 60.7% of interactions were monospecific. Therefore, interactions were highly specialized. The wasp *Z. percontatoria* was an exception, being recorded parasitizing eight spider species.

Among spider host genera ($n = 68$), 20.2% of the interactions involved three spider genera: *Anelosimus* ($n = 12$), *Araneus* ($n = 12$), and *Cyclosa* ($n = 11$).

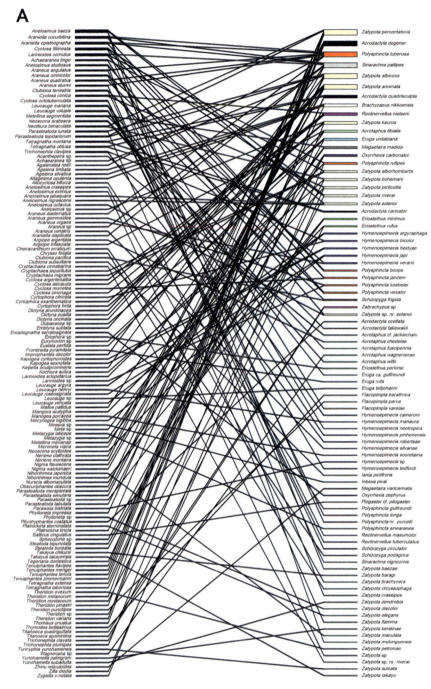

Fig. 5 Bipartite network with parasitoid species (*right*) and their spider hosts (*left*) at three taxonomic levels: (A) species, (B) genus, and (C) family. Each line represents an interaction between species. For networks with genera and families of spiders, the thickness of the line corresponds to the number of interactions with different parasitoid species.

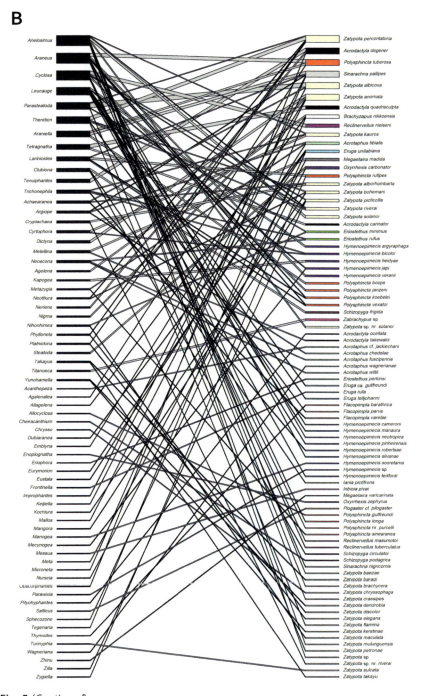

Fig. 5 (Continued)

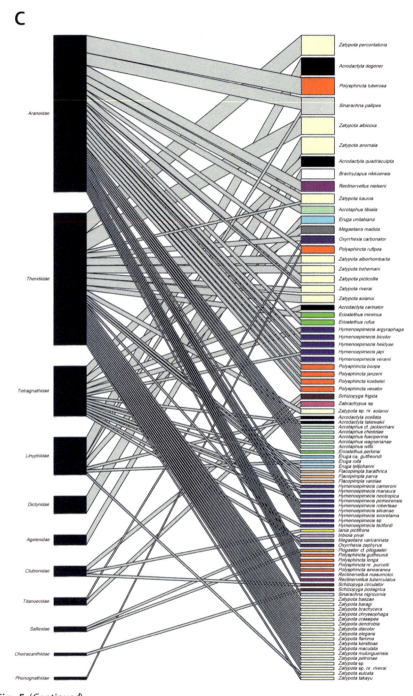

Fig. 5 (Continued)

The network also had low weighted connectance (C = 0.02), low clustering (Cw = 0.01), and low nestedness ($WNODF$ = 1.75). We found, on average, 0.83 links per species. Wasps shared 0.04 spider genera, while hosts shared 0.03 parasitoid species. The generality of parasitoid species (1.95) and the vulnerability of spider genera were similar (3.31) to the species level network. Specialization, however, decreased considerably (H_2' = 0.44).

At family level, wasps parasitized 11 spider families, in which 78.6% of interactions included three host families: Araneidae (n = 63), Theridiidae (n = 53), and Tetragnathidae (n = 20). The weighted connectance (C = 0.10), clustering (Cw = 0.09), and nestedness ($WNODF$ = 6.32) increased slightly when compared with the species level network. There was 0.95 links per species on average. Wasps shared 0.29 spider genera, while spiders shared 0.11 parasitoid species. The generality for parasitoids was similarly low (1.11), but the vulnerability of spider families increased (19.2) when compared with the species level network. Specialization was still high (H_2' = 0.90).

When investigating specialization degree (d') of parasitoid species at the three taxonomic levels of hosts, we found only four species with d' lower than 0.3: *Polysphincta* nr. *purcelli*, *Polysphincta vexator*, *Zatypota baezae*, and *Zatypota mulunguensis* (Table 2). These species exhibited associations with a limited number of hosts, but these host spiders showed broader associations. We observed a high degree of specialization at the species and genus levels, with d' values exceeding 0.5. However, when examining host specialization at the family taxonomic level, we found that only 10 parasitoid species (11.2%) exhibited a high degree of specialization (>0.5). Although the associations of polysphinctines are restricted to just 10 families, our results emphasize that specificity is low within this group.

The specific characteristics of host selection may be associated with phylogenetic, behavioral, and morphological traits. Phylogenetic and behavioral traits of spider hosts may be associated to structural aspects of webs and morphological characters, which may be relevant during the attack and immobilization processes. In addition, host body size usually has a positive effect on the number of parasite species that hosts may harbor. It happens because larger species tend to offer more space and resources for the parasites, increasing the likelihood of encounters through contact or food availability (Kamiya, O'Dwyer, Nakagawa, & Poulin, 2014). In this scenario, it is possible that the size of the hosts also represents an important factor influencing specialization in parasitoid wasps. In the next sections, we discuss how each of these factors can influence the emergence of the pattern of high specificity in interactions between spiders and polysphinctine wasps.

Table 2 Values of specialization degree (d') of parasitoid species for three different taxonomic levels of hosts (species, genus, and family). We highlighted in bold the species with d' < 0.3 in the three levels as the generalist parasitoid species across taxonomic levels.

Species level		Genus level		Family level	
Parasitoid species	**d'**	**Parasitoid species**	**d'**	**Parasitoid species**	**d'**
Zatypota baezae	**0.00**	Hymenoepimecis neotropica	0.00	Acrotaphus cf. jackiechani	0.00
Zatypota mulunguensis	**0.00**	Hymenoepimecis silvanae	0.00	Acrotaphus chedelae	0.00
Polysphincta boops	0.12	Polysphincta longa	0.00	Acrotaphus fuscipennis	0.00
Polysphincta nr. purcelli	**0.21**	Sinarachna nigricornis	0.00	Acrotaphus wagnerianae	0.00
Polysphincta vexator	**0.28**	**Zatypota baezae**	**0.00**	Acrotaphus wiltii	0.00
Zatypota riverai	0.31	Zatypota brachycera	0.00	Eriostethus perkinsi	0.00
Polysphincta tuberosa	0.40	Zatypota crassipes	0.00	Hymenoepimecis neotropica	0.00
Acrodactyla carinator	0.44	**Zatypota mulunguensis**	**0.00**	Hymenoepimecis robertsae	0.00
Acrodactyla takewakii	0.50	Zatypota sp.	0.00	Hymenoepimecis silvanae	0.00
Acrotaphus fuscipennis	0.50	**Polysphincta nr. purcelli**	**0.04**	Hymenoepimecis sooretama	0.00
Acrotaphus wiltii	0.50	Reclinervellus masumotoi	0.04	Hymenoepimecis sp.	0.00
Eruga ca. gutfreundi	0.50	Reclinervellus tuberculatus	0.04	Polysphincta gutfreundi	0.00
Flacopimpla varelae	0.50	Zatypota riverai	0.06	Polysphincta longa	0.00

Hymenoepimecis camereni	0.50	Eruga ca. gutfreundi	0.12	***Polysphincta* nr. *purcelli***	**0.00**
Hymenoepimecis neotropica	0.50	Eruga telljohanni	0.12	Polysphincta sinearanea	0.00
Hymenoepimecis pinheirensis	0.50	Hymenoepimecis cameroni	0.12	Reclinervellus masumotoi	0.00
Hymenoepimecis robertsae	0.50	Hymenoepimecis manaura	0.12	Reclinervellus tuberculatus	0.00
Hymenoepimecis tedforai	0.50	Hymenoepimecis pinheirensis	0.12	Sinarachna nigricornis	0.00
Polysphincta longa	0.50	Hymenoepimecis tedfordi	0.12	Zatypota riverai	0.04
Reclinervellus masumotoi	0.50	Flacopimpla parva	0.16	Flacopimpla barathrica	0.04
Reclinervellus tuberculatus	0.50	Zatypota flamma	0.16	Flacopimpla parva	0.04
Schizopyga circulator	0.50	Zatypota petronae	0.16	Flacopimpla varelae	0.04
Sinarachna nigricornis	0.50	Polysphincta koebelei	0.18	Oxyrrhexis zephyrus	0.04
Zatypota crassipes	0.50	**Polysphincta vexator**	**0.18**	**Zatypota baezae**	**0.04**
Zatypota flamma	0.50	Hymenoepimecis veranii	0.28	Zatypota baragi	0.04
Sinarachna pallipes	0.54	Zatypota sp. nr. Solanoi	0.28	Zatypota brachycera	0.04
Polysphincta janzeni	0.56	Polysphincta janzeni	0.31	Zatypota chryssophaga	0.04
Zatypota solanoi	0.61	Hymenoepimecis argyraphaga	0.39	Zatypota crassipes	0.04

(continued)

Table 2 Values of specialization degree (d') of parasitoid species for three different taxonomic levels of hosts (species, genus, and family). We highlighted in bold the species with d' 0.3 in the three levels as the generalist parasitoid species across taxonomic levels. (cont'd)

Species level		Genus level		Family level	
Parasitoid species	d'	Parasitoid species	d'	Parasitoid species	d'
Polysphincta rufipes	0.69	Zatypota solanoi	0.44	Zatypota dendrobia	0.04
Acrodactyla quadrisculpta	0.70	Eriostethus minimus	0.44	Zatypota discolor	0.04
Hymenoepimecis bicolor	0.72	Hymenoepimecis robertsae	0.44	Zatypota elegans	0.04
Hymenoepimecis veranii	0.72	Iania pictifrons	0.44	Zatypota flamma	0.04
Schizopyga frigida	0.72	Schizopyga circulator	0.44	Zatypota kerstinae	0.04
Zatypota nr. solanoi	0.72	Polysphincta boops	0.50	Zatypota maculata	0.04
Megaetaira madida	0.81	Eriostethus rufus	0.50	**Zatypota mulunguensis**	**0.04**
Zatypota albicoxa	0.81	Hymenoepimecis bicolor	0.50	Zatypota petronae	0.04
Zatypota alborhombarta	0.81	Zatypota kauros	0.51	Zatypota sp.	0.04
Zatypota bohemani	0.81	Acrodactyla carinator	0.56	Zatypota sp. nr. riverai	0.04
Zatypota picticollis	0.81	Acrodactyla takewakii	0.56	Zatypota takayu	0.04
Zatypota percontatoria	0.82	Acrotaphus chedelae	0.56	Zatypota kauros	0.05
Reclinervellus nielseni	0.85	Acrotaphus fuscipennis	0.56	Hymenoepimecis japi	0.12

Acrodactyla degener	1.00	Acrotaphus wiltii	0.56	Eriostethus rufus	0.15
Acrodactyla ocellata	1.00	Flacopimpla varelae	0.56	Hymenoepimecis bicolor	0.15
Acrotaphus cf. jackiechani	1.00	Hymenoepimecis japi	0.56	Hymenoepimecis heidyae	0.15
Acrotaphus chedelae	1.00	Zatypota sp. nr. riverai	0.56	Hymenoepimecis veranii	0.15
Acrotaphus tibialis	1.00	Polysphincta tuberosa	0.56	Polysphincta boops	0.15
Acrotaphus wagnerianae	1.00	Reclinervellus nielseni	0.58	Polysphincta janzeni	0.15
Brachyzapus nikkoensis	1.00	Zatypota percontatoria	0.60	Polysphincta koebelei	0.15
Eriostethus minimus	1.00	Zatypota bohemani	0.62	**Polysphincta vexator**	**0.15**
Eriostethus perkinsi	1.00	Sinarachna pallipes	0.66	Acrotaphus tibialis	0.18
Eriostethus rufus	1.00	Zatypota picticollis	0.67	Zatypota picticollis	0.18
Eruga rufa	1.00	Polysphincta sinearanea	0.72	Eriostethus minimus	0.19
Eruga telljohanni	1.00	Schizopyga frigida	0.72	Zatypota sp. nr. solanoi	0.19
Eruga unilabiana	1.00	Zatypota baragi	0.72	Reclinervellus nielseni	0.20
Flacopimpla barathrica	1.00	Zatypota dendrobia	0.72	Sinarachna pallipes	0.22
Flacopimpla parva	1.00	Zatypota discolor	0.72	Zatypota alborhombarta	0.22

(continued)

Table 2 Values of specialization degree (d') of parasitoid species for three different taxonomic levels of hosts (species, genus, and family). We highlighted in bold the species with d' 0.3 in the three levels as the generalist parasitoid species across taxonomic levels. (*cont'd*)

Species level		Genus level		Family level	
Parasitoid species	**d'**	**Parasitoid species**	**d'**	**Parasitoid species**	**d'**
Hymenoepimecis argyraphaga	1.00	*Zatypota elegans*	0.72	*Zatypota bohemani*	0.22
Hymenoepimecis heidyae	1.00	*Zatypota kerstinae*	0.72	*Zatypota solanoi*	0.22
Hymenoepimecis japi	1.00	*Zatypota maculata*	0.72	*Acrodactyla takewakii*	0.28
Hymenoepimecis manaura	1.00	*Zatypota takayu*	0.72	*Eruga* ca. *gutfreundi*	0.28
Hymenoepimecis silvanae	1.00	*Zatypota alborhombarta*	0.74	*Eruga telljohanni*	0.28
Hymenoepimecis sooretama	1.00	*Polysphincta rufipes*	0.75	*Hymenoepimecis cameroni*	0.28
Hymenoepimecis sp.	1.00	*Acrotaphus tibialis*	0.76	*Hymenoepimecis manaura*	0.28
Iania pictifrons	1.00	*Zatypota albicoxa*	0.78	*Hymenoepimecis pinheirensis*	0.28
Inbioia pivai	1.00	*Acrodactyla quadrisculpta*	0.83	*Hymenoepimecis tedfordi*	0.28
Megaetaira varicarinata	1.00	*Megaetaira madida*	0.89	*Megaetaira varicarinata*	0.28
Oxyrrhexis carbonator	1.00	*Acrodactyla degener*	1.00	*Polysphincta tuberosa*	0.28
Oxyrrhexis zephyrus	1.00	*Acrodactyla ocellata*	1.00	*Oxyrrhexis carbonator*	0.31
Piogaster cf. *pilogaster*	1.00	*Acrotaphus* cf. *jackiechani*	1.00	*Zatypota albicoxa*	0.34

Polysphincta gutfreundi	1.00	*Acrotaphus wagnerianae*	1.00	*Acrodactyla ocellata*	0.35
Polysphincta koebelei	1.00	*Brachyzapus nikkoensis*	1.00	*Eruga rufa*	0.35
Polysphincta sinearanea	1.00	*Eriostethus perkinsi*	1.00	*Zatypota sulcata*	0.35
Schizopyga podagrica	1.00	*Eruga rufa*	1.00	*Zatypota percontatoria*	0.35
Zabrachypus sp.	1.00	*Eruga unilabiana*	1.00	*Polysphincta rufipes*	0.38
Zatypota anómala	1.00	*Flacopimpla barathrica*	1.00	*Acrodactyla carinator*	0.43
Zatypota baragi	1.00	*Hymenoepimecis heidyae*	1.00	*Hymenoepimecis argyraphaga*	0.43
Zatypota brachycera	1.00	*Hymenoepimecis sooretama*	1.00	*Megaetaira madida*	0.49
Zatypota chryssophaga	1.00	*Hymenoepimecis* sp.	1.00	*Acrodactyla quadrisculpta*	0.54
Zatypota dendrobia	1.00	*Inbioia pivai*	1.00	*Eruga unilabiana*	0.57
Zatypota discolor	1.00	*Megaetaira varicarinata*	1.00	*Iania pictifrons*	0.67
Zatypota elegans	1.00	*Oxyrrhexis carbonator*	1.00	*Schizopyga circulator*	0.67
Zatypota kauros	1.00	*Oxyrrhexis zephyrus*	1.00	*Acrodactyla degener*	0.75
Zatypota kerstinae	1.00	*Piogaster* cf. *pilogaster*	1.00	*Schizopyga frigida*	0.83
Zatypota maculata	1.00	*Polysphincta gutfreundi*	1.00	*Inbioia pivai*	0.83

(continued)

Table 2 Values of specialization degree (d') of parasitoid species for three different taxonomic levels of hosts (species, genus, and family). We highlighted in bold the species with d' 0.3 in the three levels as the generalist parasitoid species across taxonomic levels. (cont'd)

Species level		Genus level		Family level	
Parasitoid species	d'	Parasitoid species	d'	Parasitoid species	d'
Zatypota petronae	1.00	Schizopyga podagrica	1.00	Piogaster cf. pilogaster	0.83
Zatypota sp.	1.00	Zabrachypus sp.	1.00	Zabrachypus sp.	0.90
Zatypota nr. riverai	1.00	Zatypota anomala	1.00	Brachyzapus nikkoensis	1.00
Zatypota sulcata	1.00	Zatypota chryssophaga	1.00	Schizopyga podagrica	1.00
Zatypota takayu	1.00	Zatypota sulcata	1.00	Zatypota anomala	1.00

6. Factors influencing specificity patterns
6.1 Phylogenetic constraints

The two major clades proposed in the molecular phylogeny conducted by Matsumoto (2016), the *Schizopyga* subgroup and the *Acrodactyla* + *Polysphincta* subgroup, differ in essential aspects that may influence their host ranges. They have two distinct oviposition stances (dorsal vs. ventral-press, reflecting which side of the ovipositor is in contact with the host) and attack different taxonomic groups of spiders. The *Schizopyga* subgroup attacks spiders included in the RTA clade (sensu Coddington & Levi, 1991), such as Agelenidae, Salticidae, Titanoecidae, and Clubionidae. These wasps always deposit their eggs on the cephalothorax of their hosts. According to Takasuka et al. (2018), the placement of eggs on this position may reduce their exposure to physical damage in spiders that actively run on substrates and hide themselves in crevices or tubular retreats. This risk is not relevant for the eggs of wasps belonging to the *Acrodactyla* + *Polysphincta* subgroup, which deposit their eggs on the abdomen of aerial web weaving spiders of the superfamily Araneoidea.

Takasuka et al. (2018) emphasize that the shift from one group of hosts (RTA clade) to another (Araneoidea) apparently promoted a stronger radiation and/or survival among wasps included in the *Acrodactyla* + *Polysphincta* subgroup. This subgroup is currently composed of 18 genera and more than 200 species, while the *Schizopyga* subgroup has only 7 genera and less than 50 species. This difference is attributed by the authors to feeding advantages for the larvae and easier location of the relatively conspicuous webs of Araneoidea, despite the greater species richness of spiders from the RTA clade (Dimitrov & Hormiga, 2021).

Differences between these two subgroups of polysphinctines constitute the first restriction to generalized patterns of host-parasitoid association, with each group being able to efficiently attack only specific spider taxa. We observed that the specialization degree of parasitoids tends to vary less and be higher in parasitoid species of the *Schizopyga* subgroup (Table 2). Despite the fewer representative species interactions in this group, we noted that the level of specialization at the species level for *Schizopyga* species exceeded d′ = 0.5 (*S. circulator* = 0.50, *S. frigida* = 0.72, and *S. podagrica* = 1.00), while *Piogaster* and *Brachyzapus* exhibited maximum specialization (d′ = 1.00). It is possible that the behavior of species of *Schizopyga* subgroup, depositing their eggs in spiders of the RTA clade, resulted in an increase in host specificity within this subgroup compared to parasitoids of the *Acrodactyla* + *Polysphincta* subgroup. However, this hypothesis remains open and represents an interesting investigation for further research on the evolutionary biology of the polysphinctine wasps.

6.2 Web structures, shelters, and other defenses

The architecture patterns of spider aerial webs are highly variable even within families, between genera and species (Eberhard 2020, Fig. 6). For example, in the two most parasitized spider families (Araneidae and Theridiidae), the webs can be relatively simple structures, such as bidimensional orb-webs, or may include barrier threads, silk or detritus stabilimenta, refuges and complex aggregations (Fig. 6). All these components were previously associated with defense against predators and parasitoids, reducing the conspicuity, acting as physical barriers, and/or allowing the existence of an early warning effect (Cloudsley-Thompson, 1995; Gonzaga & Vasconcellos-Neto, 2012; Manicom, Schwarzkopf, Alford, & Schoener, 2008; Uetz, Boyle, Hieber, & Wilcox, 2002). The three-dimensional tangle or sheet webs may be even more effective, at least against hunting wasps (e.g., Sphecidae and Crabronidae), in reducing the efficiency of the attacks (Blackledge, Coddington, & Gillespie, 2003). All of these defensive strategies are inefficient against polysphinctines. Each defensive structure involving webs, shelters, or complex collective aggregations is vulnerable to some attacking strategy of a parasitoid wasp. However, if distinct webs demand specific attacking behaviors, they may constitute another restriction for wasps to use multiple hosts.

Most polysphinctines (all those included in the *Acrodactyla* + *Polysphincta* subgroup, see Takasuka et al., 2018) attack web-weaver spiders. Spiders that construct three-dimensional web structures are especially attacked by some genera (e.g., *Zatypota*) and orb-weavers are especially attacked by others (e.g., *Polysphincta* and *Hymenoepimecis*). In interactions with multiple hosts, we observed that parasitoids could utilize webs with significant structural variation in only five cases (Table 1). We observed that the parasitoids *H. japi*, *Zatypota kaurus*, *Zatypota riverai*, as well as *Hymenoepimecis bicolor* (Gonzaga, Pádua, & Quero, 2022; Gonzaga, Sobczak, Penteado-Dias, & Eberhard, 2010; Korenko et al., 2018b; Messas, Sobczak, & Vasconcellos-Neto, 2017; Sobczak, Loffredo, Penteado-Dias, & Gonzaga, 2009; Sobczak, Messas et al., 2017; Sobczak, Paiva Arruda et al., 2019; Villanueva-Bonilla et al., 2021), exhibit the ability to attack and utilize spiders with different web architectures, ranging from orb webs to sheet and tangled webs. Furthermore, the parasitoid *Acrotaphus tibialis*, despite attacking orb-weaving spiders, utilizes species with completely distinct habits and webs. This parasitoid utilizes the

Fig. 6 Normal host webs. (A) Horizontal orb web of *Leucauge volupis*. (B) Vertical orb web of *Cyclosa fililineata* with a linear detritus stabilimentum on the upper side of the web. (C) Vertical orb web of *Trichonephila clavipes* including barrier threads. (D) Vertical orb web of *Araneus omnicolor* with a shelter constructed using a dry leaf. (E) Web of
(Continued)

Fig. 6—Cont'd *Cyrtophora citricola* composed of a dense three-dimensional structure of supporting threads and a horizontal sheet. (F) Webs of *Manogea porracea*. The inferior horizontal sheet and the three-dimensional structure above was constructed by the female, and the superior horizontal sheet was constructed by the male. The couple maintains cooperatively the integrity of the entire structure during the reproductive period. (G) Web of *Achaearanea tingo* with a leaf shelter protected by a complex three-dimensional silk structure. (H) Individual web of *Anelosimus nigriscens* surrounding leaves and stems of a plant. (I) Large colonial web of *Anelosimus dubiosus*, including a region with several dry leaves used as shelters and external dense mesh of silk.

spider *Argiope trifasciata* (Eberhard, 2013), which has a three-dimensional orb-web with barrier threads surrounding the orb, but it also attacks *Eustala perfida*, which constructs an orb web without barriers, placed always parallel to tree trunks (Messas, 2014). However, the incredible ability to subdue hosts with such distinct webs represents exceptions within the polysphinctines.

We also observed that most parasitoid pupae develop in visually exposed areas of the modified webs, but it is rare for the same parasitoid to utilize host webs with and without shelters for pupal development. The observation of pupae from the same parasitoid developing in webs with and without shelter was only noted in three interactions (Table 1). In the webs of the spider *Nihonhimea mundula*, the wasp *Eriostethus minimus* develops within shelters, while in the webs of the alternative host, *Parasteatoda* sp., the pupa remains exposed in the modified structure (Korenko et al., 2018a). A similar pattern is observed in the modified webs induced by the wasps *Eruga unilabiana* and *Z. riverai* (Pereira, Villanueva-Bonilla, Azevedo, & Sobczak, 2022; Sobczak et al., 2017; Sobczak, Villanueva-Bonilla, Pádua, & Messas, 2017; Villanueva-Bonilla et al., 2021). The rarity of variation in the pupal development sites suggests that parasitoids seldom manage to attack and utilize alternative hosts with significant architectural variations in their webs. This may be related to the absence of behavioral adaptations to target spiders with and without shelters, for example. However, the influence of the structural characteristics of host spider webs, such as the presence of shelters, on the specificity of interactions can only be addressed with improved descriptions of the behavioral routines involved in polysphinctine wasps.

6.3 Morphological and chemical host traits

Regarding morphological traits, we observed that parasitoids capable of utilizing more than one host spider typically parasitize spiders of different sizes (Table 1). *Hymenoepimecis bicolor*, for example, parasitizes individuals of the spider *Trichonephila clavipes* with a body length that can reach 24.8 mm, but also females of *Cyrtophora citricola* of about 8.8 mm (Gonzaga et al., 2010; Gonzaga et al., 2022). This variation directly impacts sex determination (Takasuka, Matsumoto, & Ohbayashi, 2009; Sobczak et al., 2023). Female parasitoids allocate unfertilized eggs to smaller hosts, producing male parasitoid larvae, while fertilized eggs are assigned to larger hosts, resulting in female production (Takasuka et al., 2009; Sobczak et al., 2023). Moreover, parasitoids modify their preference for host body size according to seasonal changes in the abundance of host spiders (Korenko, Michalková, Zwakhals, & Pekár, 2011). This suggests that the selection of alternative hosts with distinct sizes may have consequences for the sex ratio of parasitoids in the environment. Furthermore, it suggests that host switching may have been selected for in accordance with seasonal variations in host availability.

The large variation in body size between species used by the same parasitoids indicates that this variable may be less restrictive to the expansion of host range than other factors, such as host's web structure. This may be explained as a consequence of nutrient acquisition by the wasp larva during the period of development from egg to the third instar, when it becomes ready for pupation. It would be interesting to evaluate the importance of the nutrients acquired after this period (i.e., the host biomass consumed by the third instar larvae just before pupation) to the success of pupal development and adult emergence. The biomass ingested by larvae in their final instar may be less important than the nutrition obtained during larval growth, when the spider is still alive and consuming the prey captured in normal, unmodified webs. Despite this possibility and the number of described interactions, information on host size variation is scarce in the literature, hindering a robust analysis.

While some variation in body size may be tolerable, other morphological traits might be critical for determining the susceptibility of spiders to the attacks. For instance, despite the high incidence of associations between polysphinctine wasps and spiders of the family Araneidae, no records have been obtained for species included in the subfamilies Micratheninae (genera *Xylethrus* and *Micrathena*, totalizing 125 species widespread in the New World—see Scharff & Coddington, 1997; WSC, 2023) and Gastheracanthinae (genera *Gastroxya*, *Augusta*, *Macracantha*, *Isoxya*, *Austracantha*, *Togacantha*, *Gasteracantha* and *Aetrocantha*, totalizing 116 species broadly distributed in the Old World—see Scharff & Coddington, 1997; WSC, 2023). Individuals of these two subfamilies are covered by a strong exoskeletal cuticle and an armature of strong, sharp spines. It is suggested that this morphology may be important in avoiding predation by birds and hunting wasps (Cloudsley-Thompson, 1995). However, the absence of parasitism by polysphinctine wasps may be related to their larvae's inability to pierce the abdomen of these spiders for feeding. Nonetheless, the adaptations of the abdomen may also provide protection during the immobilization and oviposition processes carried out by the wasps. The protective function of the spines, as well as other traits of the exo-, endo-, and mesocuticles of the many groups of spiders ignored and attacked by parasitoids (Machałowski, Amemiya, & Jesionowski, 2020), remains an interesting and poorly known area of research.

Finally, another noteworthy fact is that several species of *Polysphincta*, such as *P. janzeni*, *P. purcelli*, and *P. sinaeranea*, are observed attacking their hosts during the night (Kloss et al., 2016, 2018). The ability to detect a host during the night suggests adaptations in the chemical receptors of their antennae to identify host cues, which could be relevant in the evolution of specificity. Adaptations in chemical receptors found in sphecid wasps may explain the higher incidence of attacks on spiders with two-dimensional webs compared to three-dimensional webs. For instance, Uma & Weiss (2010) discovered that the higher incidence of attacks by a sphecid species on two-dimensional webs was not related to the greater protection offered by three-dimensional webs, but rather to the ability to recognize chemical cues from spiders that build two-dimensional webs. The development of specificity in parasitoids through chemical recognition of host spiders is still completely unknown at this point but may be a factor that explains the association patterns reported here.

6.4 Variation in the attack behavior of polysphinctine wasps on spiders

Within the polysphinctines, there is a high interspecific and, at least in some cases, intraspecific variation in attacking behaviors used for wasps to intercept and immobilize their hosts prior to egg laying (Figs. 7, 8). Unfortunately, records of the complete behavioral sequences performed during the attacks are available for a few species (Takasuka, Matsumoto, & Maeto, 2019; Table 3), and fewer were observed more than once, which is necessary for the analysis of variation in the strategies used to subdue their hosts. One remarkable exception is *Z. albicoxa*. This species presents at least four attacking modes against one of its host species, the theridiid spider *Parasteatoda tepidariorum* (Fig. 7A–D). According to Takasuka & Matsumoto (2011b), these variations include: (a) *aggressive mimicry*, involving being voluntarily trapped by an

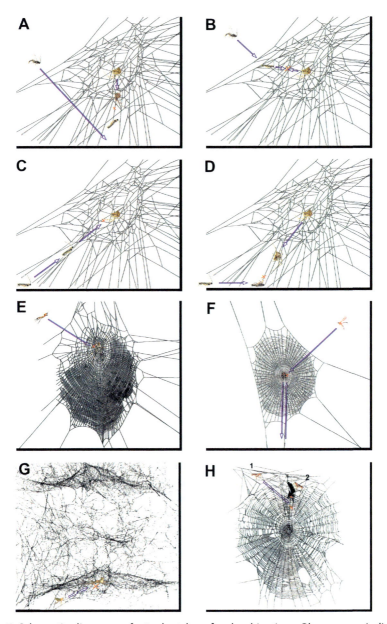

Fig. 7 Schematic diagrams of attack styles of polysphinctines. Blue arrows indicate the movements of spiders and wasps. The red cross indicates the interaction location. (A–D) *Zatypota albicoxa* attacking *Parasteatoda tepidariorum* (after Takasuka, K., & Matsumoto, R. (2011b). Lying on the dorsum: Unique host-attacking behaviour of *Zatypota albicoxa* (Hymenoptera, Ichneumonidae). *Journal of Ethology, 29*(2), 203–207. https://doi.org/10.1007/s10164-010-0263-8): strategy involvig aggressive mimicry.
(Continued)

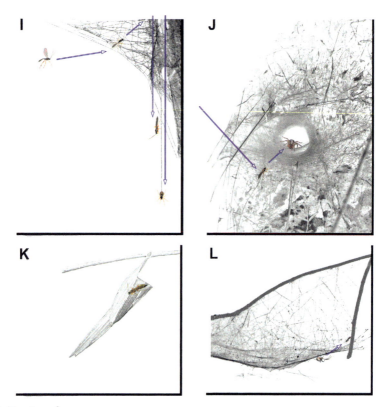

Fig. 7 (Continued)

Fig. 7—Cont'd (A) The wasp flies in and perches on the middle of the vertical gumfooted threads to be lifted up by the spider. (B) The wasp flies in and perches on the middle of the web. The spider is attracted by its movements. (C) *Climbing-style*. The wasp climbs up a non-sticky frame thread. (D) *Reclining style*. The wasp wanders under the web and lays down on her dorsum, pulling at the gumfooted thread or leans against the thread motionlessly with both legs touching the gumfoot. After this behavior, the spider climbs down and is attacked. (E) Abrupt plunge. This direct attack was observed in interactions between *Hymenoepimecis bicolor* and *Trichonephila clavipes* (M.O. Gonzaga pers. obs.). The wasp flies around the spider for a few seconds and makes a direct attack, attempting to grab its potential host still at the center of the web and inject its venom. It has been observed that the host can jump, and in this case, it is immobilized on the ground. Similar sequences were reported in other species (Table 3). (F) Ambush (*Lie-in-wait style*). This specific attack was reported, for example, in interactions involving *Polysphincta* sp. nr. *purcelli* and *Cyclosa fililineata*, and *P. janzeni* and *C. morretes*. The wasp initially lands on a position close to the web hub. The spider then jumps to the ground and the wasp remains motionless (for periods up to 14 h) at the web hub until its potential host returns to be attacked (Kloss et al., 2016b).

Hymenoepimecis cameroni was also observed waiting for the return of its host, but in a distinct position (see Fig. 9G). (G) *Chasing style*. This behavior was observed in *Zatypota* sp. attacking *Anelosimus* spp. (M.O. Gonzaga, pers. obs.) and *Hymenoepimecis soor-etama* attacking *Manogea porracea* (Sobczak et al., 2009). The initial phase is similar to the *ambush-style* described in (B). The wasp lands on vegetation or on supporting threads of the web and walks until the position occupied by the spider, but the wasp chases the potential host after reaching its position. (H) Two variations observed in the attacks of *Hymenoepimecis veranii* on *Araneus omnicolor*: (1) Ambush (*opportunistic style*), in which the wasp lands on barrier threads and waits for the spider to leave the shelter during a foraging event; (2) Aggressive intrusion, in which the wasp lands on the curled leaf used by the spider as a shelter and paralyzes the host within this structure (Gonzaga & Sobczak, 2007; M.O. Gonzaga, pers. obs.). (I) *Chasing style*. This variation of the *chasing style* described in (G) includes the initial approaching towards the spider's resting position and subsequent persecution using the drop line produced by the host. It was described only in *Acrodactyla degener* attacking *Obscuriphantes obscurus* (Bignell, 1898). (J) Aggressive mimicry used by *Brachyzapus nikkoensis* attacking *Agelena silvatica*. The wasp promotes movements to attack the spider from its funnel retreat. (K) Aggressive intrusion performed by *Schizopyga circulator* against *Clubiona riparia*. The wasp forces its entrance into the retreat composed of a silk binding folded blade of grass. (L) Aggressive mimicry of *Longitibia* sp. during the attack against *Neriene fusca*. The wasp promotes vibrations from a position above the sheet of its potential host, waiting for the spider approximation to attack.

adhesive thread and lifted up by the spider (Fig. 8A), or hanging motionlessly at the mid-height of the web, waiting for the spider to come within range before attacking it or perching threads at this position (Takasuka, 2009; Fig. 7B), (b) a climb*ing-style* in which the wasp climbs up a non-sticky thread and moves along the web until it finds the potential host; and (c) a curious variation of aggressive mimicry described as being a *reclining-style*, in which the wasp lies on her back on the ground and grasps one of the vertical gumfoot threads with her legs, feigning a captured and struggling prey (Takasuka & Matsumoto, 2011b). This parasitoid species attacks several spider species, but exclusively those of the genus *Parasteatoda* (Takasuka, Yoshida, Nugroho, & Matsumoto, 2011) with webs consisting of gumfooted vertical threads and dried frame threads (*Achaearanea*-type sensu Benjamin & Zschokke, 2003). There is no information on the strategies used during the immobilization process of the other hosts, but the restriction to the genus *Parasteatoda* as hosts (despite the wide geographical distribution of the parasitoid species) indicates that all behavioral variations are well adapted to the specific responses demonstrated by spiders of this genus.

The presence of multiple attacking modes was also observed in the wasps *Hymenoepimecis cameroni* and *Polysphincta gutfreundi* (Eberhard & Gonzaga, 2019; Gaione-Costa et al., 2022). *H. cameroni* primary strategy is

Fig. 8 (A) *Hymenoepimecis veranii* waiting for *Araneus omnicolor* to leave its shelter. (B) *Hymenoepimecis veranii* using the alternative strategy of invading *A. omnicolor*

shelter to attack. (C) *Zatypota* sp. walking on web threads of *Anelosimus jabaquara* to reach the spiders concealed within the mass of leaves used as refuges. (D) *Polysphincta* sp. nr. *purcelli* waiting on the hub of a web of *Cyclosa fililineata* for the return of the host spider previously attacked. (E) *Hymenoepimecis bicolor* laying one egg on the abdomen of a *Trichonephila clavipes* female previously directly attacked and immobilized. (F) *Hymenoepimecis cameroni* immobilizing the spider *Leucauge volupis*. (G) *Hymenoepimecis cameroni* hanging from the hub of the horizontal orb-web using their hind legs.

to engage in a direct darting attack against its host, the spider *Leucauge volupis*. This approach often prompts the spider to escape into the nearby vegetation. However, in cases where the spider seeks refuge in the vegetation, *H. cameroni* individuals employ a second strategy by hanging from the web hub using their hind legs until the spider returns (Gaione-Costa et al., 2022). Similarly, the wasp *P. gutfreundi* utilizes three basic hunting tactics to subdue the host spider *Allocyclosa bifurca*: (a) striking the spider at its resting site at the hub of its orb web;(b) landing in the sticky spiral of the web, struggling, and then attacking the spider when it approaches; and (c) waiting motionless at the hub for the return of a spider that had fled (see *lie-and-wait style* described below). This adaptation suggests that females of *H. cameroni* and *P. gutfreundi* can adjust their oviposition strategy following an unsuccessful initial attack mode (Eberhard & Gonzaga, 2019).

The attacking behavior of *H. bicolor* on the host *T. clavipes* is similar to the direct attack of *H. cameroni*, involving a simple sequence (Fig. 7E). In the *darting-style* of this species, the wasp flies around the spider, possibly assessing the size of the potential host, and launches a direct attack by throwing itself at the host's body and attempting to grasp it. If successful, the wasp inserts its ovipositor into the spider's mouth and secretes venom, immobilizing it. Eventually, the wasp and the spider fall to the ground after the attack, and the entire process of immobilization and oviposition takes place at this location. Gonzaga et al. (2022) reported *H. bicolor* parasitizing another host species, the araneid *C. citricola*, introduced in Brazil (Álvares & De Maria, 2004). The first record of this spider in Brazil was made in 2004, indicating that the wasp recently included *C. citricola* as a new host. The authors did not observe the attacking behaviors, but the complexity of the web of this new host species would almost certainly make a direct attack unfeasible.

The attacking behavior of *Polysphincta* sp. nr. *purcelli* on *C. fililineata* and *P. janzeni* on *Cyclosa morretes* also includes a distinctive characteristic. Kloss et al. (2016a), Kloss, Gonzaga, Roxinol, and Sperber (2016b) referred to

Table 3 Offensive behaviors of Polysphinctine wasps against their hosts. The behaviors were categorized according to their general patterns, but each case may involve specific variations.

Wasp species	Spider species	Attacking behavior	Type of attack	Reference
Acrodactyla degener	*Obscuriphantes obscurus*	The wasp approaches and chases the spider when it drops on a silk thread.	Active chasing	Bignell (1898)
Brachyzapus nikkoensis	*Agelena silvatica*	The female attracts the spider by promoting movements on the sheet web similar to an intercept prey	Aggressive mimicry	Matsumoto (2009)
Hymenoepimecis veranii	*Araneus omnicolor*	The wasp waits for the spider at the barrier threads or invades the dry leaf used by the host as a shelter	Ambush/ Aggressive intrusion	Gonzaga & Sobczak (2007), M.O. Gonzaga pers. obs.
Hymenoepimecis argyraphaga	*Leucauge argyra*	The wasp hovers around the spider and then rapidly darts at it	Abrupt plunge	Eberhard (2000)
Hymenoepimecis bicolor	*Trichonephila clavipes*	The wasp hovers around the spider and then rapidly darts at it	Abrupt plunge	Gonzaga et al. (2017)
Hymenoepimecis cameroni	*Leucauge volupis*	The wasp darts at the spider or hangs by hind legs from the web hub, waiting for the host	Abrupt plunge/ Ambush	Gaione-Costa et al. (2022)

Hymenoepimecis sooretama	*Manogea porracea*	The wasp invades the web, moves to the position occupied by the spider, and chases the host	Active chasing	Sobczak et al. (2009)
Longitibia sp.	*Neriene fusca*	The wasp perches on web threads above the sheet, promoting vibrations that attract the spider	Aggressive mimicry	Matsumoto (2014)
Polysphincta janzeni	*Cyclosa fililineata*	The wasp waits at the hub of the web for the spider that had fled after its initial attack.	Ambush	
Polysphincta sp. nr *purcelli*	*Cyclosa morretes*	The wasp waits at the hub of the web for the spider that had fled after its initial attack.	Ambush (lie-in-wait)	Kloss et al. (2016a)
Polysphincta gutfreundi	*Allocyclosa bifurca*	The wasp strikes the spider from its resting site on the web, lands on the stick spiral, promoting vibration to attract the host, or waits at the hub of the web for the spider that had fled.	Abrupt plunge/ Aggressive mimicry/ Ambush	Eberhard (2019)

(*continued*)

Table 3 Offensive behaviors of Polysphinctine wasps against their hosts. The behaviors were categorized according to their general patterns, but each case may involve specific variations. (*cont'd*)

Wasp species	Spider species	Attacking behavior	Type of attack	Reference
Polysphincta rufipes	*Larinioides sclopetarius*	The wasp flies directly at its host position	Abrupt plunge	Schmitt et al. (2012)
Polysphincta sinearanea	*Metazygia laticeps*	The wasp remains motionless at the hub of the orb. The wasp is attacked after leaving the retreat.	Ambush	Kloss et al. (2018)
Reclinervellus tuberculatus	*Cyclosa octotuberculata*	The wasp hovers over the spider's position and then rapidly darts at it	Abrupt plunge	Matsumoto (2019)
Schizopyga podagrica	*Cheiracanthium erraticum*	The wasp bites the sheet web	Aggressive mimicry (?)	Nielsen (1935)
Schizopyga circulator	*Clubiona riparia*	The wasp bites the sheet web or opens the folded blades of grass used as shelters	Aggressive mimicry (?)/ Aggressive intrusion	Matsumoto (2014)
Zatypota albicoxa	*Parasteatoda tepidariorum*	The wasp may perch on and hang from one of the gumfooted lines, perch at mid-height on the cobweb and attract the spider, pull a gumfooted line, or climb up a non-sticky frame thread	Aggressive mimicry/ Creeping up	Takasuka & Matsumoto (2011b), Takasuka et al. (2009)

Zatypota maculata	*Nihonhimea japonica*	The wasp may dive into the sheet from above or near the web attracting the spider, or walk along the web threads until it reaches and invades the retreat	Aggressive mimicry/ Aggressive intrusion	Takasuka et al. (2019)
Zatypota sp.	*Anelosimus* spp.	The wasp invades the web, moves to the position occupied by the spider and chases the host	Active chasing	M.O. Gonzaga pers. obs.
Zatypota petronae	*Theridion evexum*	The wasp performs a direct attack after hovering in front of the curled leaf used as a retreat by the spider	Abrupt plunge	Weng & Barrantes (2007)

this particular attack sequence as *lie-and-wait style*. The initial phase of this interaction looks like a typical abrupt plunge attack against the spider located at the hub of its web, but all the spiders observed escaped from this first supposedly capturing attempt. Afterward, the wasps waited at the web's central hub for up to 14 h, anticipating the spider's return. Once the spider returned, the wasp inserted its ovipositor into its mouth, causing it to become paralyzed and motionless for at least 30 min (Fig. 7F). During this interval, the spider's body is inspected, and the egg is deposited.

The attacking behavior of an unidentified species of *Zatypota* on *Anelosimus* spp. (Theridiidae) is similar to an *ambush-style* but includes the wasp pursuing the spiders on their dense webs. In this case, the wasp lands on the edge of an individual or colonial web and effortlessly walks over the capturing threads. The wasp searches for the spiders and initiates a direct attack once in a favorable position about 1 cm away from the potential host (M.O. Gonzaga, pers. obs.). To reach this position the wasp usually pursues a focal individual host for some time. A similar behavioral sequence was reported for *Hymenoepimecis sooretama* attacking the araneid spider *Manogea porracea* (Sobczak et al., 2009). In both cases the density of web threads around the positions usually occupied by the spiders prevents direct attacks before approximation, which almost certainly would result in the wasp promoting vibrations and warning the spiders or becoming entangled and being killed.

In the interactions involving the host *Araneus omnicolor* (Araneidae) and the wasp *Hymenoepimecis veranii* (Figs. 7H, 8A, B), two distinct styles were observed. In the attacking event reported by Gonzaga and Sobczak (2007) (*opportunistic-style*), the wasp landed and remained motionless on the barrier threads until the host left its shelter to capture a fly intercepted by the viscid spiral. At this moment, the wasp quickly attacked and inserted its ovipositor within the spider's mouth, injecting the paralyzing venom and starting to search for eggs deposited by other wasps. Alternatively, this wasp species may enter the spider's shelter, attacking the potential host within the curled dry leaf (M.O. Gonzaga, pers. obs.; Figs. 7H, 8B). The factors determining the adoption of each strategy remain to be studied. This last behavioral category is similar to the aggressive intrusion described by Takasuka et al. (2019) studying the oviposition of *Zatypota maculata* on *Nihonhimea japonica* (Theridiidae). In this case, the wasp ascends the intricate three-dimentional cobweb and gradually advances towards the spider's hiding place, ensuring a slow approach to prevent the spider from fleeing. After a considerable duration, the wasp finally enters the retreat and delivers a venomous sting to the spider.

These descriptions represent only the initial efforts to understand the intra- and interspecific variations in attack behaviors. Some other variations are summarized in Table 3, but many others certainly remain to be discovered and there is no information available on offensive behaviors in several polysphinctine genera (*Aravenator, Chablisea, Eriostethus, Flacopimpla, Dreisbachia, Iania, Inbioia, Piogaster, Oxyrrhexis, Eruga, Lamnatibia, Megaetaira, Sinarachna, Pterinopus, Ticapimpla*, and *Zabrachypus*). While some species demonstrate the ability to employ highly distinct strategies to access their hosts, it is possible that many may have limitations to expand their host range due to the requirement of strategies that are very distinct from those used to access their usual hosts.

7. Conclusions

Based on our review of host specificity patterns in polysphinctine wasps, we concluded that:

- Even in the relatively well studied group of polysphinctine Ichneumonids, there is a strong geographical bias in the available data on host-parasitoid interactions. Most studies were conducted by a few research groups located in Europe, South and Central Americas, and in Japan. There is a significant knowledge gap on host-parasitoid interactions in Asia (except Japan) and Africa, as well as only sparse records in Oceania and North America.
- Although geographical bias may constitute a problem in the analysis of general patterns of distribution of several parasitoid wasps' groups, some conclusions are already possible with others. Timms, Schwarzfeld, and Sääksjarvi (2016), for example, suggested the existence of a significant diversity of latitudinal patterns within the family Ichneumonidae, likely influenced by the diversity and abundance of different host groups. For instance, the subfamily Pimplinae, which includes the polysphinctines, presents a broad latitudinal range and a relatively high abundance across most of the gradient from equator to higher latitudes. There is, however, a higher proportion of species that attack spiders in northern latitudes and parasitoids of Lepidoptera in southern assemblages. Others, such as Tryphoninae (parasitoids of Symphta and Lepidoptera), present a completely different pattern of latitudinal abundance, being more common in northern higher latitudes. However, our analysis demonstrates that the

number of hosts and host diversity per polysphinctine species were not influenced by latitudinal variation, which suggests that these parasitoids have a limited tolerance for a wide range of abiotic conditions. Also, we observed that some polysphinctine species were able to colonize and establish their populations across a wider longitudinal range, allowing the establishment of associations with different host spiders.

- A broad longitudinal distribution of the preferential host species may increase the chances for some parasitoids to be in contact with other potential suitable hosts. In local situations in which the alternative potential hosts became more abundant, the parasitoids may shift between host species or attack both. This may explain why polyphagous parasitoids present a broader distribution. Another possibility is the existence of a large variation in nutritional requirements between species or genera and, especially, in behavioral plasticity during approximation, subduing, and oviposition processes. For instance, while some *Zatypota* species may use several tactics to access their multiple hosts, this variability may be reduced or absent in other wasp genera, restricting their attacks to one or a few specific hosts and also their distribution.

- Parasitoids of spiders must cope with potentially lethal hosts and overcome a series of morphological, physiological, and behavioral barriers imposed by their victims in order to succeed in their attempts of approaching, immobilizing, and ovipositing. Furthermore, they need to select hosts within limits of size and other morphological characteristics, thus ensuring adequate nutrition for their larvae. It is highly likely that the local availability of potential hosts that possess similar characteristics to those of the typically attacked hosts restricts the occurrence of polyphagy in polysphinctines.

- Traits such as the structural pattern of webs and host size do not appear to be critical limiting factors determining specificity. Some species can attack hosts within a wide range of body sizes and webs varying from simple two-dimensional orbs to complex tangles. Nonetheless, we observed that other species are exclusively associated with spiders with specific defensive traits, such as the stabilimentum present in webs of the araneid genus *Cyclosa* parasitized by *Polysphincta* wasps (Kloss et al., 2016a; Kloss et al., 2016b). The rupture of these host's defenses requires highly adapted behaviors.

- Although some wasps establish associations with numerous hosts, it seems that there is a high level of specialization within polysphinctines. This specialization becomes evident when examining the connectivity levels in their interaction network and the limited number of spider families they target, in contrast to the extensive diversity of 132 spider families recognized (WSC, 2023). Additionally, only a small fraction of polysphinctine wasp species can parasitize more than one family of spiders. These observations, along with very stereotyped and specific behaviors for attacking particular hosts, support the conjecture that the specificity in this group of koinobiont manipulative parasitoids is influenced by host's defensive strategies.

Acknowledgements

We thank Stanislav Korenko, Robert Poulin, and Glauco Machado for their carefull review and valuable suggestions. We would also like to thank Amanda Vieira for her help with the elaboration of the maps and Luciana Ueda for her help with some cryptic references. This study was supported by Fundação de Amparo à Pesquisa do Estado de Minas Gerais (FAPEMIG: APQ-03316–22, APQ-02009–21, APQ-02984–17, APQ-00935–18, BIP-00193-24), Fundação de Amparo à Pesquisa do Estado de São Paulo (FAPESP: Proc. 465562/2014–0), Instituto Nacional de Ciência e Tecnologia dos Hymenoptera Parasitoides da Região Sudeste (HYMPAR/Sudeste-CNPq/CAPES/FAPESP), Conselho Nacional de Desenvolvimento Científico e Tecnológico (CNPq: Proc. 310477/2020–4, 314518/2023-1, 441225/2016-0), Universidade do Estado de Minas Gerais (Pesquisador Produtividade da UEMG—PQ/UEMG), Coordenação de Aperfeiçoamento de Pessoal de Nível Superior (CAPES - Demanda Social: 88887.686570/2022-00), and Coordenação de Aperfeiçoamento de Pessoal de Nível Superior (CAPES: Finance Code 001).

Appendix A. Supporting information

Supplementary data associated with this article can be found in the online version at https://doi.org/10.1016/bs.asb.2024.02.002.

References

Adamo, S. A. (1997). How parasites alter the behavior of their insect hosts. In N. E. Beckage (Ed.). *Parasites and pathogens* (pp. 231–245). Boston, Massachusetts, United States: Springer. https://doi.org/10.1007/978-1-4615-5983-2_12.

Agnarsson, I. (2006). A revision of the New World *eximius* lineage of *Anelosimus* (Araneae, Theridiidae) and a phylogenetic analysis using worldwide exemplars. *Zoological Journal of the Linnean Society, 146*(4), 453–593. https://doi.org/10.1111/j.1096-3642.2006.00213.x.

Aguirre, H., de Almeida, L. P., Shaw, S. R., & Sarmiento, C. E. (2015). An illustrated key to Neotropical species of the genus Meteorus Haliday (Hymenoptera, Braconidae, Euphorinae). *Zookeys, 489*, 33–94. https://doi.org/10.3897/zookeys.489.9258.

Almeida, L. F. V., & Dias, A. M. P. (2015). Five new species of *Meteorus* Haliday (Hymenoptera: Braconidae: Euphorinae) from Brazil. *Zootaxa, 4057*(2), 231–247. https://doi.org/10.11646/zootaxa.4057.2.4.

Almeida, S. S., Mendes-Pereira, T., & Kloss, T. G. (2020). Zombies in safe places? Modified webs with leaf shelters do not increase the survival of spider parasitoids. *Anais do VI Congresso Latino-Americano de Aracnologia, 328–329.*

Almquist, S. (2005). Swedish Araneae, Part 1—families Atypidae to Hahniidae (Linyphiidae excluded). *Insect Systematics & Evolution, 62*, 1–284.

Althoff, D. M. (2003). Does parasitoid attack strategy influence host specificity? A test with New World braconids. *Ecological Entomology, 28*, 500–502. https://doi.org/10.1046/j.1365-2311.2003.00533.x.

Álvares, E. S. S., & De Maria, M. (2004). First record of *Cyrtophora citricola* (Forskål) in Brazil (Araneae, Araneidae). *Revista Brasileira de Zoologia, 21*(1), 155–156.

Andow, D. A., & Imura, O. (1994). Specialization of phytophagous arthropod communities on introduced plants. *Ecology, 75*, 296–300. https://doi.org/10.2307/1939535.

Araujo, G., & Moura, R. R. (2022). Individual specialization and generalization in predator-prey dynamics: The determinant role of predation efficiency and prey reproductive rates. *Journal of Theoretical Biololgy, 537*, 111026. https://doi.org/10.1016/j.jtbi.2022.111026.

Arias-Penna, C. D., Whitfield, J. B., Janzen, D. H., Hallwachs, W., Dyer, L. A., Smith, M. A., et al. (2019). A species-level taxonomic review and host associations of *Glyptapanteles* (Hymenoptera, Braconidae, Microgastrinae) with an emphasis on 136 new reared species from Costa Rica and Ecuador. *Zookeys, 890*, 1–685. https://doi.org/10.3897/zookeys.890.35786.

Askew, R. R., & Shaw, M. R. (1986). Parasitoid communities: Their size, structure and development. In J. Waage, & D. Greathead (Eds.). *Insect parasitoids* (pp. 225–264). London: Academic Press.

Bánki, O., Roskov, Y., Döring, M., Ower, G., Vandepitte, L., Hobern, D., Remsen, D., et al. (2023). Catalogue of life checklist (version 2023-05-15). *Catalogue of Life.* https://doi.org/10.48580/dfs6.

Bayram, A., & Ünal, M. (2002). A new record for the Turkish spider fauna: *Cyclosa conica* Pallas (Araneae, Araneidae). *Turkish Journal of Zoology, 26*, 173–175.

Benjamin, S. P., & Zschokke, S. (2003). Webs of theridiid spiders: Construction, structure and evolution. *Biological Journal of the Linnean Society, 78*, 293–305. https://doi.org/10.1046/j.1095-8312.2003.00110.x.

Bignell, G. C. (1898). The Ichneumonidae (parasitic flies) of the south of Devon. *Report and Transactions of the Devonshire Association for the Advancement of Science Literature and Art, 30*, 458–504.

Blackledge, T. A., Coddington, J. A., & Gillespie, R. G. (2003). Are three-dimensional spider webs defensive adaptations. *Ecology Letters, 6*(1), 13–18. https://doi.org/10.1046/j.1461-0248.2003.00384.x.

Blackwall, J. (1843). I. Account of a species of ichneumon whose larva is parasitic on spiders. *Annals and Magazine of Natural History, 11*, 1–4.

Blaimer, B. B., Santos, B. F., Cruaud, A., Gates, M. W., Kula, R. R., Mikó, I., et al. (2023). Key innovations and the diversification of Hymenoptera. *Nature Communications, 14*(1212), 1–18. https://doi.org/10.1038/s41467-023-36868-4.

Bösenberg, W., & Strand, E. (1906). Japanische Spinnen. *Abhandlungen der Senckenbergischen Naturforschenden Gesellschaft, 30*, 93–422.

Bradley, G. A. (1974). Parasites of forest Lepidoptera in Canada: Subfamilies Metopiinae and Pimplinae (Hymenoptera: Ichneumonidae). Publications No. 1336. Environment Canada, Canadian Forestry Service, Ottawa, Canada.

Brooks Mollie, E., Kristensen, K., Benthem Koen, J. V., Magnusson, A., Berg Casper, W., ... Bolker Benjamin, M. (2017). glmmTMB: Balances speed and flexibility among packages for zero-inflated generalized linear mixed modeling. *The R Journal, 9*(2), 378. https://doi.org/10.32614/RJ-2017-066.

Brown, J. (1984). On the relationship between abundance and distribution of species. *The American Naturalist, 124*, 255–279.

Chamberlain, S., Barve, V., Mcglinn, D., Oldoni, D., Desmet, P., Geffert, L., Ram, K. (2023). Rgbif: Interface to the GlobalBiodiversity Information Facility API. R package version 3.7.5, https://CRAN.R-project.org/package=rgbif.

Cloudsley-Thompson, J. L. (1995). A review of the anti-predator devices of spiders. *Bulletin of the British Arachnological Society, 10*(3), 81–96.

Coddington, J. A., & Levi, H. W. (1991). Systematics and evolution of spiders (Araneae). *Annual Review of Ecology and Systematics, 22*(1), 565–592.

Cuny, M. A. C., & Poelman, E. H. (2022). Evolution of koinobiont parasitoid host regulation and consequences for indirect plant defence. *Evolutionary Ecology, 36*, 299–319. https://doi.org/10.1007/s10682-022-10180-x.

De Geer, C. (1771). *Memoires pour servir à l'histoire des insects.* Stockholm, Sweden: French Grefing and Hesselberg.

Dimitrov, D., & Hormiga, G. (2021). Spider diversification through space and time. *Annual Review of Entomology, 66*, 225–241. https://doi.org/10.1146/annurev-ento-061520-083414.

Dormann, C. F., Gruber, B., & Fruend, J. (2008). Introducing the bipartite package: Analysing ecological networks. *R News, 8*(2), 8–11.

Dormann, C. F., & Strauss, R. (2014). A method for detecting modules in quantitative bipartite networks. *Methods in Ecology and Evolution, 5*, 90–98. https://doi.org/10.1111/2041-210X.12139.

Eberhard, W. G. (2000a). Spider manipulation by a wasp larva. *Nature, 406*, 225–226. https://doi.org/10.1038/35018636.

Eberhard, W. G. (2001). Under the influence: Webs and building behavior of *Plesiometa argyra* (Araneae, Tetragnathidae) when parasitized by *Hymenoepimecis argyraphaga* (Hymenoptera, Ichneumonidae). *Journal of Arachnology, 29*(3), 354–366. https://doi.org/10.1636/0161-8202(2001)029[0354:UTIWAB]2.0.CO;2.

Eberhard, W. G. (2013). The Polysphinctine Wasps *Acrotaphus tibialis, Eruga* ca. *gutfreundi,* and *Hymenoepimecis tedfordi* (Hymenoptera, Ichneumonidae, Pimplinae) induce their host spiders to build modified webs. *Annals of the Entomological Society of America, 106*(5), 652–660. https://doi.org/10.1603/AN12147.

Eberhard, W. G., & Gonzaga, M. O. (2019). Evidence that Polysphincta-group wasps (Hymenoptera: Ichneumonidae) use ecdysteroids to manipulate the web-construction behaviour of their spider hosts. *Biological Journal of the Linnean Society, 127*(2), 429–471. https://doi.org/10.1093/biolinnean/blz044.

Eberhard, W. G. (2010b). New types of behavioral manipulation of host spiders by a parasitoid wasp. *Psyche: A Journal of Entomology, 2010*(1), 1–4. https://doi.org/10.1155/2010/950614.

Felix, G. M., Pinheiro, R. B. P., Poulin, R., Krasnov, B. R., & Mello, M. A. R. (2022). The compound topology of host–parasite networks is explained by the integrative hypothesis of specialization. *Oikos, 2022*(1), e08462. https://doi.org/10.1111/oik.08462.

Fitch, E. A. (1882). External parasites of spiders. *The Entomologist, 15*, 169–175.

Fitton, M. G., Shaw, M. R., & Gauld, I. D. (1988). Pimplinae Ichneumon-flies. Hymenoptera Ichneumonidae (Pimplinae). In P. C. Barnard, & R. R. Askew (Eds.). *Handbooks for the identification of british insects vol. 7, part 1* (pp. 1–110). Cromwell Road, London, United Kingom: Royal Entomological Society of London.

Futuyma, D., & Moreno, G. (1988). The evolution of ecological specialization. *Annual Review of Ecology and Systematics, 19*, 207–233. https://doi.org/10.1146/annurev.es.19.110188.001231.

Gadallah, N. S., & El-Hennawy, H. K. (2017). First record of the genus *Oxyrrhexis* Foerster, 1869 (Hymenoptera: Ichneumonidae: Pimplinae, Ephialtini) for the fauna of Egypt, with an unexpected new host record. *Zootaxa, 4318*(1), 1–6. https://doi.org/10.11646/zootaxa.4318.1.11.

Gaione-Costa, A., Pádua, D. G., Delazari, Í. M., Santos, A. R. S., & Kloss, T. G. (2022). Redescription and oviposition behavior of an orb-weaver spider parasitoid *Hymenoepimecis cameroni* Townes, 1966 (Hymenoptera: Ichneumonidae). *Zootaxa, 5134*(3), 415–425. https://doi.org/10.11646/zootaxa.5134.3.5.

Gaston, K. J., Blackburn, T. M., Greenwood, J. J., Gregory, R. D., Quinn, R. M., & Lawton, J. H. (2000). Abundance–occupancy relationships. *Journal of Applied Ecology, 37*, 39–59.

Gaston, K. J., Blackburn, T. M., & Lawton, J. H. (1997). Interspecific abundance-range size relationships: An appraisal of mechanisms. *Journal of Animal Ecology, 66*(4), 579–601. https://doi.org/10.2307/5951.

Gauld, I. D., & Dubois, J. (2006). Phylogeny of the Polysphincta group of genera (Hymenoptera: Ichneumonidae; Pimplinae): A taxonomic revision of spider ectoparasitoids. *Systematic Entomology, 31*, 529–564.

Gonzaga, M. O., & Vasconcellos-Neto, J. (2012). Variation in the stabilimenta of *Cyclosa fililineata* Hingston, 1932, and *Cyclosa morretes* Levi, 1999 (Araneae: Araneidae), in Southeastern Brazil. *Psyche: A Journal of Entomology, 2012*, 396594. https://doi.org/10.1155/2012/396594.

Gonzaga, M. O., & Sobczak, J. F. (2007). Parasitoid-induced mortality of *Araneus omnicolor* (Araneae, Araneidae) by *Hymenoepimecis sp.* (Hymenoptera, Ichneumonidae) in southeastern Brazil. *Die Naturwissenschaften, 94*(3), 223–227. https://doi.org/10.1007/s00114-006-0177-z.

Gonzaga, M. O., Sobczak, J. F., Penteado-Dias, A. M., & Eberhard, W. G. (2010). Modification of *Nephila clavipes* (Araneae Nephilidae) webs induced by the parasitoids *Hymenoepimecis bicolor* and *H. robertsae* (Hymenoptera Ichneumonidae). *Ethology Ecology & Evolution, 22*(2), 151–165. https://doi.org/10.1080/03949371003707836.

Gonzaga, M. O., Pádua, D. G., & Quero, A. (2022). Inclusion of an alien species in the host range of the Neotropical parasitoid *Hymenoepimecis bicolor* (Brullé, 1846) (Hymenoptera, Ichneumonidae). *Journal of Hymenoptera Research, 89*, 9–18. https://doi.org/10.3897/jhr.89.76620.

Gonzaga, M. O., Cardoso, J. C. F., & Vasconcellos-Neto, J. (2015b). Do parasitoids explain differential abundance of two syntopic orb-weaver spiders (Araneae: Araneidae)? *Acta Oecologica, 69*(1), 113–120. https://doi.org/10.1016/j.actao.2015.10.001.

Gonzaga, M. O., Loffredo, A. P., Penteado-Dias, A. M., & Cardoso, J. C. F. (2016). Host behavior modification of *Achaearanea tingo* (Araneae: Theridiidae) induced by the parasitoid wasp *Zatypota alborhombarta* (Hymenoptera: Ichneumonidae): Behavioral manipulation of *A. tingo*. *Entomological Science, 19*(2), 133–137. https://doi.org/10.1111/ens.12178.

Gonzaga, M. O., Kloss, T. G., & Sobczak, J. F. (2017). Host behavioural manipulation of spiders by ichneumonid wasps. In C. Viera, & M. O. Gonzaga (Eds.). *Behaviour and ecology of spiders* (pp. 417–437). New York: Springer.

Grosman, A. H., Jessen, A., de Brito, E. F., Cordeiro, E. G., Colares, F., Fonseca, J. O., et al. (2008). Parasitoid increases survival of its pupae by inducing hosts to fight predators. *PLoS One, 3*(6), e2276. https://doi.org/10.1371/journal.pone.0002276.

Hartig, F. (2022). DHARMa: Residual diagnostics for hierarchical (multi-level/mixed) regression models. R package version 0.4.6, https://CRAN.R-project.org/package=DHARMa.

Harvey, J. A. (2005). Factors affecting the evolution of development strategies in parasitoid wasps: The importance of functional constraints and incorporating complexity. *Entomologia Experimentalis et Applicata, 117*(1), 1–13. https://doi.org/10.1111/j.1570-7458.2005.00348.x.

Harvey, J. A., & Strand, M. R. (2002). The developmental strategies of endoparasitoid wasps vary with host feeding ecology. *Ecology, 83*, 2439–2451. https://doi.org/10.2307/3071805.

Harvey, J. A., Kadash, K., & Strand, M. R. (2000). Differences in larval feeding behavior correlate with altered developmental strategies in two parasitic wasps: Implications for the size-fitness hypothesis. *Oikos, 88*(1), 621–629.

Hijmans, R. (2022). Geosphere: Spherical trigonometry. R package version, 1, 5–18. https://CRAN.R-project.org/package=geosphere.

Holt, B. G., Lessard, J.-P., Borregaard, M. K., Fritz, S. A., Araújo, A. B., Dimitrov, D., et al. (2013). An update of Wallace's zoogeographic regions of the World. *Science (New York, N. Y.), 339*, 74–78. https://doi.org/10.1126/science.1228282.

Howard, L. O. (1982). The hymenopterous parasites of spiders. *Entomological Society of Washington, 2*, 290–302.

Hu, J. L. (2001). *Spiders in Qinghai-Tibet Plateau of China*. Henan Science and Technology Publishing House. pp. 658.

Kamiya, T., O'Dwyer, K., Nakagawa, S., & Poulin, R. (2014). Host diversity drives parasite diversity: Meta-analytical insights into patterns and causal mechanisms. *Ecography, 37*(7), 689–997. https://doi.org/10.1111/j.1600-0587.2013.00571.x.

Keesing, F., Holt, R., & Ostfeld, R. (2006). Effects of species diversity on disease risk. *Ecology Letters, 9*(4), 485–498. https://doi.org/10.1111/j.1461-0248.2006.00885.x.

Khoramabadi, A. M.-, Talebi, A., Broad, G. R., & Zwakhals, K. (2022). A study of the genus *Zabrachypus* Cushman, 1920 (Hymenoptera Ichneumonidae Pimplinae) from Iran with descriptions of two new species. *Journal of Zoology, 105*(1), 29–36. https://doi.org/10.19263/REDIA-105.22.05.

Kloss, T. G., Gonzaga, M. O., Oliveira, L. L., & Sperber, C. F. (2017). Proximate mechanism of behavioral manipulation of an orb-weaver spider host by a parasitoid wasp. *PLoS One, 12*(2), e0174146. https://doi.org/10.1371/journal.pone.0171336.

Kloss, T. G., Gonzaga, M. O., Roxinol, J. A. M., & Sperber, C. F. (2016a). Host behavioural manipulation of two orb-weaver spiders by parasitoid wasps. *Animal Behaviour, 111*, 289–296. https://doi.org/10.1016/j.anbehav.2015.11.001.

Kloss, T. G., Gonzaga, M. O., Roxinol, J. A. M., & Sperber, C. F. (2016b). Attack behavior of two wasp species of the *Polysphincta* genus group (Hymenoptera, Ichneumonidae) on their orb-weaver spider hosts (Araneae, Araneidae). *Journal of Insect Behavior, 29*(3), 315–324. https://doi.org/10.1007/s10905-016-9560-6.

Kloss, T. G., Pádua, D. G., Almeida, S. S., Penteado-Dias, A. M., Mendes-Pereira, T., Sobzack, J. F., et al. (2022). A new Darwin wasp (Hymenoptera: Ichneumonidae) and new records of behavioral manipulation of the host spider *Leucauge volupis* (Araneae: Tetragnathidae). *Neotropical Entomology, 51*, 821–829. https://doi.org/10.1007/s13744-022-00991-6.

Kloss, T. G., Pádua, D. G., Lacerda, F. G., Oliveira, L. S., Cossolin, J. F. S., Serrão, J. E., et al. (2018). Suppression of orb-web building behavior of the spider *Metazygia laticeps* (O. Pickard-Cambridge, 1889) (Araneae: Araneidae) by a new parasitoid wasp. *Zoologischer Anzeiger, 276*, 100–106. https://doi.org/10.1016/j.jcz.2018.06.005.

Korenko, S. (2022). *Sinarachna nigricornis* and genus-specific host utilization of *Araneus* spiders by the genus *Sinarachna* (Hymenoptera: Ichneumonidae). *The Journal of Arachnology, 50*(1), 51–55. https://doi.org/10.1636/JoA-S-21-012.

Korenko, S., & Giovanni, F. D. (2019). Spider parasitoids of the tribe ephialtini (Hymenoptera: Ichneumonidae: Pimplinae) in Italy and their host association. *Acta Zoologica Bulgarica, 71*(4), 473–486.

Korenko, S., & Pekar, S. (2011). A parasitoid wasp induces overwintering behaviour in its spider host. *PlosOne, 6*(9), 1–5. https://doi.org/10.1371/journal.pone.0024628.

Korenko, S., Michalková, V., Zwakhals, K., & Pekár, S. (2011). Host specificity and temporal and seasonal shifts in host preference of a web-spider parasitoid *Zatypota percontatoria*. *Journal of Insect Science, 11*, 1–12. https://doi.org/10.1673/031.011.10101.

Korenko, S., Hamouzová, K., Kysilková, K., Kolářová, M., Kloss, T. G., Takasuka, K., & Pekár, S. (2018a). Divergence in host utilisation by two spider ectoparasitoids within the genus Eriostethus (Ichneumonidae, Pimplinae). *Zoologischer Anzeiger, 272*, 1–5. https://doi.org/10.1016/j.jcz.2017.11.006.

Korenko, S., Spasojevic, T., Pekár, S., Walter, G. H., Korenková, V., Hamouzová, K., et al. (2018b). One generalist or several specialist species? Wide host range and diverse manipulations of the hosts' web-building behaviour in the true spider parasitoid *Zatypota kauros* (Hymenoptera: Ichneumonidae). *Insect Conservation and Diversity, 11*(6), 587–599. https://doi.org/10.1111/icad.12307.

Korenko, S., Isaia, M., Satrapová, J., & Pekár, S. (2014). Parasitoid genus-specific manipulation of orb-web host spiders (Araneae, Araneidae): Parasitoid genus-specific manipulation of orb-web spiders. *Ecological Entomology, 39*(1), 30–38. https://doi.org/10.1111/een.12067.

Korenko, S., Kysilková, K., & Černecká, L. (2017). Further records of two spider-parasitoids of the genus *Polysphincta* (Hymenoptera, Ichneumonidae, Ephialtini) from Central Europe, with notes on their host interactions. *Arachnologische Mitteilungen, 54*, 28–32. https://doi.org/10.5431/aramit5406.

Korenko, S., Satrapová, J., & Zwakhals, K. (2015b). Manipulation of araneid spider web architecture by the polysphinctine parasitoid *Zatypota picticollis* (Hymenoptera: Ichneumonidae: Pimplinae): Manipulation by *Zatypota picticollis. Entomological Science, 18*(3), 383–388. https://doi.org/10.1111/ens.12132.

Krasnov, B. R., Poulin, R., Shenbrot, G. I., Mouillot, D., & Khokhlova, I. S. (2004). Ectoparasitic "jacks-of-all-trades": Relationship between abundance and host specificity in fleas (Siphonaptera) parasitic on small mammals. *The American Naturalist, 164*, 506–516. https://doi.org/10.1086/423716.

Kruitwagen, A., Beukeboom, L. W., Wertheim, B., & van Doorn, G. S. (2021). Evolution of host preference and performance in response to an invasive host acting as evolutionary trap. *Ecology and Evolution, 12*(7), e9030. https://doi.org/10.1002/ece3.9030.

Kuntner, M., Hamilton, C. A., Cheng, R. C., Gregorič, M., Lupse, N., Lokovsek, T., et al. (2019). Golden orbweavers ignore biological rules: Phylogenomic and comparative analyses unravel a complex evolution of sexual size dimorphism. *Systematic Biology, 68*(4), 555–572. https://doi.org/10.1093/sysbio/syy082.

Kuris, A. M., & Lafferty, K. D. (2000). Parasite-host modeling meets reality: Adaptive peaks and their ecological attributes. In R. Poulin, S. Morand, & A. Skorping (Eds.). *Evolutionary biology of host-parasite relationships: Theory meets reality* (pp. 9–26). Amsterdam: Elsevier Science.

Lafferty, K. D., Dobson, A. P., & Kuris, A. M. (2006). Parasites dominate food web links. *PNAS, 103*(30), 11211–11216. https://doi.org/10.1073/pnas.0604755103.

Levi, H. W. (1963). American spiders of the genus *Achaearanea* and the new genus *Echinotheridion* (Araneae, Theridiidae). *Bulletin of the Museum of Comparative Zoology, 129*, 187–240.

Levi, H. W. (1991). The Neotropical and Mexican species of the orb-weaver genera *Araneus, Dubiepeira,* and *Aculepeira* (Araneae: Araneidae). *Bulletin of the Museum of Comparative Zoology, 152*, 167–315.

Levi, H. W. (1999). The Neotropical and Mexican Orb Weavers of the genera *Cyclosa* and *Allocyclosa* (Araneae: Araneidae). *Bulletin of the Museum of Comparative Zoology, 155*, 299–379.

Levi, H. W. (2004). Comments and new records for the American genera *Gea* and *Argiope* with the description of new species (Araneae: Araneidae). *Bulletin of the Museum of Comparative Zoology, 158*, 47–65.

Levy, G. (1987). Spiders of the genera *Araniella, Zygiella, Zilla* and *Mangora* (Araneae, Araneidae) from Israel, with notes on *Metellina* species from Lebanon. *Zoologica Scripta, 16*(3), 243–257. https://doi.org/10.1111/j.1463-6409.1987.tb00071.x.

Maeto, K. (2018). Polyphagous koinobiosis: The biology and biocontrol potential of a braconid endoparasitoid of exophytic caterpillars. *Applied Entomology and Zoology, 53*, 433–446. https://doi.org/10.1007/s13355-018-0581-9.

MacArthur, R. H., & Pianka, E. R. (1966). On optimal use of a patchy environment. *The American Naturalist, 100*, 603–609.

Machałowski, T., Amemiya, C., & Jesionowski, T. (2020). Chitin of Araeae: Structural features and biomimetic applications: A review. *Applied Physics A, 126*, 678. https://doi.org/10.1007/s00339-020-03867-x.

Manicom, C., Schwarzkopf, L., Alford, R. A., & Schoener, T. W. (2008). Self-made shelters protect spiders from predation. *Proceedings of the National Academy of Sciences, 105*(39), 14903–14907. https://doi.org/10.1073/pnas.0807107105.

Manuel, R. L. (1976). *Biology of the spider Frontinella pyramitela (Walckenaer, 1841) (Arachnida: Linyphydae) with special reference to predation. [Doctoral Thesis, Departament of Entomology.* Canada, Montreal: McDonal College of McGill University, pp. 185.

Matsumoto, R. (2009). Veils" against predators: Modified web structure of a host spider induced by an ichneumonid parasitoid, *Brachyzapus nikkoensis* (Uchida) (Hymenoptera). *Journal of Insect Behavior, 22*(1), 39–48. https://doi.org/10.1007/s10905-008-9152-1.

Matsumoto, R., & Takasuka, K. (2010). A revision of the genus *Zatypota* Förster of Japan, with descriptions of nine new species and notes on their hosts (Hymenoptera: Ichneumonidae: Pimplinae). *Zootaxa, 2522*(1), 1–43. https://doi.org/10.11646/zootaxa.2522.1.1.

Matsumoto, R. (2016). Molecular phylogeny and systematics of the *Polysphincta* group of genera (Hymenoptera, Ichneumonidae, Pimplinae). *Systematic Entomology, 41*, 854–864. https://doi.org/10.1111/syen.12196.

Matsumoto, R. (2014). Natural history of the Polysphincta group of genera (Ichneumonidae: Hymenoptera) (in Japanese) *Acta Arachnologica, 63*, 41–53. https://doi.org/10.2476/asjaa.63.41.

Matsumoto, R., & Konishi, K. (2007). Life histories of two ichneumonid parasitoids of *Cyclosa octotuberculata* (Araneae): *Reclinervellus tuberculatus* (Uchida) and its new sympatric congener (Hymenoptera: Ichneumonidae: Pimplinae). *Entomological Science, 10*(3), 267–278. https://doi.org/10.1111/j.1479-8298.2007.00223.x.

Mello-Leitão, C. F. (1943). Catálogo das aranhas do Rio Grande do Sul. *Arquivos do Museu Nacional do Rio de Janeiro, 37*, 147–245.

Messas, Y. F. (2014). História natural e ecologia populacional de *Eustala perfida* Mello Leitão, 1947 (Araneae, Araneidae) na Serra do Japi, Jundiaí, São Paulo – Brazil. *[Master's dissertation, Animal Biology Institute, Campinas State University, Brazil, São Paulo,* 102 pp. (in. eng.)].

Messas, Y. F., Sobczak, J. F., & Vasconcellos-Neto, J. (2017). An alternative host of *Hymenoepimecis japi* (Hymenoptera, Ichneumonidae) on a novel family (Araneae, Araneidae), with notes on behavioral manipulations. *Journal of Hymenoptera Research, 60*, 111–118. https://doi.org/10.3897/jhr.60.14817.

Nakagawa, S., & Schielzeth, H. (2013). A general and simple method for obtaining R^2 from generalized linear mixed-effects models. *Methods in Ecology and Evolution, 4*, 133–142. https://doi.org/10.1111/j.2041-210x.2012.00261.x.

Nielsen, E. (1923). Contributions to the life history of the Pimpline spider parasites (*Polysphincta, Zaglyptus, Tromatobia*) (Hymenoptera: Ichneumonidae). *Entomologiske Meddeslelser, 14*, 137–205.

Novotny, V., Miller, S. E., Cizek, L., Leps, J., Janda, M., Basset, Y., et al. (2003). Colonising aliens: Caterpillars (Lepidoptera) feeding on *Piper aduncum* and *P. umbellatum* in rainforests of Papua New Guinea. *Ecological Entomology, 28*, 704–716. https://doi.org/10.1111/j.1365-2311.2003.00558.x.

Pádua, D. G., Kloss, T. G., Tavares, M. T., Santos, B. F., Araujo, R. O., Shoeninger, K., ... Gonzaga, M. O. (2022). Hyperparasitoids of polysphinctine Darwin wasps (Hymenoptera: Ichneumonidae) in South America. *Austral Entomology, 61*(2), 170–186. https://doi.org/10.1111/aen.12593.

Pereira, L. C., Villanueva-Bonilla, G. A., Azevedo, R., & Sobczak, J. F. (2022). Behavioral manipulation in two sheet web weaver-spider by the parasitoid wasp, *Eruga unilabiana* Pádua & Sobczak, 2018 (Hymenoptera: Ichneumonidae). *Entomological Science, 25*(4), 1–12. https://doi.org/10.1111/ens.12523.

Peters, R., Krogmann, L., Mayer, C., Donath, A., Gunkel, S., Meusemann, K., et al. (2017). Evolutionary history of the hymenoptera. *Current Biology, 27*(7), 1013–1018. https://doi.org/10.1016/j.cub.2017.01.027.

Poeta, M. R. M., Marques, M. A. L., & Buckup, E. H. (2010). Sobre algumas espécies do gênero *Eustala* (Araneae, Araneidae) do Brasil. *Iheringia, Série Zoologia, 100*, 267–274.

Quicke, D. L. J., Laurenne, N. M., Fitton, M. G., & Broad, G. R. (2009). A thousand and one wasps: A 28S and morphological phylogeny of the Ichneumonidae (Insecta: Hymenoptera) with an investigation into alignment parameter space and elision. *Journal of Natural History, 43*, 1305–1421. https://doi.org/10.1080/00222930902807783.

R Development Core Team, R. (2023). R: A language and environment for statistical computing (4.2.3). https://www.r-project.org/.

Santos, A. M. C., & Quicke, D. L. J. (2011). Large-scale diversity patterns of parasitoid insects: Parasitoid diversity patterns. *Entomological Science, 14*, 371–382. https://doi.org/10.1111/j.1479-8298.2011.00481.x.

Schaack, S., Gilbert, C., & Feschotte, C. (2010). Promiscuous DNA: Horizontal transfer of transposable elements and why it matters for eukaryotic evolution. *Trends in Ecology & Evolution, 25(9)*, 537–546. https://doi.org/10.1016/j.tree.2010.06.001.

Scharff, N., & Coddington, J. A. (1997). A phylogenetic analysis of the orb-weaving spider family Araneidae (Arachnida, Araneae). *Zoological Journal of the Linnean Society, 120*, 355–434.

Schmitt, M., Richter, D., Göbel, D., & Zwakhals, K. (2012). Beobachtungen zur Parasitierung von Radnetzspinnen (Araneidae) durch *Polysphincta rufipes* (Hymenoptera: Ichneumonidae). *Arachnologische Mitteilungen, 44*, 1–6. https://doi.org/10.5431/aramit4401.

Shaw, M. R., & Huddleston, T. (1991). Classification and biology of braconid wasps (Hymenoptera: Braconidae). In W. R. Dolling, & R. R. Shaw (Eds.). *Handbooks for the identification of british insects 7, part 11* (pp. 1–126). London: Royal Entomological Society of London.

Sheehan, W., & Hawkins, B. A. (1991). Attack strategy as an indicator of host range in metopiine and pimpline Ichneumonidae (Hymenoptera). *Ecological Entomology, 16*, 129–131. https://doi.org/10.1111/j.1365-2311.1991.tb00200.x.

Shirai, S., & Maeto, K. (2009). Suspending cocoons to evade ant predation in Meteorus pulchricornis, a braconid parasitoid of exposed-living lepidopteran larvae. *Entomological Science, 12*, 107–109. https://doi.org/10.1111/j.1479-8298.2009.00301.x.

Sobczak, J., Loffredo, A., Penteado-Dias, A., & Gonzaga, M. O. (2009). Two new species of Hymenoepimecis (Hymenoptera: Ichneumonidae: Pimplinae) with notes on their spider hosts and behaviour manipulation. *Journal of Natural History, 43*(1), 43–44. https://doi.org/10.1080/00222930903244010.

Sobczak, J. F., Messas, Y. F., & Pádua, D. G. D. (2017). Parasitism of *Zatypota riverai* Gauld (Hymenoptera: Ichneumonidae: Pimplinae) on *Anelosimus baeza* Agnarsson (Araneae: Theridiidae) in northeast Brazil, with a description of the male. *Zootaxa, 4247*(1), 78–82. https://doi.org/10.11646/zootaxa.4247.1.11.

Sobczak, J. F., Villanueva-Bonilla, G. A., Pádua, D. G., & Messas, Y. F. (2017). The wasp *Flacopimpla varelae* Gauld (Ichneumonidae: Pimplinae), parasitoid of the spider *Achaearanea tingo* Levi (Theridiidae: Theridiinae), with description of the male wasp. *Zootaxa, 4365*(5), 594–599. https://doi.org/10.11646/zootaxa.4365.5.7.

Sobczak, J. F., Pádua, D. G., Villanueva-Bonilla, G. A., Nóbrega, F. A. S., & Messas, Y. F. (2019). Two new species of Zatypota (Hymenoptera: Ichneumonidae, Pimplinae) sharing the same host spider in Northeast Brazil. *Zootaxa, 4609*(1), 169–177. https://doi.org/10.11646/zootaxa.4609.1.9.

Sobczak, J. F., Paiva Arruda, I. D., De Pádua, D. G., & Villanueva-Bonilla, G. A. (2019). Parasitism in *Theridion sp.* (Araneae: Theridiidae) by *Zatypota riverai* Gauld, 1991 (Hymenoptera: Ichneumonidae: Pimplinae). *The Journal of Arachnology, 47*(2), 266–270.

Sobczak, J. F., Xavier, G. M., Gonzaga, M. O., & Penteado-Dias, A. M. (2023). Host size selection and progeny sex determination in *Hymenoepimecis bicolor* (Hymenoptera, Ichneumonidae, Pimplinae). *Ethology, 129*(6), 280–287. https://doi.org/10.1111/eth.13365.

Sobczak, J. F., Pádua, D. G., Costa, L. F. A., Carvalho, J. L. V. R., Ferreira, J. P. S., Sobczak, J. C. M. S. M., & Messas, Y. S. (2017c). The parasitoid wasp *Eruga unilabiana* Pádua & Sobczak, sp. nov. (Hymenoptera: Ichneumonidae) induces behavioral modification in its spider host: A new wasp species and its host spider. *Entomological Science, 21*(1), 59–65. https://doi.org/10.1111/ens.12278.

Sobczak, J. F., Sobczak, J. C. M. S. M., Messas, Y. F., Souza, H. D. S., & Vasconcellos-Neto, J. (2014). A new record of a host-parasitoid interaction: *Hymenoepimecis veranii* Lofredo & Penteado-Dias, 2009 (Hymenoptera: Ichneumonidae) parasitizing *Araneus orgaos* Levi, 1991 (Araneae: Araneidae). *Journal of Insect Behavior, 27*(6), 753–758. https://doi.org/10.1636/JoA-S-18-103.

Stireman, J. O., & Singer, M. S. (2003). What determines host range in parasitoids? An analysis of a tachinid parasitoid community. *Oecologia, 135*(4), 629–638. https://doi.org/10.1007/s00442-003-0235-2.

Suzuki, M., Miura, K., & Tanaka, T. (2008). The virus-like particles of a braconid endoparasitoid wasp, *Meteorus pulchricornis*, inhibit hemocyte spreading in its noctuid host, *Pseudaletia separata*. *Journal of Insect Physiology, 54*, 1015–1022. https://doi.org/10.1016/j.jinsphys.2008.03.013.

Takasuka, K. (2009). *Zatypota albicoxa* attacking her host *Achaearanea tepidariorum* under the artificial condition. *Movie Archives of Animal Behavior Data No.: Momo.* 090727za02a. http://www.momo-p.com/showdetail-e.php?movieid=momo090727za02a.

Takasuka, K., & Matsumoto, R. (2011b). Lying on the dorsum: Unique host-attacking behaviour of *Zatypota albicoxa* (Hymenoptera, Ichneumonidae). *Journal of Ethology, 29*(2), 203–207. https://doi.org/10.1007/s10164-010-0263-8.

Takasuka, K., Matsumoto, R., & Maeto, K. (2019). Oviposition behaviour by a spider-ectoparasitoid, *Zatypota maculata* exploits the specialized prey capture technique of its spider host. *Journal of Zoology, 308*(3), 221–230. https://doi.org/10.1111/jzo.12668.

Takasuka, K., Matsumoto, R., & Ohbayashi, N. (2009). Oviposition behavior of *Zatypota albicoxa* (Hymenoptera, Ichneumonidae), an ectoparasitoid of *Achaearanea tepidariorum* (Araneae, Theridiidae). *Entomological Science, 12*(3), 232–237. https://doi.org/10.1111/j.1479-8298.2009.00338.x.

Takasuka, K., Yasui, T., Ishigami, T., Nakata, K., Matsumoto, R., Ikeda, K., et al. (2015). Host manipulation by an ichneumonid spider ectoparasitoid that takes advantage of preprogrammed web-building behaviour for its cocoon protection. *Journal of Experimental Biology, 218*(15), 2326–2332. https://doi.org/10.1242/jeb.122739.

Takasuka, K., Yoshida, H., Nugroho, P., & Matsumoto, R. (2011). A new record of *Zatypota albicoxa* (Hymenoptera: Ichneumonidae) from Indonesia, with description of a new species of its host spider (Araneae: Theridiidae). *Zootaxa, 2910*(1), 63–68. https://doi.org/10.11646/zootaxa.2910.1.3.

Takasuka, K., Fritzén, N. R., Tanaka, Y., Matsumoto, R., Maeto, K., & Shaw, M. R. (2018). The changing use of the ovipositor in host shifts by ichneumonid ectoparasitoids of spiders (Hymenoptera, Ichneumonidae, Pimplinae). *Parasite (Paris, France), 25*, 17. https://doi.org/10.1051/parasite/2018011.

Takasuka, K. (2019a). Evaluation of manipulative effects by an ichneumonid spider-ecto-parasitoid larva upon an orb-weaving spider host (Araneidae: *Cyclosa argenteoalba*) by means of surgical removal and transplantation. *The Journal of Arachnology, 47*(2), 181–189. https://doi.org/10.1636/JoA-S-18-082.

Takasuka, Korenko, K., Kysilková, S., Štefánik, K., Černecká, M., Mihál, I., et al. (2017). Host utilization of koinobiont spider-ectoparasitoids (Ichneumonidae, Ephialtini, Polysphincta genus-group) associated with *Cyclosa* spp. (Araneae, Araneidae) across the Palaearctic. *Zoologischer Anzeiger, 267*, 8–14. https://doi.org/10.1016/j.jcz.2017.01.001.

Tanikawa, A. (1992). A revisional study of the Japanese spiders of the genus *Cyclosa* (Araneae: Araneidae). *Acta Arachnologica, 41*(1), 11–85. https://doi.org/10.2476/asjaa.41.11.

Timms, L. L., Schwarzfeld, M., & Sääksjarvi, I. E. (2016). Extending understanding of latitudinal patterns in parasitoid wasp diversity. *Insect Conservation and Diversity, 9*, 74–86. https://doi.org/10.1111/icad.12144.

Uetz, G. W., Boyle, J., Hieber, C. S., & Wilcox, R. S. (2002). Antipredator benefits of group living in colonial web-building spiders: The 'early warning' effect. *Animal Behaviour, 63*(3), 445–452. https://doi.org/10.1006/anbe.2001.1918.

Uma, D. B., & Weiss, M. R. (2010). Chemical mediation of prey recognition by spider-hunting wasps. *Ethology: Formerly Zeitschrift fur Tierpsychologie, 116*(1), 85–95. https://doi.org/10.1111/j.1439-0310.2009.01715.x.

Villanueva-Bonilla, G. A., Faustino, M. L., Dos Santos, W. R., Pereira, L. C., De Pádua, D. G., & Sobczak, J. F. (2021). Behavioral manipulation of a "Trashline Orb-weaving spider" *Cyclosa fililineata* (Araneidae) by the parasitoid wasp *Zatypota riverai* (Ichneumonidae: Pimplinae). *The Journal of Arachnology, 49*(1), 146–150. https://doi.org/10.1636/JoA-S-20-043.

Webb, B. A., Strand, M. R., Dickey, S. E., Beck, M., Hilgarth, R., Barney, W. E., et al. (2006). Polydnavirus genomes reflect their dual roles as mutualists and pathogens. *Virology, 1*(347), 160–174. https://doi.org/10.1016/j.virol.2005.11.010.

Weng, J. L., & Barrantes, G. (2007). Natural history and larval behavior of the parasitoid *Zatypota petronae* (Hymenoptera: Ichneumonidae). *Journal of Hymenoptera Research, 16*(2), 326–335.

World Spider Catalog. (2023). World Spider Catalog. Version 24. Natural History Museum Bern http://wsc.nmbe.ch, Accessed 02.2023. 10.24436/2.

Yin, C. M., Peng, X. J., Yan, H. M., Bao, Y. H., Xu, X., Tang, G., et al. (2012). *Fauna Hunan: Araneae in Hunan, China.* Changsha, China: Hunan Science and Technology Press, pp. 1590.

Zizka, A., Silvestro, D., Andermann, T., Azevedo, J., Duarte Ritter, C., Edler, D., et al. (2019). CoordinateCleaner: Standardized cleaning of occurrence records from biological collection databases. *Methods in Ecology and Evolution, 7*. https://doi.org/10.1111/2041-210X.13152.

Zitani, N. M., & Shaw, S. R. (2002). From meteors to death stars: Variations on a silk thread (Hymenoptera: Braconidae: Meteorinae). *American Entomologist, 48*, 228–235. https://doi.org/10.1093/ae/48.4.228.

CHAPTER FOUR

Orb web construction in a new generation of behavioral analysis: A user's guide

William G. Eberhard[a,b,c,*]

[a]Smithsonian Tropical Research Institute, Balboa, Panama
[b]Escuela de Biologia, Universidad de Costa Rica, Ciudad Universitaria, Costa Rica
[c]Museum of Natural Science, Louisiana State University, Baton Rouge, Louisiana, USA
*Corresponding author. e-mail address: william.eberhard@gmail.com

Contents

1. Introduction	156
2. A brief introduction to orb construction behavior	157
2.1 Operations (tasks)	160
2.2 Detailed movements	160
2.3 Cues guiding decisions regarding sticky spiral spacing	162
2.4 Potential cues that are *not* used	171
3. Additional decisions during sticky spiral construction	175
4. Uniformity of cues used in different families of orb weavers	176
4.1 The spider's agility and precision	179
4.2 "Rigid flexibility"? Pre-programmed versus flexible, open-ended responses to cues	180
5. Learning and maturation	184
6. Coordination and independence of flexible adjustments of web variables	186
6.1 Memory of preceding stages and insightful solutions to problems	188
7. Do spiders have expectations regarding the sites and orientations of web lines?	193
7.1 Modularity: Categories of behavior that are biologically real	194
7.2 Topics of general interest for future research	197
8. Conclusion: The promise of orbs for new directions of behavioral research	204
Acknowledgments	206
References	206
Further Reading	211

Abstract

The flexible execution of highly repeated, discrete, and easily recorded tasks makes orb web construction an attractive model for a new generation of general questions concerning complex, flexible behavior by small, apparently simple animals. Accumulated data make it profitable to focus attention on one type of decision that is repeated over and over in each orb: where to attach the sticky spiral to each

Advances in the Study of Behavior, Volume 56
ISSN 0065-3454, https://doi.org/10.1016/bs.asb.2024.02.001
Copyright © 2024 Elsevier Inc. All rights are reserved, including those for text and data mining, AI training, and similar technologies.

155

radius that it crosses. Spiders use at least ten cues to make this decision. Combining this progress with new neurobiological techniques and concepts makes it possible to address new questions concerning higher levels of behavioral organization, including behavioral imprecision (errors), attention and lack of attention, mental maps, open-ended versus rigidly flexible behavioral rules, and the effects of psychoactive drugs. I discuss these and other promising lines for future research. Some data suggest that at least rudimentary higher-level analytical processes occur in orb weavers.

1. Introduction

Orb web construction played an historic role in early attempts to understand the characteristics and limits of innate behavior. It was an iconic example of complex, precise, pre-programmed behavior by "simple", small-brained animals that is executed with little or no learning (e.g., Fabre, 1912; Hingston, 1920, 1929). That image gradually faded as evidence accumulated that orb construction behavior is highly flexible and is adjusted to many different variables. This progress, especially concerning sticky-spiral construction (the major focus of this review), has also cleared away confusion regarding several possible confounding variables that are *not* used by spiders.

The first detailed review of more than a century of research on orb web construction behavior brought the study of the cues guiding sticky spiral construction to the threshold of a new age, in which orb webs can again play an important role in answering a new generation of questions (Eberhard, 2020). Topics of general importance that may now be accessible include the following: behavioral imprecision (errors) at higher levels of behavioral organization; attention (and momentary lapses of attention); solving novel problems that may involve animal insight; flexibility in the rules by which different stimuli interact to guide behavioral decisions; rules for converting intentions into actions; the possibility that spiders consult mental models of their webs, rather than using simple rules to respond reflexively to specific stimuli to produce complex outcomes (e.g., Braitenberg, 1984); position–dependent rules for producing standardized results such as relatively uniform spacing between loops of sticky spiral (the spider receives widely variable stimuli from different legs in different parts of the web); the ability to trace an approximately circular path centered on the hub regardless of the lines encountered along the way; the existence of expectations of finding lines in particular circumstances; and the effects of psychoactive drugs on both information processing and motor responses.

The goal of this review is to provide a springboard for a new round of studies of complex behavior by these "simple" animals. I emphasize fine details of sticky spiral construction because the variables that affect this behavior are complex, experimentally accessible, and especially well documented, and are thus especially promising for future studies. I also point out several promising points for future growth. Other stages of web construction, such as temporary spiral construction (see Eberhard, 1988a; Gotts & Vollrath, 1991, 1992) have some of the same advantages, and the guiding cues are probably quite different (Eberhard, 2020; Hesselberg, 2015; Vollrath, 1988), but they are much less well-studied.

2. A brief introduction to orb construction behavior

A few terms require explanation (Fig. 1). I refer to the spider's legs by their positions on the spider's body (leg I, leg II, leg III, leg IV, from anterior to posterior), and distinguish the legs located on the side of the spider's body nearest the "outside" edge of the web (oI, oII, oIII, oIV) from the "inside" legs nearest the hub (iI, iII, iIII, iIIII). "Sticky" lines carry a coat of liquid or a fibrous adhesive; non-sticky lines lack such additions (Foelix, 2011). Spiders have exquisitely sensitive sense organs ("slit sense organs" or "lyriform organs") that sense stress in the cuticle, and that can thus sense a leg's position and the forces on it. A spider's metatarsal lyriform organ can respond to displacements on the order of only 10 Å (Barth, 2002).

Spiders that build orb webs are currently classified in six to eight different families, depending on the criteria for recognizing families (Kulkarni et al., 2021; Kuntner et al., 2023); all but one belong to the group Araneoidea; the other, Uloboridae, belongs to Deinopoidea. The orb webs of these families are geometrically uniform, both in the regularly spaced non-sticky radii that are joined at a central hub, and the more or less circular and parallel sticky spiral lines with regular spaces between them. Both types of regularity are probably ancient, and roughly similar patterns have evolved in various combinations in several other spider non-orb weaving families (Ramírez et al., 2023). Both the cues and responses that guide orb construction are highly conserved in orb weavers (Eberhard & Barrantes, 2015), so I have combined data from the different species observed. I use the araneid *Micrathena duodecimspinosa* for many examples, as this species is relatively well-studied and is the one with which I am most familiar; other workhorse species are the European araneids *Araneus diadematus* and *Zygiella x-notata*, the tetragnathid

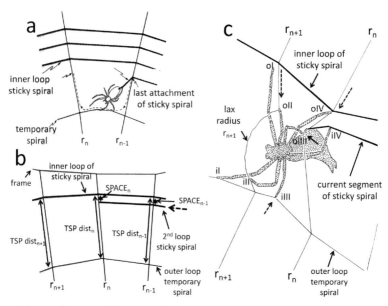

Fig. 1 These schematic drawings illustrate terms used in the text, including a simplified version of the path of a spider as she moves from one attachment of the sticky spiral to the next (A), the terms used to designate the different radii, the spaces between sticky spiral lines, and the distances between the outer loop of temporary spiral and the inner loop of sticky spiral during sticky spiral construction (B), and the positions of her outside (oI, oII, oIII, oIV) and inside (iI, iII, iIII, iIV) legs and the forces they exert (dashed arrows) while she is attaching a sticky spiral line to a radius (C) (after Eberhard, 2020).

Leucauge mariana, and the uloborid *Uloborus diversus*. To facilitate clearer behavioral descriptions, I indulge in the fiction, as in the arachnological literature in Spanish, French and German, that all web building spiders are female. In fact, nearly all published observations of orb web construction behavior are of mature females. More detailed discussions and more extensive references for most of the topics I discuss below are available in Eberhard (2020), including discussions of web building by juveniles and males.

It was established long ago (e.g., Fabre, 1912; Hingston, 1920) that orb-weaving spiders use the following sequence of major operations in building their webs:

1. Exploration and placement of the earliest radii and anchor lines;
2. Addition of frame lines, and more anchors and radii;
3. Construction of the widely-spaced non-sticky temporary (or "auxiliary") spiral, starting at the hub and working outward;

4. Laying sticky rather than non-sticky lines that are closely spaced and in an approximate spiral, starting at the edge and working inward. During sticky spiral construction the spider makes hundreds of decisions regarding where she should attach the sticky line that she is producing to each radius that she encounters. She breaks the temporary spiral, segment by segment, while she is building the sticky spiral.

Although the order is relatively rigid (e.g., Hingston, 1920; König, 1951), there are a few exceptions (Eberhard, 2020; König, 1951). The construction stages are generally not mixed, and at any one time the spider is usually clearly engaged in a particular task. Generally speaking, the earlier the stage, the poorer the current understanding of the cues that guide the spider's behavior. The latter stages of construction are increasingly isolated from variations in the web's surroundings, and the spider's behavior is increasingly guided by the lines of the web itself, and increasingly stereotyped (Witt, 1965). The major focus of this review is on sticky spiral construction, and on the decisions that determine how far apart successive loops of the sticky spiral are spaced. This trait has obviously been under selection that favored relative uniformity in spacing; additional consistent, fine-scale adjustments are superimposed in the outer versus inner and the upper versus lower portions of the web (Eberhard, 2014; Nakata & Zschokke, 2010; Zschokke & Nakata, 2015).

Nearly nothing is known regarding the roles of different parts of the spider's central nervous system (CNS) in orb construction. A preliminary comparison found no differences in the degree of imprecision in sticky spiral spacing when spiders with large differences in absolute brain sizes were compared (Eberhard, 2007). Comparisons of the CNSs of different-sized conspecifics that build similar orbs (and make similar complex adjustments in orb design to being confined in different-sized spaces in which to build) found that both small and large individuals had similar estimated numbers of neurons, as a result of smaller individuals having smaller neurons and relatively larger CNS sizes (Quesada, Barrantes, & Eberhard, 2021). This suggests that the number of neurons may be important for building orbs, because this relatively large investment in nervous tissue by small individuals is likely to be costly (Eberhard & Wcislo, 2011). Additional studies that distinguish recently active neurons before, during and after construction using pS6 RNA-immunoprecipitation techniques (e.g., Baran & Streelman, 2020), could serve to fill this vacuum.

For convenience, I will analyze sticky spiral construction behavior at two levels of organization: the operations or tasks that the spider performs, and the detailed movements of the different parts of her body that she uses to accomplish these tasks. These two levels contrast starkly in their degrees of variation: the operations are highly uniform; but they are produced by a perhaps infinite variety of detailed movements.

2.1 Operations (tasks)

The operations in sticky spiral construction are, at one level, simple and highly repetitive. The spider attaches the sticky line she is producing to a radius, moves inward along this radius to reach the temporary spiral, then along the temporary spiral and out along the next radius until she reaches the inner loop of spiral that is already in place. She then attaches the sticky spiral a more or less constant distance inward from the previous loop (Fig. 1) and moves on to the next radius.

In addition to deciding where to attach the sticky line, the spider makes decisions regarding the physical characteristics of the lines themselves (e.g., the amount of adhesive material placed on the line, the possible mechanical properties of the line). In *Cyclosa* the amount of glue added to the sticky spiral line and thus the diameters of the droplets of glue on the line varied within a given web, and diameters were larger when the spider was better-fed (Crews & Opell, 2006), and when the web was built following several windy days (Liao, Chi, & Tso, 2009; Wu et al., 2013).

In addition, the spider decides whether to double back (to begin to spiral around the web in the opposite direction). Turnbacks (or "reverses") function to improve the uniformity of spaces between sticky lines when the form of the web is asymmetrical (Eberhard, 1969; Hingston, 1920; Le Guelte, 1966; Zschokke, 1993). In at least one species the decision to turn back is made before the sticky line is attached to the radius (Eberhard, 1969). The cues guiding turnback decisions are poorly known. Only two variables were needed to produce superficially typical orb-like patterns of turnbacks in a simulation study, but it is not clear which cues are used by spiders (Eberhard, 1969). Caffeine induced spiders to build rounder webs that needed fewer turnbacks (Hesselberg & Vollrath, 2004). Whatever the turnback cues are, they are sometimes over-ridden by memories of lines encountered previously in other parts of the web (Eberhard, 2019; see below).

2.2 Detailed movements

The details of the movements that the spider executes to accomplish the operations involved in making an attachment are reviewed in Table 1; they show much variation, some of which will be described in the sections below.

Table 1 The sequence of operations or behavioral tasks involved in making each attachment of sticky spiral to a radius and the detailed movements used to accomplish these tasks (summary in Eberhard, 2020). The point where the spiral will be attached to the radius, and thus the decision regarding the sticky spiral spacing (the major focus of this review), is determined by the sites gripped by legs oIII and oIV (step #4), perhaps in combination with step #5 (it is not known whether the space between the point touched by the spinnerets is consistent with respect to the positions of legs oIII and oIV). This list of detailed movements is highly simplified, as it ignores all movements needed to move and to support the spider as it performs these tasks, the variations in these movements associated with different sites in the web, and the decision whether or not to double back after making the attachment (#7).

1. Locate the next radius, using probing movements of a leg (usually leg I or II)
2. Pass this radius to more posterior legs (grip it successively a more posterior leg and release the grip with the more anterior leg)
3. Move outward along the radius (or reel it in), making probing movements with a leg to locate the innermost loop of sticky spiral already in place
4. After locating the inner loop, grip the radius with leg oIII just inside the future attachment site and with oIV just outside the future attachment site
5. Pull the radius toward the abdomen and/or lower the abdomen toward the radius, thus placing the radius in the very middle of the group of spinnerets on the abdomen
6. Initiate and then terminate production of special lines and glue (from the piriform glands) to fasten the sticky spiral to the radius with brief, brisk spinneret movements
7. Move inward and continue circling along the temporary spiral, searching for the next radius.

Nevertheless, they also show several patterns. The spider generally uses exploratory tapping movements with her anterior legs (e.g., leg I or leg II) in lateral and anterior directions to find the non-sticky web lines (radii and temporary spiral) that she uses to support herself as she moves during sticky spiral construction. After finding and grasping a line with a leg (a "leading" leg), she often then passes this line to the next more posterior ("following") leg on the same side of her body (i.e., oI often leads, and is followed by oII) (Eberhard, 2017). The following leg moves relatively directly (with little tapping) to grasp the line that is being held by the leading leg, and grasps it near the point being held by the leading leg's tarsus; presumably its movement is guided by information from the leading leg. Soon after the following leg arrives to grasp the line, the more anterior leg releases its hold and moves on to search for another line. In some cases, more posterior legs then follow, successively grasping the same line (Eberhard, 2017). These details resolve a question posed long ago by Peters (1954): spiders do not explore with some legs to find the precise sites that they will grasp later with other legs; rather the following legs grasp points that are near to but not the same as the points grasped by leading legs.

There are also consistent patterns in the lateral components of the movements of both leading and following legs. As a leg moves to grasp a line, it moves laterally toward the side where its asymmetrically placed median tarsal claw projects (the prolateral side on legs I and II, the retrolateral side on legs III and IV) (Eberhard, 2017). These lateral movements facilitate snagging the line with the median claw. As an orb weaver moves across her web, she probably also constantly adjusts the rotation of each leg so as to align its middle claw more nearly perpendicular to the line that it is grasping (Eberhard, 2017). Because the different lines that she encounters make highly variable angles with her path, these adjustments likely result in variable leg positions.

Before making each attachment of the sticky spiral to a radius (r_n in Fig. 1), most orb weavers execute specialized movements whose name, "inner loop localization behavior," is justified by both design and context. The spider extends her leg and taps toward the inner loop of sticky spiral that is already in place while she is moving outward along the radius prior to attaching. She terminates this exploratory behavior as soon as she touches the inner loop, and immediately turns and attaches the sticky line, leaving a space between new attachment and the inner loop.

Another consistent detail is that when the spider has arrived at the point where she will make the next attachment of the sticky line, leg oIII grasps the radius just inside the point where the attachment will be made, and leg oIV then grasps it just outside this point (Fig. 1C). The spider then flexes these legs, simultaneously bringing the radius toward her abdomen and moving her abdomen toward the line. As a result, the radius is positioned very precisely, running through the center of the cluster of spinnerets at the tip of her abdomen (Fig. 1C). With a brief burst of brisk movements of her spinnerets, the spider then attaches the sticky spiral to the radius, initiating and then almost immediately terminating the production of a set of fine lines and glue from her piriform glands (in *M. duodecimspinosa* this burst of spinneret movements lasts on the order of only 0.03 s).

2.3 Cues guiding decisions regarding sticky spiral spacing

Abundant evidence shows that the spaces between sequential loops of sticky spiral vary substantially, even in a single orb (Eberhard, 2020; Herberstein & Tso, 2011; Zschokke, 1993). This variability results, at least in large part, from adjustments made by the spider to a host of variables. The different variables that are thought to guide sticky spiral spacing are listed in Table 2, where they are classified according to the probable times when the spider senses them.

2.3.1 "Reference point" variables

At one extreme are the "reference point" variables that the spider evaluates each time she makes an attachment: the site of the inner loop of sticky spiral; and the distance between this inner loop and the outer loop of temporary spiral (the "TSP distance"). Their use as cues has been established by consistent responses to experimental manipulations of lines (Fig. 2B). The spider senses the site of the inner loop using "inner loop localization behavior" (Eberhard, 1982).

In addition, correlations in unmanipulated webs indicate that a short-term memory of the TSP distance that the spider experienced at the previous attachment modulates the response to the current TSP distance; the greater the difference with the current distance, the weaker the response to the current distance. This memory-based response tends to smooth out the path of the sticky spiral by "buffering" or reducing responses to especially large changes in the TSP distance. Other possible but less consistently used or less confidently demonstrated reference point cues are the separation between adjacent radii, the length of the current segment of sticky line, and the directions in which sticky and temporary spirals coil (Table 2A).

In two families (Theridiosomatidae and Anapidae), no clear inner loop localization behavior occurs (Eberhard, 1982, 1987). Nevertheless, the spider always stops short before contacting the inner loop as she moves out the radius, and spaces between sticky spiral attachments to each radius are highly consistent. These spiders probably use an ideothetic sense, measuring the distance they move outward along the radius. Path integration using ideo-thetic cues is an ancient trait in spiders and other arachnids (Eberhard, 2020; Hesselberg, 2015) and is relatively simple to produce in artificial nerve networks (Chittka & Niven, 2009). It thus seems likely that even in the other groups that perform clear inner loop localization tapping behavior (Araneidae, Tetragnathidae, Uloboridae), the spider also senses the TSP distance (in effect, she has two cues available; see Table 2). In some cases, when another leg maintains its hold on the temporary spiral at the same time (this is especially common in the inner portions of the orb), the TSP distance may be sensed directly from the positions of her leg or legs that are holding the temporary spiral at the moment when the exploring leg touches the inner loop.

Table 2 Variables that orb weaving spiders are thought to use in making decisions that determine the spacing between loops of the sticky spiral. Data from different species are combined here, because of the general taxonomic uniformity of cues used to guide sticky spiral construction (Eberhard & Barrantes, 2015). Variables that correlate strongly with each other and that may represent a single cue sensed by the spider are marked with the same italicized letter; those cues most convincingly demonstrated to be likely of general importance are marked with "*". Two general orientation abilities that may not depend on external cues from particular web lines are included (in D). The references include only especially extensive studies; more exhaustive references, and more complete discussions of the techniques used to document the effects of different variables, and possible limitations in the support for different cues, are summarized in Eberhard (2020).

A. "Reference point" cues (sensed anew at each attachment)	Major references
*1. Site of inner loop of sticky spiral (see "Hingston experiment" in Fig. 3)	Hingston (1920); Peters (1939); Eberhard and Hesselberg (2012)
*2. Distance between the inner loop of sticky spiral and the outer loop of temporary spiral ("TSP distance") (see Fig. 3)	Eberhard (2012); Eberhard and Hesselberg (2012)
*3. Memory of the distance on the previous radius between the inner loop of sticky spiral and the outer loop of temporary spiral	Eberhard and Hesselberg (2012)
Less certain possibilities: distance between radii(A)[a]; length of current segment of sticky spiral(A); and direction of coiling of temporary and sticky spirals	Peters (1939); Eberhard (2020); unpub. data; Zschokke (1993)
B. Intermediate cues (possibly not sensed anew at each attachment)	
*4. Amount of silk available (especially sticky silk) versus area yet to be covered	Witt et al. (1968); Reed et al. (1969, 1970); Eberhard (1988a); Zschokke (1997); Hesselberg (2015)
*5(A). Distance from hub[b]	Eberhard (2014, 2020)
*6. Orientation with respect to the hub[b] (above, below, etc.) and angle of radius (vector) with gravity	Lopardo, Giribet, and Hormiga (2011); Vollrath (1988)

7. Memory of sharp changes in the TSP distance up to about 1 min previously at other sites in the orb	Eberhard (2020)
Less certain possibility: memory of a sharp change in the TSP distance encountered 30–60 s previously	Eberhard (2020)
C. "Prior settings" (probably sensed only once before beginning construction)	
*8. Body (leg) size	Vollrath (1987)
*9(**B**). Body weight	Christiansen et al. (1962)
*10(**B**). Recent total intake of food	summary Herberstein and Tso (2011)
11. Recent intake of specific prey[c]	Tso, Wu, and Hwang, (2005); Tso, Chiang, and Blackledge (2007); Blamires, Chao, and Tso (2010); Blamires et al. (2010)
12. Presence of predators (?)[c]	Li and Lee (2004); Nakata and Mori (2016)
13. Wind velocity	Liao et al. (2009)
14(**B**). Impending oviposition	
15. Sites in previous web where prey were captured or escaped[c]	Heiling and Herberstein (1999); Nakata (2007)
16. Time of day	Buskirk (1975)
17. Season of year	Sandoval (1994)
*18. Whether previous webs were built at this site[d]	Zschokke and Vollrath (2000)
19. Temperature	Vollrath et al. (1997)
20. Humidity	Vollrath et al. (1997); Opell, Schwend, and Vito (2011)

(*continued*)

Table 2 Variables that orb weaving spiders are thought to use in making decisions that determine the spacing between loops of the sticky spiral. Data from different species are combined here, because of the general taxonomic uniformity of cues used to guide sticky spiral construction (Eberhard Barrantes, 2015). Variables that correlate strongly with each other and that may represent a single cue sensed by the spider are marked with the same italicized letter; those cues most convincingly demonstrated to be likely of general importance are marked with "*". Two general orientation abilities that may not depend on external cues from particular web lines are included (in D). The references include only especially extensive studies; more exhaustive references, and more complete discussions of the techniques used to document the effects of different variables, and possible limitations in the support for different cues, are summarized in Eberhard (2020). (cont'd)

A. "Reference point" cues (sensed anew at each attachment)	Major references
*21. Amount of silk (probably sticky silk) in glands compared with size of web[e]	
D. Internal sources of orientation in web	
Distinguish the direction of the hub from the direction of the edge of the web[f]	Hingston (1920); König (1951); Vollrath (1988); Eberhard (2017)
Trace spiral path (around hub) independent of web lines encountered	Eberhard (2017)

[a]*A. diadematus* and *Z. x-notata* usually responded to experimental increases in distances between radii, but not always; responses in *L. mariana* were consistent.
[b]Implies that the spider knows the direction of the hub (see Vollrath, 1988).
[c]Conflicting data and controversy regarding this possible cue are summarized in Eberhard (2020).
[d]The second web is larger and has more sticky spiral loops; it is not known whether the spaces between loops are also different.
[e]Long-term effect of silk reserves on the size of the entire web and average sticky spiral spacing; contrast with "local" changes in the last few attachments as the spider runs out of silk (#4).
[f]Implicit in use of cues #1, #2, #5 and #6, and by the tendency to flee toward the hub when disturbed during temporary spiral and sticky spiral construction (Hingston, 1920; König, 1951; W. Eberhard unpub. on *M. duodecimspinosa*, *L. mariana*).

It is important to note that the spider's weight distorts her web, in some cases quite severely in slanted and vertical orbs. Thus sensing, grasping, and responding precisely to the positions of web lines in her vicinity probably requires complex behavioral adjustments by the spider. In addition, determining the angles that lines will have in the finished web is probably impossible (Eberhard, 2020). The possible consequences of this weight effect and possible compensations by the spider for this effect could be tested by measuring the precision of sticky spiral spacing after experimentally adding

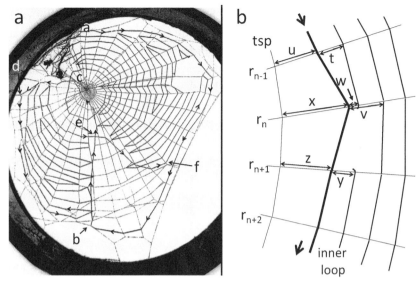

Fig. 2 Two types of evidence that confirm the impression obtained from direct observations of the "inner loop localization" leg movements during construction that the site of the inner loop has a strong influence on the locations of subsequent loops. In the *Uloborus diversus* web (A) (sticky lines are darker than non-sticky lines; arrowheads on dark lines indicate the direction in which the spider moved while laying the sticky lines), the spider wandered briefly during sticky spiral construction, laying deviant sticky lines that influenced the placement of subsequent sticky lines. After initiating the sticky line at point 1, she circled the web along its periphery until arriving at 2, where she turned inward (perhaps mistaking this radius for a temporary spiral line and vice versa) until she reached the hub (3). She then returned to the edge of the web (4) and began filling in the sector between 2 and 4, turning back each time she encountered a radially oriented sticky line. As she neared the hub, she finally crossed the sticky line at 5, and immediately moved again to the edge of the web (6) and began to fill in the sector between 6 and 1, using the sticky line she had laid earlier as an "inner loop". She resumed turning back each time she encountered a sticky line running more or less perpendicular to her path. The drawing (B) summarizes a second type of evidence based on "Hingston experiments" that were performed with the tetragnathid *Leucauge mariana*; a similar experiment was first performed by Hingston (1920). Thin lines are non-sticky; thicker lines are sticky; the thickest lines are the experimental loop; the large arrows show the spider's direction of movement; the double-headed arrows show distances between attachments of lines. The segment of the inner loop of sticky spiral between radii r_n and r_{n+1} was removed experimentally while the spider was on the opposite side of the web. When she next arrived at radius r_n to lay the experimental loop, her exploratory movements of leg oI to locate the inner loop of sticky spiral between radii r_n and r_{n+1} resulted in her contacting the loop that had been laid previously, and her attachment of the experimental loop was displaced outward (sticky spiral space t>sticky spiral space w in the drawing) (after Eberhard, 2020; Hingston, 1920).

weight to the spider's body (e.g., Christiansen et al., 1962), and by comparing vertical webs (where complex adjustments would be needed) with horizontal webs (where only smaller adjustments would be needed).

One consequence of the pattern of always attaching the new sticky line on the inward side of the inner loop is that the spider effectively follows a strict "do-not-cross-a-sticky-line" rule during sticky spiral construction. The effect of this rule on sticky spiral placement is especially dramatic in webs in which the spider wandered briefly earlier while building the sticky spiral, and then repeatedly turns back rather than cross it (Fig. 2A and Eberhard, 1969 on a uloborid; similar patterns occur in the araneid *A. diadematus*; see Vollrath, 1986, 1988). This do-not-cross-a-sticky-line rule is crucial in evaluating behavior in other contexts (see below).

2.3.2 The first loop of sticky spiral
The first loop of sticky spiral is a special case, because there is no inner loop of sticky spiral for the spider to use as a reference point. Several lines of evidence indicate that instead spiders use the outer loop of temporary spiral as a reference point (Eberhard & Hesselberg, 2012; Peters, 1937; Zschokke, 1993). Experimental modification of the outline of the outer loop of the temporary spiral in *Z. x-notata* (produced by rotating the web just before temporary spiral construction began) resulted in a change in the form of the outer loop of sticky spiral to follow the modified outline of the temporary spiral (Peters, 1937). In *M. duodecimspinosa,* an additional cue from the frame line to which the radius is attached is superimposed on this cue in some cases, when the distance between the frame and the outer loop of sticky spiral is below a certain threshold value (Eberhard, 2012).

The outline of the outermost loop of temporary spiral is thus determined to some extent by the spacing of previous loops of temporary spiral. This spacing varies in different parts of the web, and the function of these differences may be to produce a certain outline of the capture zone (the area bearing sticky lines) (for instance larger in the lower part of the web) (Eberhard, 2020).

2.3.3 "Intermediate", gradually changing variables
"Intermediate" variables that change more gradually during sticky spiral construction also influence sticky spiral attachment decisions. The spider may sense these variables less often. though the timing has not been confidently established. These cues include the following: the relative distance from the hub vs the distance to the edge of the web; her relative

position in the web above, below or to the side of the hub; memory of sharp changes in the TSP distance that were encountered up to approximately 1 min previously; and her relative silk reserves (presumably in terms of the relative degree to which her silk glands are full in comparison with the silk needed to fill the open area that is yet to be covered with sticky lines). The reserves of sticky spiral silk (from the aggregate and flagelliform glands in araneoids) rather than those of non-sticky silk (from the ampullate glands) may be most important (Table 2B). Surprisingly, the absolute size of these glands (which would seem more difficult for the spider to sense) may also have an effect (Reed, Witt, Scarboro, & Peakall, 1970). The consistent similarity between the direction of coiling (clockwise vs counterclockwise) of the temporary spiral and the sticky spiral in *A. diadematus* (Zschokke, 1993) (but not some other species—Eberhard, 2020; Zschokke, 1993) suggests that an additional, as yet unknown cue may also be used to guide sticky spiral spacing.

There are no data on how any of these variables are sensed. One possibility is that the spider may sense the area yet to be covered by comparing an estimate of the area already covered with sticky lines (using, perhaps path integration or the amount of sticky silk laid) with the total area of the web (Eberhard, 2020); this area is probably sensed using idiothetic cues and path integration during exploration (Eberhard, 2020; Hesselberg, 2015). This interpretation, however, is only speculative.

2.3.4 "Prior settings" variables

Finally, there are many additional (up to 14) "prior settings" variables that the spider may sense only once, some perhaps even before she initiates the orb; these remain relatively constant throughout sticky spiral construction. They involve a wide variety of factors, including the following: the spider's leg length; her body weight; her recent total intake of food; her recent intake of particular prey species; the presence of predators; memory of wind velocities on previous days; the proximity of oviposition; memories of particular sites in previous webs where prey were captured; the overall size of the web (possibly sensed using some sort of cognitive map formed during the exploration stage) (Hesselberg, 2015); the time of day; temperature; humidity; and the season of the year (in one species) (Table 2C). The spider's history of webs at the site may also have an effect, as the second web built at a site tends to be larger and have more loops of sticky spiral than the first (the effect on sticky spiral spacing is not known) (Zschokke & Vollrath, 2000).

The strength of empirical support linking these different variables to sticky spiral spacing varies substantially (see Eberhard, 2020 for critical evaluations of the evidence), and no single species has been tested for its responses to all of these cues (Table 2). It may be that the spider evaluates some of these cues repeatedly rather than only once; the timing has not demonstrated for any of them.

2.3.5 Other likely cues

The spider probably perceives and responds to two further variables during sticky spiral placement (Table 2): the direction of the hub (as opposed to the web's edge); and the direction that she would need to move to make a roughly circular path around the hub (independent of cues from the web lines that she encounters). Knowledge of the direction of the hub is implicit in cues #'s 5 and 6 in Table 2. The existence of this knowledge during sticky spiral construction is supported by the fact that the spider's usual response when she is disturbed during sticky spiral construction is to move directly to the hub (rather than to the edge of the web or elsewhere) (Ades, 1986; W. G. Eberhard, unpub. data). Spiders also return frequently to the hub during normal orb construction, even in the very early stages, and also remember the hub location in other contexts (e.g., Le Guelte, 1969) The ability to circle the web is supported by less extensive evidence from the paths of spiders of several species in exceptional circumstances (e.g., Fig. 2A; see also Eberhard, 2020).

2.3.6 Independence of different cues

Some of the cues just mentioned are probably correlated (see, for instance, italicized letters *A* and *B* in Table 2; also, body weight is determined to some extent by both recent feeding history and impending oviposition). There are inevitably strong correlations between many different aspects of an orb because of the geometric regularity of its design, and most studies did not check all possibly correlated variables. These associations introduce doubt regarding those conclusions based only on evidence from correlations. For instance, the area of an orb is correlated with the number of radii, the number of radii is correlated with the number of sticky spiral loops, and the number of sticky spiral loops is correlated with the spaces between them. Does the correlation between the web area and sticky spiral spacing in experimental *L. mariana* webs (Barrantes & Eberhard, 2012) mean that the web area was used as a "prior settings" cue by the spider to determine the spaces between loops of sticky spiral? Or was this correlation with web area only incidental, or due to some other unknown factor?

Appropriate experimental manipulations and careful statistical analyses (e.g., Zschokke, 2011) can discriminate between incidental correlations and cause-effect relationships, but are lacking in some cases. Most studies have analyzed only a limited subset of the possible variables, and the multivariate statistical techniques that are needed to discriminate between first order and more incidental correlations lose power as the number of variables increases.

Nevertheless, even considering these limitations and others (reviewed in Eberhard, 2020), it is very likely that at least 10 of the variables in Table 2 influence each attachment, and the number may be as high as 15 in some cases. Whatever the total number of independent cues may to be, it is now clear that these "simple" animals integrate a great variety of cues in as yet incompletely understood ways. It is profoundly misleading to conceive of orb weavers as simple automatons that execute the same behavior over and over when building their webs.

I have not attempted to review the numbers of cues that other animals use to guide particular behavioral decisions. But I suspect that the high number of cues guiding sticky spiral attachment behavior is probably unusual, if not unique for a single behavioral act, at least in an arthropod. It is nevertheless also possible that the large number of documented cues in orb weaving spiders is an artifact of the ease with which their decisions can be studied (see the final section).

2.4 Potential cues that are *not* used

While a surprisingly high number of variables influence the spider during sticky spiral construction, it is important to note, especially in the context of future possible studies, that additional data clearly eliminate several other types of possible cues. In *U. diversus*, for instance, possible gradients in light, temperature, vibration, wind, humidity, and gravity were eliminated in captivity and the spiders still spun apparently normal horizontal orbs (Eberhard, 1969). Visual cues from the web itself can also be confidently ruled out, as orb weavers' eyes have poor resolution, and are directed dorsally while their web lines are consistently ventral to the spider during orb construction; and most species build in darkness (Eberhard, 2020). The web strands' small diameters and light weight make it very unlikely that spiders could perceive their vibrations transmitted through the air (Wirth & Barth, 1992). Finally, possible chemical signals from distant lines in the web are highly unlikely to be useful because of their lack of resolution, especially in a wind.

A further set of possibilities is that the spider senses local chemical differences between apparently similar lines by touch. For example, perhaps radii of different lengths have different chemical coatings. Or perhaps the spider guides sticky spiral placement using memories of the shape of the array of non-sticky lines that she has just finished building. Both of these possibilities are largely ruled out by unusual webs like that in Fig. 2A, where an alteration of the path of a single sticky line (due to a brief period of "wandering") resulted in multiple changes in the sites of subsequent lines (see also Eberhard, 1969, 2020). "Wandering" could be induced by shining a bright light on the spider during sticky spiral construction (Eberhard, 1969). Similarly, when a sticky line was experimentally added to webs of *M. duodecimspinosa* during sticky spiral construction, the path of the subsequent sticky spiral was altered (Eberhard, 2020). One possible chemical signal may be important, however, when they use the positions of previously laid sticky lines to guide sticky spiral placement (Figs. 2 and 3): spiders clearly distinguish sticky from non-sticky lines, possibly by chemical cues.

Still another possibility, which has been mentioned repeatedly (e.g., Eberhard, 1969; Hingston, 1920) is that sticky spiral construction is guided by differences in the tensions or tension-dependent cues such as the extensibility or the resonant vibrations of web lines. Nevertheless, several lines of evidence contradict such tension hypotheses. Most importantly, experimental reductions and increases in the tensions on radii have consistently failed to produce changes in sticky spiral spacing (summary in Eberhard, 2020). This lack of effect indicates that neither radius tension nor tension-dependent variables influence sticky spiral spacing decisions. Reductions in radius tensions are occasionally made spontaneously by *M. duodecimspinosa,* when the spider interrupts sticky spiral construction, goes to the hub and removes the center of the hub (thus relaxing all radii), and then resumes construction; these tension changes also have no obvious effects on sticky spiral spacing (W.G. Eberhard unpub. data).

On further reflection, the lack of use of tension-related cues is not surprising, because these variables would, in practice, constitute extremely unreliable cues. In the first place, the spider's own weight causes large changes in the tensions on lines in her immediate vicinity, and these changes vary dramatically in different parts of the web. For instance, when she is below the hub, her weight will tense the "inside" portion of the radius (on hub side) and relax the "outside" portion (on the side nearer the web's edge). When she is above the hub, the situation will be reversed, with increased tension on the outside portion and reduced tension on the

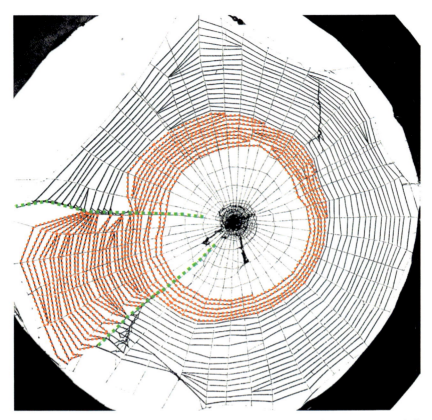

Fig. 3 This *Zosis geniculata* web provides an experimental demonstration of the importance of sticky rather than non-sticky lines in guiding sticky spiral construction. The spider had interrupted sticky spiral construction on the first night without finishing, leaving a central area with no sticky lines and about three loops of temporary spiral intact. The 7:00–9:00 sector of this web was then broken experimentally (dotted green lines); the lateral edges of the outer portion of this sector contained sticky lines, but the edges in the more internal portion lacked sticky lines. On the following night, the spider built six new radii in the damaged sector, and then partially filled it with zig-zag sticky spiral lines, starting at the outer edge of the repair sector and working inward (the dotted red lines). She stopped before finishing, leaving the central area with no sticky lines and about two loops of temporary spiral intact. While filling the outer portion of the repair sector, she turned back each time she encountered the edge of the intact web, which contained sticky lines. In the inner portion, however, she ceased turning back at the edge of the repair sector where the border did not contain sticky lines, thus demonstrating that the do-not-cross rule applies to lines containing sticky silk but not to lines that lack sticky silk (after Eberhard, 2019).

inside portion (Fig. 1C). On a more nearly horizontal radius these effects will be more balanced, but will vary in complex ways depending on the angle of the radius with horizontal, and on nearby connections with the temporary spiral.

A further complication for using tension-related cues arises from the fact that the substrates to which anchor lines are attached sometimes move (Mulder, Mortimer, & Vollrath, 2021), causing variable, unpredictable transient changes tensions in web lines. Even in webs that are attached to rigid supports, changes in wind speed and direction, and in the properties of the silk in radial lines when exposed to different humidity, especially the "super-contraction" that occurs under higher humidity (e.g., Blackledge et al., 2009), could also result in changes in radius tensions. In addition, both direct measurements and analyzes of angles between lines in finished orbs show that the tensions on radial lines vary substantially, by a factor of about 8 (Denny, 1976) in an *Larinioides sclopetarius* (Clerck, 1757) orb, and just over 4 (Wirth & Barth, 1992) in an *A. diadematus* orb. Radii in the upper portions of *Zygiella x-notata* (Clerck, 1757) web were also under more tension than others (LeGuelte, 1966). The tension on a radius even varies along the length of the radius itself because the spiral lines attached to it pull it inward (Eberhard, 1969).

The conclusion that tension-related variables are not used as cues has important consequences for studies of orb construction behavior. It means that, just as one can deduce what a blind man is attempting to locate by observing the behavior of his cane, one can deduce what information is available to the spider by observing which legs she is waving in which directions, and thus her intentions and her the likely direction in which she will move. For instance, the fact that inner loop localization behavior usually results in only a single contact with the inner loop (the spider turns immediately to attach the sticky line after this single touch) implies that the spider probably only senses the location of this line, and not the direction in which it runs. Contact with two points on the line would be needed to sense its direction (the directions of a non-sticky line might be sensed after only a single contact, however, if the tarsus grasps it). The fact that tension-related cues are not used to guide sticky spiral spacing decisions does not mean, of course, that they are not used to guide other stages of orb construction.

In sum, an orb-weaving spider flexibly adjusts sticky spiral spacing on the basis of multiple cues. The cues that she uses are tactile cues from the web lines that she encounters in her immediate vicinity, short-term memories of distances she has traveled, and general "settings" cues such as the approximate size of the web and information on her internal state (silk reserves, etc.). This extensive knowledge of the variables that spiders do and do not use as cues during sticky spiral construction makes it possible for future studies to ask new questions by focusing on relevant cues. The gradual realization that tension-related cues are not used to guide sticky spiral construction amounts to a breakthrough in understanding sticky spiral construction, because it means that it is possible to use the positions of lines in the spider's immediate vicinity and the spider's own leg movements to deduce which cues, she used to make any given decision. In addition, experimental manipulations of the positions of these lines can be used to explore the effects of additional manipulations such as psychoactive drugs and experimental interruption of the spider's attention.

3. Additional decisions during sticky spiral construction

In addition to deciding where on the radius to attach the sticky spiral, the spider also makes other, less well-studied decisions each time she encounters a radius. One decision is whether or not to double back and begin circling the web in the opposite direction. Doubling back allows the spider to fill in the larger portions of an asymmetrical space before circling inward to fill the rest of her orb (Hingston, 1920; Le Guelte, 1966; Peters, 1937; Zschokke, 1993). In *U. diversus*, the turnback decision is probably made before the spider attaches the sticky line, and turning back may also sometimes be associated with a decision to attach to an earlier radius than she would have otherwise (Eberhard, 1969). A simulation study indicated that the doubling back decisions might be based on the angles that the current sticky spiral line makes with the radius and with the inner loop, but did not demonstrate that spiders actually use these cues (Eberhard, 1969).

A second response, which may involve multiple decisions, concerns the characteristics of the lines the spider is producing. The amount of aggregate gland glue applied to the sticky line being produced varies, even in a given web, perhaps on the basis of available silk (Crews & Opell, 2006). It also varies between webs, depending on the wind velocity experienced on previous days (Wu et al., 2013). The thickness and rigidity of other web lines also varies on the basis of previously experienced wind (Liao et al., 2009) and the spider's weight (Christiansen et al., 1962).

4. Uniformity of cues used in different families of orb weavers

Some of the cues mentioned above may only be used by a subset of orb weaver species. At one extreme, early morning rains from June to September induced the Brazilian araneid *Parawixia bistriata* to build more widely-spaced sticky spirals in orbs that were apparently designed to capture the weak-flying termite reproductives that flew in large numbers only on such mornings (Sandoval, 1994). This response is unknown in any other species. Cues that elicit turnbacks in *A. diadematus* may also differ from those used by the araneids *Z. x-notata* and *Gasteracantha* sp. and some uloborids (Zschokke, 1993). And some species may give different weights to the same cues. For instance, *M. duodecimspinosa* seems less likely to turn back when the TSP distance decreases abruptly than are some other species such as *A. diadematus* (Zschokke, 1993, pers. comm.; W.G. Eberhard unpub. data).

Nevertheless, despite these minor differences, there is a general uniformity in both the cues that spiders use and their responses to them. Even though experimental tests of the use of different cues in different species are far from complete, experimental manipulation of a potential cue that produced a given response in one species often produce the same response when performed with other species (Eberhard, 2020; Eberhard & Barrantes, 2015). A particularly striking example is the similarity in changes in at least seven conservatively distinguished, statistically distinct web traits (including hub, radii, frame lines, and sticky spiral variables) that changed when two species (the araneoid *L. argyra* and the deinopoid *Zosis geniculata*) were obliged to build webs in very small spaces (Table 3). Several of the responses seen in these experiments appear to be extensions of trends in field webs of *L. argyra* (Table 3).

This similarity has important consequences for the old, still-unresolved debate concerning whether orb webs arose independently in Araneoidea and Deinopoidea. The similarity in the two groups in both the cues that are used to guide orb construction behavior and the responses that spiders give to these cues argues in favor of monophyly; 20 shared derived behavioral traits with feasible alternatives are known (Eberhard, 2022a) (the feasibility of alternatives for one was subsequently questioned, see above). This uniformity typifies sticky spiral construction as well as other stages of orb construction (Eberhard, 1982, 2020; Eberhard & Barrantes, 2015). In contrast, however, recent phylogenies based on molecular data suggest that

Table 3 Changes in the designs of orb webs built by species in different families, *Zosis geniculata* (Uloboridae) and *Leucauge argyra* (Tetragnathidae), when the spiders were confined to cages that were much smaller than the sizes of their normal webs (definitions of variables and explanation of classifications of the independent decisions are given Eberhard & Barrantes, 2015).

Changes in webs built in small exptl. spaces				Same trend in field webs of *L. argyra*?
Web traits	Decision	*Zosis geniculata*	*Leucage argyra*	
Relative areas				
Capture area	—[a]	Smaller	Smaller	Yes
Hub area	C	Smaller	Smaller	Yes
Free zone area	G	Smaller	Smaller	Yes
Overall symmetry	D	?	Reduced	No
Radii, frames, anchors				
Number of radii	B	Smaller	Smaller	Yes
Length of radii		Shorter	Shorter	Yes?
Number of frame lines	A	Smaller	Smaller	Yes
Proportion of radii attached to substrate	A	Larger	Larger	No
Proportion of frame lines with only one radius attached to them	A	Larger	Larger	No

(continued)

Table 3 Changes in the designs of orb webs built by species in different families, *Zosis geniculata* (Uloboridae) and *Leucauge argyra* (Tetragnathidae), when the spiders were confined to cages that were much smaller than the sizes of their normal webs (definitions of variables and explanation of classifications of the independent decisions are given Eberhard Barrantes, 2015). (*cont'd*)

Changes in webs built in small exptl. spaces				Same trend in field webs of *L. argyra*?
Number radii/number frame lines	A	Smaller	Smaller	Yes
Proportion of radii ending in a "V"	A	Larger	Larger	No
Sticky spiral				
Distance from outer loop of sticky spiral to frame	E	Smaller	Smaller	No
Number of loops of sticky spiral	F	Smaller	Smaller	Yes
Spaces between loops of sticky spiral on longest radius	F	Smaller	Smaller	Yes
Distance from outer to inner sticky spiral loop	G	Smaller	Smaller	Yes
Consistency of spaces between sticky spiral loops	?	No change	No change	Yes
Hub				
Number of loops of hub spiral	?	?	No change	Yes

[a]Directly imposed by experimental treatment rather than by decision of the spider.

orb webs have originated three to five different times (Kulkani et al., 2021), and possibly ancestral basic aspects of regularity are known in the webs of several non-orb groups (Eberhard, 2021; Ramírez et al., 2023). The contrasting, monophyly hypothesis (e.g., Coddington et al., 2019) argues that orbs evolved only once, in the common ancestor of uloborids and araneoids. It is supported by the similarity in cues and responses in orb weavers, and by the fact that several alternative types of cues that could have provided spiders with sufficient information to guide construction behavior, due to the geometric regularity of orbs, are not used in either group. This controversy is currently unresolved.

In sum, both the cues and the spiders' responses to them are apparently ancient, and they have been evolutionarily conservative. There is no sign in modern species of a gradual evolutionary process of perfecting the ability to build an orb. This uniformity contrasts with the abundant evidence of independent, gradual losses of responses to cues that have occurred in lineages in which orbs have been lost or modified (Eberhard, 2018).

4.1 The spider's agility and precision

The smooth flow of rapid, precise movements by a spider building her orb gives the impression of simplicity. Her operations during sticky spiral construction seem especially uncomplicated and uniform: she moves outward, attaches, moves inward and onward along the temporary spiral to the next radius, then moves outward along this radius to attach again; and she repeats this process over and over and over. But the uniformity of this verbal description of sticky spiral construction conceals a possibly infinite variety of different leg and body movements and forces that she exerts when she performs these "repetitive" movements (Eberhard, 2020). The leg and body movements that are needed to accomplish the different, tightly coordinated tasks that are executed each time the spider attaches the sticky spiral to a radius include coordination between the movements and forces exercised by different legs, coordination between leg and spinneret movements, and the nearly instantaneous initiation and termination of silk production from the piriform glands (Table 1). Even the path that the spider follows (and thus the lines she contacts) varies (Fig. 4): it follows the temporary spiral more closely in the outer than in the inner portion of her orb (König, 1951), and when she is moving upward rather than downward in her web (Zschokke & Vollrath, 1995).

Building a sticky spiral is also physically challenging, making the spiders' sustained coordination even more impressive. For instance, during the

Fig. 4 The lines trace the path followed by the body of a *Larinioides sclopetarius* as she circled in a clockwise direction while she built the sticky spiral in a more or less vertical web, starting at the outer edge and working inward. The path illustrates both consistent patterns and clear variations on that in the simplified drawing in Fig. 1A. The path forms "bundles" where the spider repeatedly used the temporary spiral as a bridge to get from one radius to the next. This bundling pattern was clearer near the web's outer edge throughout the web, and also when the spider was ascending (left side of the figure). But when she was descending (right side of the figure), she tended to move more directly from one attachment to the next, using gravity rather than the temporary spiral bridge to move from one radius to the next; this difference was more pronounced in more central portions of the orb (unpublished figure courtesy of S. Zschokke).

15–20 min that *M. duodecimspinosa* spends building the sticky spiral, she moves in human terms (correcting for relative body sizes) the equivalent of about 7–8 km, much of this upward and downward (Eberhard, 2020). Orb construction requires substantial physical endurance as well as agile and precise coordination.

4.2 "Rigid flexibility"? Pre-programmed versus flexible, open-ended responses to cues

The old "automaton" image of orb weavers has given way to the realization that they respond flexibly to a number of different stimuli. It is nevertheless possible that spiders are automaton-like, in that they may give invariable,

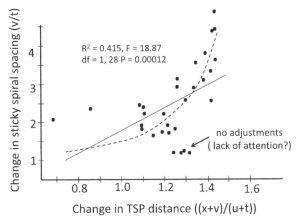

Fig. 5 The sizes of the adjustments in sticky spiral spacing that *Leucauge mariana* spiders made in different "Hingston experiments" varied widely. It was related to the difference when the experimental space compared with the immediately preceding control space (t/v in Fig. 2B) was compared with the change in the TSP distance ((u + t)/(x + v) in Fig. 1B) (units are standardized in terms of the mean values in each web). The sizes of the adjustments ranged from close to no change (v/t = 1.0) to increases in which v was several times the value of t. In general, the increase in spacing (v/t) was greater when the difference between the TSP distance on radii r_{n-1} and r_n ((u + t)/(w + x)) was greater (the lack of certainty whether the TSP distance effect was linear or curvilinear is indicated by including the straight regression line and a hand-fitted dashed line). There was, however, a group of points in which the spider made essentially no adjustment, perhaps due to lack of attention to the TSP distance (after Eberhard, 2020).

automatic responses to guiding stimuli. This possibility of "rigid flexibility", is contrasted below with the alternative of "open-ended" flexibility at two levels of organization of sticky spiral construction behavior.

4.2.1 Operations (tasks)

Sticky spiral construction shows substantial flexibility, and the spider adjusts the spaces between loops in response to many different variables. There is generally a great deal of scatter in the relations between sticky spiral spacing and any given variable. For instance, the coefficients of correlation between the normalized spaces between the first two loops of sticky spiral and the standardized TSP distance was only $R = 0.31$ in the 18 webs of *L. mariana*, and $R = 0.41$ in 16 webs of *M. duodecimspinosa* (Eberhard & Hesselberg, 2012). Similarly, calculations of relative "imprecision values" (based on the ratios of absolute values of the differences between the spaces between adjacent loops of sticky spiral in particular small areas of the orb) showed values between 0.15 and 0.22 (Eberhard, 2007) (with 0 indicating no variation).

The source of this variation is not entirely clear. Some variation in the responses to a given variable is undoubtedly due to the effects of other variables, and it could be that the variations are due to rigidly pre-programmed responses to these variables. The adjustments to the variables listed in Table 2 could all be due to tightly programmed rigid flexibility, and variations in these responses could be due to other tightly programmed responses to simultaneous variation in other variables. Alternatively, the spider's responses to a given variable may be less reliable, and more open-ended. For instance, variations might be due to occasional failures to pay attention to a particular variable (Fig. 5), to "errors" caused by imprecision in the nervous system itself (Calvin, 1983; Eberhard, 1990), or to gradually accumulated memories of earlier lessons. Most studies of orb weavers have presumed rigid flexibility in responses, and alternative possibilities are usually not even considered. The special traits of sticky spiral construction behavior make possible studies of additional questions of general importance, such as attention and inattention, nervous system imprecision, and the spider's expectations.

4.2.2 Detailed movements

The question of rigid versus open-ended flexibility has to my knowledge never been addressed specifically at the level of detailed movements in orb weavers. But I believe it is nevertheless easily answered: true, open-ended flexibility is almost certainly the rule. While the operations involved in sticky spiral production are relatively constant, this uniformity is the result of a "roiling sea of variation" in the combinations of the detailed movements of the different legs (Eberhard, 2020). The details of how the legs move, their coordination, and the forces that they exercise vary dramatically in different parts of a single orb (see section on mechanical agility above); the combinations of leg movements and their coordination are probably infinitely variable. The fact that under near-zero gravity conditions (an evolutionarily novel situation for which spiders surely have not evolved appropriate hard-wired responses) at least some individuals of both the araneid *A. diadematus* and the nephilid *Trichonephila clavipes* performed novel, appropriate, coordinated leg movements that enabled them to build highly uniform sticky spiral spacing (Witt, Scarboro, Daniels, Peakall, & Gause, 1977; Zschokke, Countryman, & Cushing, 2021) confirms such open-ended flexibility.

What processes underlie such open-ended variation? This question has no empirically justified answer for orb-weaving spiders at the moment.

I will, however, outline two speculative hypotheses to illustrate the exciting directions in which orb web studies could lead. One possibility, originally proposed on the basis of orb web repair behavior (Eberhard, 2017), is that the spider is a least vaguely conscious of both the goals of its building behavior, and of the consequences that the particular actions that it might make could have for accomplishing these goals. Novel behaviors could arise when the spider employs a novel set of movements in an attempt to accomplish a given task under novel conditions.

A second possibility, involving only lower-level mental processes, is inspired by analyses of vertebrate nervous system processes (Edelman & Tononi, 2000). It could be that multiple, interactive functional groups of neurons that control leg movements have reentry connections, i.e., reciprocal interconnections between functionally segregated neuron groups (Edelman & Tononi, 2000). Perhaps some of these interconnections would be similar to the "synergy" interneurons that activate different groups of muscle fibers in the vertebrate spinal cord (Bizzi & Ajemian, 2015). Each function could be adjusted in a continuous fashion to variables such as the actions of other legs, the locations of lines, the stresses on the legs, the angles with gravity, and also to one or more neurological "value systems" (Edelman & Tononi, 2000) that indicate that a particular stage of web construction is in progress. Such a value system could result from the activity of small neuronal "centers" or nodes that have diffuse projections in the brain. The spider's movements and their timing and coordination could thus vary continuously rather than being discrete. The reentry connections could result in harmonious coordination of the movements of different legs to accomplish a given task (e.g., a reaching forward movement of leg II and its details would be elicited and modulated by the ipsilateral leg I having already found and grasped a line, by the weight-sustaining positions of other legs, and by the spider being engaged in the process of moving forward to search for another line).

A possible illustration of how it may be possible to distinguish rigid from open-ended flexibility in detailed behavior comes from the ability of some orb weavers to adjust to the loss of a leg by altering the behavior of her remaining legs. Compensations for leg loss have only been studied in a preliminary manner (Jacobi-Kleemann, 1953 and Reed, Witt, & Jones,1965 on leg I of the araneid *A. diadematus*; Pasquet, Anotaux, & Leborgne, 2011 on *Z. x-notata*; Eberhard, 2020 on leg IV of *T. clavipes*). The question of whether these adjustments are the result of rigid or open-ended flexibility could be addressed by comparing the responses of species in orb weaving taxa such as these species, which frequently lose legs in nature as a defense against predators, with the responses of species in other groups such as tetragnathids that do not naturally lose their legs (Roth & Roth, 1984). Rigid flexibility would predict that tetragnathids would not compensate as effectively for such a loss, because such adjustments are seldom if ever needed in nature and thus specific, pre-programmed flexibility would be unlikely to evolve (Soley, Rodríguez, Hoebel, & Eberhard, 2021). In contrast, open-ended flexibility would predict that tetragnathids would make successful adjustments of similar efficacy to those made by araneids and nephilines. Experimental tests remain to be done.

5. Learning and maturation

Orb web designs change during the spider's lifetime in several species (summaries in Hesselberg, 2010; Witt, Reed, & Peakall, 1968; Eberhard, 2020). These changes could be due to maturation of the spider or to learning. Orb web spiders clearly have the ability to learn (Ades, Da Cunha, & Tiedemann, 1993; Bays, 1962; Hénaut, Machkour-M'Rabet, & Lachaud, 2014; Le Guelte, 1967). Nevertheless, ontogeny and changes in the relative development of silk glands (Reed et al., 1970) are thought to explain most changes in web designs (e.g., Eberhard, 2020; Rawlings & Witt, 1973; Witt et al., 1968).

The classic study of *Z. x-notata* by Petrusewiczowa (1938) found that learning was not responsible for the typical acquisition of an "open sector" (a sector lacking sticky spiral lines and with a signal line running through it from the hub to the spider's retreat beyond the edge of the orb) in the orbs of older individuals. Young individuals laid sticky spirals in the open sector, and then later removed them when they built the signal line; older individuals sometimes left the sector empty of sticky lines by turning back at its edges during sticky spiral construction (Mayer, 1952). The adults of another araneid, *Eustala illicita*, also build more open sectors than do spiderlings (Hesselberg, 2010). Petrusewiczowa (1938) found that when she reared *Z. x-notata* nymphs to maturity in small containers, and thus prevented them from building orbs, they nevertheless built open sectors and signal lines when they were given a chance to build orbs in a larger container. These results were later questioned by the finding of Peters (1969) that *Z. x-notata* spiderlings built an open sector even in their first orbs. There is also variation between the webs of adults (Gregorič, Kostanjšek, & Kuntner, 2010), and some individuals use both techniques in different webs (S. Zschokke pers. comm.). This behavior merits further study.

The webs of lab-raised *Argiope aurantia* that were deprived of web building experience showed several other, quantitative design changes that were also apparently not due to learning, but rather to maturational changes in the CNS and to different degrees of development of the spider's silk glands whose size correlates with previous demand for silk; glands were smaller in lab individuals prevented from building webs and whose demand for silk was thus smaller (Reed et al., 1969, 1970). Other studies have also generally indicated that learning does not have a large role in determining changes in orb designs (Eberhard, 2020). For instance, the adjustments in the designs of *Eustala illicita* orbs to different sizes and shapes of spaces in which the webs were built did not change with practice (Hesselberg, 2014).

I know of only three cases in which learning seemed to affect web design. One was the gradual improvement in the ability of *Argiope argentata* to build horizontal orbs when imprisoned in a horizontal open space (Ades et al., 1993; Da Cunha-Nogueira & Ades, 2012). This apparently complex ability is not used in nature, because the orbs of this species are generally more or less vertical. The general ability to learn that was demonstrated in this experiment might, however, have evolved to enable adjustment to other factors, and deserves further study. A second case is the possible gradual improvement in locomotory and web-building skills in *A. diadematus* under weightless conditions in space, though the data in this case are very fragmentary (Witt et al., 1977). Finally, *A. diadematus* gradually built more perfectly planar and vertical orbs when several were built at the same site (Zschokke & Vollrath, 2000). In this case, however, the possibility of more thorough exploration of the website for the second web as opposed to learning was not eliminated. In none of these cases was it clear what immediate reward or eventual payoff the spider might obtain from an "improved" performance. Recent advances in automated recording of details of building behavior (Corver, Wilkerson, Miller, & Gordus, 2021) could facilitate tests of learning in more detailed aspects of construction behavior.

One possible reward that could reinforce learning of particular behavioral details would be increased prey capture. But given the highly stochastic arrival of prey in the web, there are no obvious immediate payoffs to a spider for learning any of the particular abilities that have been studied. Altering a design detail, such as for example the orb's vertical asymmetry (which changes during the spider's lifetime in some species), is likely to correlate only very loosely (if at all) with greater prey capture from one web to the next of a given spider. In addition, the timing of such rewards (often hours after she has built her web) is unlikely to result in the spider perceiving associations (Eberhard, 2019; Heiling & Herberstein, 1999).

A different possible reward that a spider might be more reasonably expected to perceive is a savings in effort; this could result from improved precision or coordination of her construction behavior. The rewards for such "practice makes perfect" learning could be reductions in the time or effort expended in building. This hypothesis is not supported, however, by the few available data. The adjustments of adult *E. illicita* to different-shaped spaces for their webs did not improve with experience (Hesselberg, 2015). In addition, in several species the spaces between adjacent loops of sticky spiral were not less consistent in the webs early instar spiderlings than in the webs of conspecific adults (Barrantes & Eberhard, 2012; Eberhard, 2007; Hesselberg, 2010; Quesada et al., 2021).

The lack of an important role for learning is not surprising considering the natural history of orb weavers. Immediate behavioral competence, without any learning period, is likely crucial for the survival of newly emerged spiderlings that depend on their webs to survive. Young spiders probably cannot afford the luxury of only gradually learning how to build an orb.

In summary, changes in orb designs often occur during the lifetime of an individual that could be due to ontogenetic changes or to learning. Although few species have been studied in sufficient detail, evidence of several sorts indicates that learning is generally of little importance, and there are also theoretical reasons to expect that learning is seldom important. One apparent case of learning of what may be a complex lesson deserves further study.

6. Coordination and independence of flexible adjustments of web variables

The patterns of lines in an orb are the result of many different decisions made at different stages of construction; nevertheless, they constitute a physically coherent whole in the finished web. At least some coordination exists between different decisions made during sticky spiral construction. A simple example is the interaction between the cues #1, #2 and #3 in Table 2. In most situations all three influence the decision where to attach. But when the site of the inner loop is especially distant from the temporary spiral, cue #2 apparently tends to over-ride #1 and #3 (Eberhard & Hesselberg, 2012). Similarly, *Neoscona nautica* used cue #1 in the outer part of its web but not near the hub (Hingston, 1920).

More complex coordination occurred in the araneid *M. sexspinosa* and the tetragnathid *L. mariana* when the spider's reserves of sticky spiral silk (in the flagelliform and aggregate glands) were experimentally altered. Each spider replaced the orb that she had built early the same morning when it was severely damaged by breaking all but the frame lines and three radii. Control spiders were allowed to finish the sticky spiral in the first web, thus more or less depleting their glands of sticky spiral silk. In contrast, the first web of each experimental spider was destroyed when the spider had only just begun sticky spiral construction, thus leaving her stores of sticky spiral silk more or less intact. When the spiders then rebuilt their webs later that morning, the replacement orbs of the control (depleted) spiders differed from their original orbs in being smaller, having fewer radii and fewer loops of sticky spiral. The replacement orbs of experimental spiders, in contrast, were not smaller and did not have fewer radii than their original webs. In both control and experimental webs the spaces between sticky spiral loops were unaltered (Eberhard, 1988b). In *Leucauge*, this flexibility is itself flexible. When *L. argyra* was induced experimentally to build in very tightly constrained spaces, spiders made similar adjustments in most of these variables (reduced web area, number of radii, and number of sticky spiral loops); but the spaces between sticky spiral loops were also reduced (Barrantes & Eberhard, 2012).

Similar coordinated flexibility occurs in other species. The orbs of *A. diadematus* spiders that built four webs in the space of 24 h (and presumably had depleted silk reserves for the later web) became successively smaller and had fewer radii and a shorter sticky spiral with larger spaces between loops (Vollrath, Downes, & Krackow, 1997). The araneid *Cyclosa mulmeinensis* showed a coordinated, multivariable response to high wind velocity on previous days: webs were smaller, and had larger spaces between sticky spiral loops, shorter total lengths of silk, and larger droplets of adhesive on the sticky spiral lines (Liao et al., 2009). Some similar adjustments to wind also occur in *A. diadematus* (Vollrath et al., 1997). The multidimensional coordination revealed by these experiments is probably a normal part of orb construction that occurs each time an orb is initiated. The spider likely adjusts multiple aspects of the web that she will build on the basis of the information that she perceives during the exploration stage (Eberhard, 2020; Hesselberg, 2015; Krink & Vollrath, 1999; Vollrath, 1992).

It might seem that the ability to make such integrated multidimensional flexible decisions stems from "rigid flexibility", because the calculations that would be required in order to make functionally appropriate, open-ended adjustments seem far too complex. But open-ended flexibility is a feasible possibility even for such multiple, interacting adjustments if there are reentry connections of the type described above. The susceptibility of these decisions to experimental manipulations that might distinguish between rigid and open-ended flexibility (for example, distracting stimuli, drug treatments) remains to be determined.

How many different, independent web traits are coordinated by an orb weaver? I cannot give a confident numerical answer. One analysis gave a conservative estimate of at least seven different independent adjustments in the webs of *L. argyra* when spiders built orbs in very small spaces (about 7% of the area of a typical field web), based on multivariate statistical analyzes that demonstrated changes in 15 design variables (Barrantes & Eberhard, 2012) (Table 3). Seven may be an underestimate, however, because more than one decision may have been involved in the changes seen in five of these variables (Barrantes & Eberhard, 2012; Eberhard, 2020). For instance, the number of loops of sticky spiral in an orb is very unlikely to result from any sort of decision regarding numbers per se by the spider. More likely, the number of loops resulted from a combination of decisions such as where to attach the outermost loop of sticky spiral, how far apart to space the subsequent loops, and when to terminate sticky spiral construction. The fact that a lack of statistical independence between different responses is not necessarily equivalent to a lack of biological independence could also lead to underestimates of the number of independent responses; aspects that have strong statistical correlations could nevertheless result from independent behavioral decisions.

These tests of independence emphasize the important evolutionary point that there can variation in one decision even after other, previous decisions have been made. Thus natural selection may act separately on the two decisions, and they can evolve independently. In some sense, these behavioral questions are related to discussions of evolutionary "constraints" or pre-existing developmental patterns, which are more often posed in the context of morphological evolution (Gould & Lewontin, 1979; Müller & Wagner, 1991; but see West-Eberhard, 2003 for behavioral examples).

6.1 Memory of preceding stages and insightful solutions to problems

Some species of orb weavers repair web damage (caused in nature by prey, detritus, wind, etc.) by rebuilding portions of their orbs. In these species it is possible to experimentally alter the size and shape of the space to be repaired, and thus to test the spider's degree of flexibility and the possible effects of her memories of recent building activities. Testing her responses to situations that seldom if ever occur under natural conditions can provide insight into the possibility that her responses are rigidly flexible, because appropriate, pre-programmed responses are unlikely to occur in evolutionarily novel situations (Eberhard, 2019; Soley et al., 2021). Because of their important implications regarding the spider's mental capabilities, I will describe some tests in detail.

To begin, it is necessary to briefly review orb repair behavior. Orb-weaving spiders make two general types of repairs to damaged webs. In "shoring up repairs", non-sticky lines are added soon after the damage occurs; these lines increase the tension on slack lines, and enable the orb to continue to function as an effective trap (Eberhard, 2022b; Tew, Adamson, & Hesselberg, 2015). The second type, "major repairs", is discussed here. Major repairs are typically not made until the next normal web-construction period, often many hours after the damage, and they involve adding sticky as well as non-sticky lines. Major repairs have been best studied in uloborids, but also occur in various araneoids (Eberhard, 2020). To make a major repair, the uloborids *U. diversus* and *Z. geniculata* often remove the hub, the inner portions of all of the radii, and often some other lines from the previous orb. The spider more or less smooths the outline of the damaged area by packing sticky and non-sticky lines together (Figs. 3, 6–8). She then builds (in order) a new hub and radii, a temporary spiral starting at the hub and working outward, and finally a sticky spiral line that starts at the edge and ends near the hub. During sticky spiral construction she typically doubles back each time she encounters the cable of sticky and non-sticky lines at the edge of a repair sector (Figs. 3, 6–8); as expected from the "do–not–cross–a–sticky–line" rule, however, she does not double back if this edge does not contain sticky lines (Fig. 3).

To test the possibly that the spider's memory of having performed the first stages of repair behavior might affect subsequent sticky spiral repair behavior, *Z. geniculata* spiders were induced to make a major repair by breaking one or two portions of a newly built orb on day 1. In "one hole" webs only one triangular sector was broken, while in "two hole" webs two triangular sectors on approximately opposite sides of the orb were broken. On the following night, the spider replaced the old hub with a new one that had new radii radiating into the repair sector or sectors, and added sticky spiral lines that originated near the outer edge of a repair sector. While laying sticky spiral in a two hole repair web, the spider was often

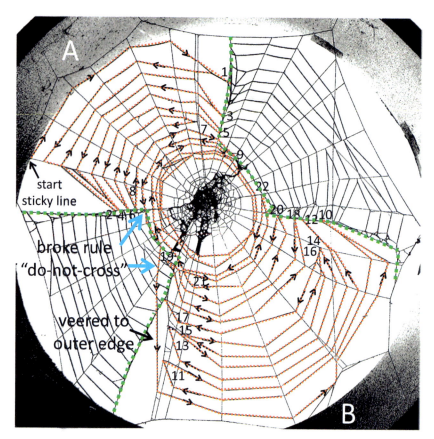

Fig. 6 This repair of a two-hole experiment illustrates how a *Zosis geniculata* broke the "do-not-cross" rule, and entered a second repair sector (the borders of repair zone are indicated with dotted green lines, the repair sticky spiral with dotted red lines, the direction the spider moved with arrowheads, and the order of the turnbacks with numbers). After building a new hub and new radii in the damaged sectors (A and B), the spider began laying zig-zag sticky spiral starting at the outer edge of sector A. She doubled back each time she encountered the lateral border of the sector (which contained sticky lines). When she neared the hub following turnback #9, however, she broke the do-not-cross rule (blue arrows), moved across an intact portion of the previous web, and then veered sharply outward to begin to lay sticky lines in sector B. Here she resumed turning back each time she encountered the edge of the repair sector. Finally, near the hub, she made a few complete, tightly-spaced loops (after Eberhard, 2019).

confronted with the following problem: she was "imprisoned" in the first repair area of her web where she initiated the sticky spiral, due to the "do-not-cross-a-sticky line" rule (see Figs. 2A, 3, and the section on short-term cues above), and was thus unable to gain access to the other repair area

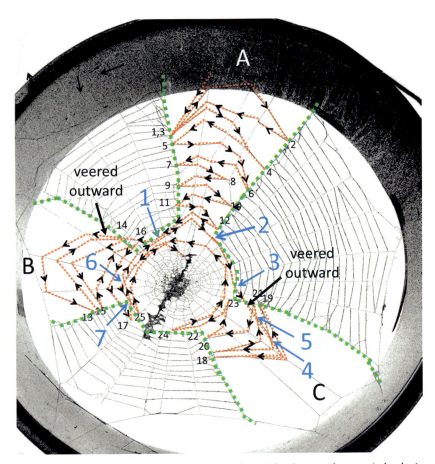

Fig. 7 In this three-hole repair experiment, the spider began the repair by laying sticky spiral in sector A, turning back consistently every time she encountered the edge of the repair (dotted green lines). When she had nearly reached the hub, following turnback #12, she broke the "do-not-cross" rule (blue arrow 1) and moved toward sector B and veered sharply outward. After again obeying the "do-not-cross" rule while filling this sector with zig-zag sticky lines, she again broke the rule (blue arrows 2 and 3 following turnback #17) to reach sector C and once again veered outward. She laid zig-zag sticky lines in this sector, breaking the rule two more times (blue arrows 4 and 5) before eventually nearly circling the web adjacent to the hub. The small arrowheads indicate the direction she moved; the turnbacks in the sticky spiral are numbered in the order they occurred (after Eberhard, 2019).

that lacked sticky lines. If she remembered having built this second repair area, she was expected to somehow break out of this prison and gain access to the second repair area, and then to move to the outer portion of this area to begin to fill it with sticky spiral lines. If, in contrast, she did not

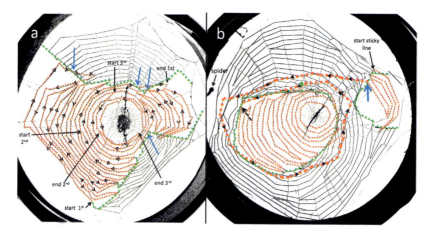

Fig. 8 (A) A two-hole repair experiment in which *Zosis geniculata* combined breaking the "do-not-cross" rule with interruption and re-initiation of sticky spiral construction (red dotted lines; arrowheads indicate the direction the spider moved) at the outer edge of the larger replacement sector (borders are marked with dotted green lines; the blue arrows mark sites where the spider broke the "do-not-cross" rule). She interrupted and then reinitiated sticky spiral construction twice. (B) This 'spontaneous' repair web of *Uloborus diversus* (the web was not manipulated) includes the longest exception to the "do-not-cross rule" seen. The spider repaired two holes (marked with dotted green lines); the spider's route while adding sticky lines is traced with arrowheads dotted red lines. The spider began by filling the outer hole with five loops of sticky spiral (light red dotted lines), turning back each time she reached the edge of the repair zone. But then broke the "do-not-cross" rule (blue arrow) and moved 540° in a more or less circular pattern (heavy red dotted line) across intact portions of the web that contained both sticky and non-sticky lines. Finally, she entered the second repair zone (dotted black arrow). Here she resumed obeying the "do-not-cross" rule, and filled this are with zig-zag loops of sticky spiral (light red dotted lines) (after Eberhard, 2019).

remember the second repair area, she was expected to leave it unfilled with sticky lines. In "one hole" control webs she was expected not to break the do-not-cross rule. The spider's decisions were deduced by tracing the paths of the sticky spiral lines (dotted red lines in Figs. 3, 6–8).

The results suggested that spiders remembered their earlier building activities. In one hole repairs the spider always followed the "do–not–cross" rule (100% of 371 encounters with sticky lines in 31 webs) and doubled back each time she encountered the sticky lines at the edge of the repair sector (Fig. 3). In contrast, spiders in two-hole repair webs almost always gained access to the second repair sector (29 of 31 webs), as expected if they remembered them. Most commonly (in 46% of 26 webs in which her path could be traced confidently) the spider gained access to the second repair sector by following the "do-not-cross" rule in the outer portion of one repair sector, but eventually breaking the rule, moving across an intact area of the web to reach the second repair sector and then veering toward its outer edge; she then added zig-zag sticky lines to this sector (Fig. 6). A second technique was to fill or nearly fill the first repair sector and then move across the free zone of an old sector to enter the second repair zone, veer toward its outer edge, and add sticky lines working inward. A third technique was to fill the first repair zone, cease sticky spiral production after filling the first sector, move to the outer portion of the second repair zone, and then resume sticky spiral production. There were no obvious individual differences, as all individuals that made more than a single web utilized at least two of the three different techniques; one individual with six webs utilized all three. Fragmentary data suggest that spiders may sometimes remember three repair zones (Fig. 7; see also Eberhard, 2019).

Facultative violations of the "do-not-cross-sticky-lines" rule that enable the spider to reach an otherwise inaccessible portion of the web also occur in *U. diversus*. The most extensive violation yet seen was a spontaneous two-hole repair by *U. diversus* (Fig. 8B): after filling one repair sector with zig-zag sticky lines, the spider moved in a more or less circular path for nearly 540° across intact portions of the web before she finally crossed into the second, larger repair zone and filled it with sticky lines.

There are reasons to doubt that either learning or pre-programmed rigid responses explain this flexibility in following the "do-not-cross" rule (see Eberhard, 2019). It may be necessary to resort to explanations that combine goal-directed motivation (e.g., to fill empty sectors of the web with sticky lines) and memories of having built such areas (similar to the mental maps that other types of evidence have suggested in orb weavers) (Eberhard, 2020; Hesselberg, 2015) to explain two- and three-hole repair behavior. It is as yet unknown whether other factors (e.g., drugs, interruptions of attention, or transfer of individuals between webs with different numbers of repair zones) influence the spider's tendency to break the "do-not-cross" rule and to veer outward in the second sector.

7. Do spiders have expectations regarding the sites and orientations of web lines?

Experiments suggest that spiders may have "expectations" during sticky spiral construction. In the most dramatic experiment, *A. diadematus* was placed in a clever "treadmill" type of situation during sticky spiral construction, in which the web rotated slowly on an axis that ran through the center of the hub and was perpendicular to the web plane. The speed of rotation was adjusted so that the spider's position in space remained static as she moved on her web. This movement maintained her orientation with respect to gravity constant. When this experiment was initiated while the spider was either descending or ascending in her web (e.g., when she remained to one side of the hub rather than above or below it), her path was altered slightly during the first 90°, but did not change substantially thereafter (Vollrath, 1986). In contrast, when the spider was above or below the hub when the experiment began, she did not alter her path on the web for about the first 90°, but then veered sharply toward the hub and never completed 360° (Vollrath, 1986, 1987). It was as if the spider anticipated that while moving horizontally in her web she would soon begin to move vertically, but that while she was moving vertically, she had no expectation that her path would change with respect to gravity.

A second indication of "expectations" during sticky spiral construction occurred when Hingston (1920) cut radii or temporary spiral lines of *N. nautica*. When the spider came to a place where lines had been cut, she paused and waved her legs; spiders also paused and appeared to search for lines that had been removed during radius and temporary spiral construction (Hingston, 1920). Evidence of expectations also occurs in other contexts: contrasts between the probing movements of the legs when *L. mariana* turns at the hub to attack a prey (Briceño & Eberhard, 2011) and when she arrives at a hub that has been partially destroyed (W.G. Eberhard unpub. data); and probing by one leg I of *M. duodecimspinosa* as the spider returns to the hub and searches for the next exit radius during secondary frame construction (Eberhard, 2020).

These apparent searching movements could result from pre-programmed rigid flexibility, but this has not been determined. The possible effects of experimental manipulations of distracting stimuli or drugs have never been tested in these contexts.

7.1 Modularity: Categories of behavior that are biologically real

Historically, orb web construction has been described as occurring in a series of semi-independent stages such as radius construction, temporary spiral construction, etc., with each stage broken down into substages during which the spider repeats a particular set of behavioral tasks over and over. These traditional labels run the risk of being artificially imposed linguistic categories that do not reflect biologically significant behavioral units. Recent summaries of several types of evidence have confirmed, however, the biological realism of several modular categories (Eberhard, 2020). The phrase "degree of modularity" to describe discreteness from other expressed traits is more appropriate than the single word "module," and it is in this sense that I use the word "modular" below. Behavioral modularity is important for future studies because it implies a physical modularity of some sort in the animal's nervous system (though not necessarily a morphological separation), and also in its genetic determination.

Several types of evidence document modularity. The simplest involves recombinations of particular traits. For instance, the webs built by *Z. geniculata* in association with their egg sacs show different combinations of lower-level modular subunits, including construction of the hub, the stabilimentum, radial lines, and sticky spiral lines that are centered on the sac, on the hub, or both (Eberhard, 2020). Other similar examples come from the resting webs of mature males, the "orb plus cone" web of *Uloborus conus*, orb-like barriers built at the sides of some orbs, and molting webs (Eberhard, 2020). In each case some aspects of the webs resemble small versions of the normal prey capture orbs of conspecific females (e.g., different hub-like structures), but some others are omitted (e.g., the sticky spiral).

A second type of evidence of modularity comes from the numerous evolutionary transitions from orbs to secondarily reduced webs. A summary of 51 behavioral transitions in 11 species (involving construction of the sticky spiral as well as other stages) revealed that just over two thirds of the transitions involved either a modular trait, or cues that direct the construction of such a trait (Eberhard, 2018). The remaining 32.7% of the transitions in the survey involved acquiring a new trait that had no clear homology with ancestral trait. Surprisingly, modular re-acquisition may have occurred in one case, the theridiosmatid *Baalzebub*: its intact hub may have been secondarily recovered following a previous loss of hubs in an ancestor (Coddington, 1986).

Even here, however, many of these "new" behavior patterns would probably, when examined at lower levels of analysis, be seen to include lower-level modular traits that were derived from modular ancestral behavior (Eberhard, 2018; Ramírez et al., 2023). One of these traits, loss of frame lines, can be induced facultatively in *L. argyra* and *Z. geniculata* by severely reducing the space in which the spider can build her orb (Barrantes & Eberhard, 2012; Eberhard & Barrantes, 2015), and is typical in other species such as anapids and *Meta* that build orbs close to the ground or other substrates (Hesselberg, Simonsen, & Juan, 2019). So, frame loss (and perhaps other traits) may have originated as a facultative behavior.

Variation in modular traits is evident during ontogeny. In *Nephilengis cruentata*, for example, the patterns of change in radius length, number of radii at the edge of the web, and the number of sticky spirals differ over the spider's lifetime and in different parts of the orb (Japyassú & Ades, 1998). Similar differences occur during the ontogeny of *Z. x-notata* (Le Guelte, 1966). Modularity is also evident in the lack of flexibility in some types of behavior. Hingston (1920) eliminated the entire temporary spiral of *N. nautica* after the temporary spiral was finished, while the spider was building the sticky spiral. He found that the spiders were unable to return to temporary spiral construction, even though the lack of temporary spiral bridges between radii severely impaired sticky spiral construction. Without the bridges, the spiders built highly deviant, irregular arrays of sticky lines.

A different confirmation of the modularity of building behaviors comes from analyzes of high-resolution videos of *U. diversus* using deep learning neural networks for image analysis, and multidimensional statistical classifications. Series of brief, stereotyped action patterns (possible "atomic" elements of behavior) were distinguished in stage-specific sequences (Corver et al., 2021). This study represents a major technical advance, as it shows that these elements can be recorded and analyzed in massive numbers with automated techniques, promising detailed analyzes of large samples of behavior in the future.

One final assay for independence and discreteness of expression is to check whether chemical probes can elicit particular behavioral modular traits. Data of this sort come from the larvae of parasitoid ichneumonid wasps, which apparently utilize the spider's molting hormone, ecdysone (or an analog) to induce the spider to build a cocoon web that is similar to the spider's normal molting web. The larva thus obtains a stable, protected support to which to attach its pupal cocoon (Gonzaga et al., 2017; Eberhard & Gonzaga, 2019; Kloss, Gonzaga, de Oliveira, & Sperber, 2017). Construction of both molting and cocoon webs involves more or less the same suite of behavioral traits (Eberhard & Gonzaga, 2019). Some details in cocoon webs (e.g., *L. argyra* when parasitized by *Hymenoepimecis argyraphaga*) are clearly not present in the spiders' normal molting webs, however, suggesting further larval effects on the spider (Eberhard & Gonzaga, 2019).

In sum, orb web construction behavior displays a high degree of modularity at higher levels of organization. While the inter-connectedness of different aspects of phenotypes sometimes limit the usefulness of the concept of a "module" (West-Eberhard, 2003), the evidence for the relative independence of many different aspects of web construction behavior is strong. The fact that orb web construction behavior is organized in modular units is of course no surprise. In general, phenotypic development is modular in that it results from hierarchies of developmental decisions in both behavior and morphology (West-Eberhard, 2003).

7.2 Topics of general interest for future research

7.2.1 When and where do orb weavers make errors?

Publications on animal behavior are often attempts to determine the effects of one or more variables on a given behavior. Nevertheless, it is also possible that some variations in animal behavior may not have an "external" or obvious cause, but instead represent errors, or inadvertent failures. Given the imprecision and inconsistency in the activities of individual neurons (Calvin, 1983), such behavioral errors seem likely. Understanding the frequencies and types of errors that animals make under natural conditions may have major importance for understanding the significance of particular behavioral performances, of patterns of activity in nervous system activities, and of how the evolution of behavior occurs. For instance, it is possible that substantial portions of the nervous system activity in reentry connections is dedicated to suppressing or correcting errors generated in other portions. The intensity of these corrective actions, and the likelihood of future evolutionary divergence are related to the selective consequences of making different types of error (Eberhard, 1990).

The potential role of errors is usually overlooked, due in part to the difficulty of actually documenting them and studying their causes. This is especially true at higher levels of analysis because it is often difficult to know with certainty all of the relevant cues that an animal is perceiving, or to have a complete understanding of its intentions. The combination of unusual traits of orb web construction (see final section), especially in the later stages when the spider is relatively isolated from the environment except for the lines in her web (Witt, 1965), opens up several as yet relatively unexplored possibilities in studying errors at higher levels of behavior.

One clear type of error in sticky spiral construction is the occasional failure to break the temporary spiral while the sticky spiral is being laid. These omissions are appropriately labeled as "errors" because they are disadvantageous: intact segments of temporary spiral cause spiders such as *M. duodecimspinosa* to leave over-sized spaces between loops of the sticky spiral (Eberhard, 2020) (apparently the spider sometimes mistakes an intact segment of temporary spiral for the inner loop of sticky spiral during inner loop localization behavior). This type of error is especially common in ulo-borids (Eberhard & Opell, 2022). Other apparent sticky spiral errors include sticky spiral lines that adhere to each other (Pasquet, Marchal, Anotaux, & Leborgne, 2013), and over-sized spaces between sticky spiral loops (Eberhard & Hesselberg, 2012; Pasquet et al., 2013). Still other types of errors that concern non-sticky lines include radii that are attached at either end to a sticky line (Pasquet et al., 2013) (due mistakes when the spider cuts a radius rather than the temporary spiral?), and occasional attachments of adjacent radii to each other during temporary spiral construction (in *T. clavipes*), creating small holes in the array of radii (Eberhard, 2020).

Nothing appears to be known regarding the causes of these errors. In fact, nothing is known of the cues that spiders use to trigger removal of the temporary spiral (presumably short TSP distances are involved), nor how the spider distinguishes temporary spiral lines from radii (I do not know of a single direct observation of a spider mistakenly breaking a radius). This general topic has yet to receive the attention that it deserves.

7.2.2 Senile behavior

The mechanisms that cause behavioral senescence in animals (gradual, irreversible decay of behavioral capabilities) are only incompletely understood (Monaghan, Charmantier, Nussey, & Ricklefs, 2008). Orb weaving spiders have promise for comparative studies, as they show multiple types of behavioral senescence. Changes associated with advanced age include partial or complete loss of sticky spiral lines, greater variation in sticky spiral spacing, and more sticky lines that adhere to each other (Bristowe, 1941; Eberhard, 1971; Anotaux et al., 2012). Senile orb forms were more common in virgin than in non-virgin female *U. diversus* (Eberhard, 1971), while *Z. x-notata* may have two classes of females that show different patterns of behavioral senescence (Anotaux et al., 2012).

Not even such simple tests as Hingston experiments (Fig. 2B) have ever been performed with senile spiders. The field is wide open for future studies, such as whether different aspects of senility are due to sensory, motor, or analytical deficits.

7.2.3 Sustained attention—where orb weavers shine

Animals receive floods of information from the environment through their sense organs, much more than their brains can process (Dukas, 2004). By filtering these stimuli, and by then only processing the information from a small subset of this input, an animal can respond more consistently, efficiently, and rapidly to those stimuli that are most relevant to its current behavioral context (Shettleworth, 2010). Attention of this sort is a well-established phenomenon in vertebrates, and there are strong indications that other animals such as insects and spiders also present "attention-like" phenomena (Nakata, 2010; Shettleworth, 2010; Eberhard & Hesselberg, 2012); there are, in fact, even cases of "selective attention" by individual neurons (Wiederman & O'Carroll, 2013). The study of attention, as well as of possible lapses in attention that are associated with behavioral errors, may help explain present-day variations in the behavior of species and individuals.

The complexity that is involved in coordinating and directing the spider's orb construction behavior brings into focus the realization that building the sticky spiral may require intense and sustained attention to choose and execute the appropriate leg movement patterns needed to produce consistent sticky spiral spacing. Orb weavers appear to maintain tightly focused attention on an extensive set of variables that may require complex adjustments (see section above on mechanical agility) for impressively long periods of time. In the course of producing a typical orb, *M. duodecimspinosa* makes about 3000 decisions regarding sites of sticky spiral attachments with few if any interruptions during 15–20 min (up to about $2\text{--}3\,\text{s}^{-1}$), with few obvious "errors" (Eberhard & Hesselberg, 2012). Sticky spiral construction by the giant, slow moving *Nephila pilipes* (= *maculata*) can last even longer (over 4.5 h, almost without interruptions) (Hingston, 1922). Each decision that determines an attachment site involves attention to multiple cues, and careful execution of multiple physical tasks, including substantial adjustments in the movements and forces exerted by the legs. Possible examples of lapses in attention during sticky spiral construction include occasional failures to remove temporary spiral segments *M. duodecimspinosa* (previous section) and failures to adjust spacing on the basis of the TSP distance on the previous radius in *L. mariana* (Fig. 5; see also Eberhard, 2020). I suspect that such sustained attention to tasks that involve so many rapid decisions and such behavioral precision may be unusual among invertebrates (and perhaps also vertebrates, for that matter), though I know of no comparisons; further study is needed.

The spider's attention can probably be manipulated experimentally using distracting stimuli, and surely this is a rich field for future studies of multiple aspects of sticky spiral construction. There is, for instance, an anecdotal suggestion that briefly shining a bright light on *U. diversus* during sticky spiral construction caused the spider to temporarily lose track of the location of the hub (Eberhard, 1969).

7.2.4 Leg loss and flexibility

Spiders use different legs for different tasks during sticky spiral construction. For instance, inner loop localization behavior during sticky spiral construction is performed by leg oI in uloborids and most araneids. Spiders occasionally lose legs in nature, however, especially in taxa in which defensive adaptations include pre-formed lines of weakness near the base of the leg that result in the leg breaking off when it is restrained (e.g., grasped by a predator; Roth & Roth, 1984). As noted in the section above on flexibility, a simple experiment to test the ability to compensate for leg loss is to observe construction behavior after a leg has been lost (Hingston, 1920; Jacobi-Kleemann, 1953; Eberhard, 2020; Pasquet et al., 2011; Reed et al., 1965). The consistent finding has been that spiders compensate for the loss of a leg by using an adjacent leg to accomplish (at least partially) the tasks of the lost leg. Thus, leg oII immediately (without practice) began to perform inner loop localization behavior when oI was lost in *A. diadematus* (Jacobi-Kleemann, 1953; Reed et al., 1965). Such compensations can reach surprising extremes: a three-legged *T. clavipes* substituted for missing legs by using her chelicerae to hold the web when she wrapped prey at the hub (Soley et al., 2021).

There are no studies, however, in which the effects of substitution of one leg for another are focused on other questions, such as how different cues are analyzed and integrated, the effects of variables such the spider's distance from the hub and her orientation with respect to the hub, the likelihood of leg loss under natural conditions (the legs of some groups are not designed to be lost; Roth & Roth, 1984) on the adjustments, the spider's responses to Hingston experiments (Fig. 2B), and how psychoactive drugs influence behavior. This is another promising area for future studies.

7.2.5 Evolutionary transitions and "task-specific" motivations

Resolving the questions concerning rigid versus open-ended flexibility and the generation of errors and error correction could have important general consequences in understanding the evolution of new behavioral traits. A new trait generally arises when natural selection acts on pre-existing variation, causing an originally scarce or newly induced variant to become common. Although textbooks on evolution often depict the source of new variations on which natural selection can act as being due to mutation, it is likely that many evolutionary transitions originate as facultative alternative forms that are the result of developmental flexibility (West-Eberhard, 2003). Such an origin is more likely because such variants, especially when complex (involving coordinated expression of components), are much more common, and require less extensive changes in intermediate forms.

Take, for instance, the following example. Spiders in different families and subfamilies use different exploratory movements to sense the location of the inner loop (cue #1 in Table 2). Araneids and uloborids tap outward with outer leg I; nephilids (and deinopids and a few araneids) use outer leg IV; tetragnathids use inner leg I; and the three theridiosomatoid families make no inner loop localization movements, and instead use the TSP distance (cue #2) (Eberhard, 1982; Kuntner et al., 2008). How is one to explain the evolutionary origin of the use of a different leg to influence a behavioral decision when the behavior within a group is consistent, and when both the leg movement and the response to the stimuli that it receives as a result of such a movement must change simultaneously for the intermediate form to be functional?

I have no confident answers, but will illustrate exciting questions that can be approached using orb web construction behavior. Take for example using leg oI (araneids, uloborids); and using leg iI (tetragnathids). For the sake of argument, suppose that using oI was derived from the using iI (the phylogenetic relations are uncertain; see Coddington et al., 2019; Eberhard, 2022a; Kulkarni et al., 2021). An intermediate form would need to execute new movements with both of its legs I; and it would also need to respond to the contacts that the leg oI makes with sticky lines in a new way (trigger the end of searching movements and initiate attachment behavior). Open-ended behavioral flexibility at the level of detailed movements that are coordinated by reentry connections could "solve" this problem by providing the original source of variation. Perhaps the intermediate stages in the evolutionary transition from using different legs for the same function involved "task-specific" motivation.

Such a transition might superficially appear to have resulted from insightful behavior to reduce the physical problems imposed by the need to locate the inner loop when the spider has a large body and makes a small-meshed orb. But the change may not require "insight" (as supposed by Eberhard, 2019). It could result from new connections between value system neurons whose activity is associated with a task-specific motivation such as "find a sticky line" and the organized modules of functional interneurons (the "synergies" of Bizzi & Ajemian, 2015) that activate particular sets of muscles in distinct proportions, and that thus control the movements of different legs. Further observations of a species like *Micrathena* sp., which facultatively changes from using leg oI to using oIV as the spider nears the hub (Eberhard, 1982), might illuminate this question.

Another possible case in which task-specific motivation could explain the use of diverse movements to accomplish the same task are the means by which spiders apparently measure the "TSP distance" (Fig. 1B): spanning the space between the inner loop and the temporary spiral with the body (Eberhard, 2020); holding the temporary spiral while reeling in the radius with legs oI and oII until they reach the inner loop; and walking away from the temporary spiral until contacting the inner loop. Different movements of different legs are even used in a single species to sense this distance; in *Gasteracantha cancriformis* the spider reels in the radius in the outer part of her orb, but spans the distance to the inner loop with her body in the inner part (Eberhard, 2020).

Some evolutionary transitions are easier to imagine, because the behavior of possible ancestral groups is variable and the physical change in movements is relatively small. For instance, the tetragnathids *L. mariana* and *L.* sp. nearly always use leg iI to locate the inner loop, but occasionally tap outward and contact the inner loop with leg oI (Kuntner et al., 2008; Eberhard, 2020). Similarly, one species of *Micrathena* uses leg oI to locate the inner loop in the outer portion of the web (as do other araneines), but changes to using leg oIV (and ceases tapping laterally with oI) when near the hub (Eberhard, 2020). In this case, the original variant movements of oIV that resulted in contact with the inner loop could have been occasional contacts of this leg with the inner loop (Fig. 9) as the leg moved to grasp the radius to make an attachment (Fig. 1C). The change would then only require initiation of the use of the information from this leg for the decision where to attach the sticky line to the radius. The use of leg IV for inner loop localization has evolved 5–6 times in other groups and is associated with large body sizes relative to the mesh size (the distances between radii and between loops of sticky spiral) (Eberhard, 2020). By using posterior legs instead of anterior legs, these species probably reduce the energy that would otherwise be expended in turning the spider's entire body each time to sense the inner loop.

7.2.6 Translating variable cues and behaviors into consistent physical results

The details of the behavioral mechanisms by which different stimuli are translated into sticky spiral spacing have received little attention. Two studies (Toscani et al., 2012; Eberhard, 2012) indicated that the positions of legs that grasp the radius just before attachment influenced the location of the attachment site. In video recordings of sticky spiral construction by

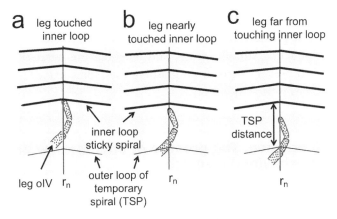

Fig. 9 Conversion of behavior (position of leg oIV) into sticky spiral spacing. The drawings show three relative positions where tarsus oIV of *Micrathena duodecimspinosa* grasped the radius just before attaching the sticky spiral: (A) at the junction with the inner loop; (B) near the junction (<diameter of tarsus); (C) farther from the junction. When the tarsal positions on two adjacent radii (r_{n-1}, r_n) were compared with the sticky spiral spaces on these same radii, sticky spiral spacing tended to be larger when the tarsus had grasped the radius farther from the inner loop (TSP distance = distance between outer loop of temporary spiral and inner loop of sticky spiral; after Eberhard, 2012).

M. duodecimspinosa, the distance of the attachment from the inner loop increased compared with the previous distance when the tarsus of leg oIV grasped the radius farther from the inner loop (Fig. 9). An additional correlation was that sticky spiral spacing was greater in those areas of the web (above the hub, near the edge) in which tarsus oIV grasped the radius farther from the inner loop (Eberhard, 2012).

These correlations were far from perfect, however, indicating that other factors, such as imprecision in leg behavior, the site grasped by leg oIII, and the positions of the legs relative to the spinnerets may also have important effects on sticky spiral spacing. The idea that spiders have greater difficulty in producing consistent sticky spiral spacing in those portions of the web in which their own weight causes lines to sag more drastically (see the sections on mechanical agility and errors) would predict that scatter should be greater in those portions of orbs, but this has not been tested. Experiments involving distracting stimuli, drugs, and blocking the tarsal claws of legs oIII or oIV to prevent them from grasping the radius (e.g., Foelix, 1970) could help clarify these questions.

8. Conclusion: The promise of orbs for new directions of behavioral research

A major goal of this review is to demonstrate the likely payoffs from a new generation of studies of orb web construction. The previous sections concentrated on showing that sufficient data have accumulated to provide a solid base for future studies. This final section demonstrates the many practical advantages that orb construction has for future studies. Orb construction has several unusual traits that facilitate observations (Ades, 1986; Eberhard, 2020; Zschokke & Vollrath, 1995) that promise to facilitate illumination of the mechanistic underpinnings of complex behavior in a simple animal.

Sticky spiral construction occurs at predictable times and places, and can be easily observed with unrestrained animals in captivity, with few if any behavioral artifacts. The spider's operations are repeated over and over again, providing ample opportunity for replicated observations and huge sample sizes. The sequence of tasks is consistent, and at any one moment the spider is usually executing a well-defined, predictable task, making it possible to confidently deduce the functions of even small details of her behavior, such as why a particular leg is waved in a particular direction at a particular moment. Spiders are functionally blind with respect to their web lines, and visual, chemical, and other potential long-distance cues do not play a role in guiding sticky spiral attachments. Some potential tactile cues from the web that are difficult to measure, such as line tensions and vibrations, also play no role in guiding sticky spiral construction. Tactile stimuli are dominant. The stimuli available to guide the spider can thus be deduced from the locations of the web lines in the spider's immediate vicinity. Even though the sticky lines do not follow the exact path that the spider followed during construction, it is certain that her spinnerets touched the radius at exactly the site of each attachment, so it is certain that she was in position to sense those lines in the immediate vicinity of each attachment.

The spider's limitation to local tactile cues has several attractive consequences. Direct behavioral observations of the positions and movements of her legs can document her ability to perceive the presence of these lines. And because some cues are sensed using specialized movements, it is possible to use the timing and orientation of these movements to deduce which cues the spider is attempting to perceive at a particular moment (recall the image of a blind man's cane). In addition, the finished web itself constitutes an exquisitely precise, easily recorded, and easily quantified record of both the cues that were available and of the decisions that were made during construction. Because of the general uniformity of orb construction behavior and the cues that are used to guide it in different taxa of orb weavers, it is also possible to deduce with unusual confidence the behavioral transitions that have occurred in evolutionary lineages that have secondarily lost orbs, and to thus evaluate the degree of modularity of different classes of behavior through evolutionary time.

This unusual combination of advantageous traits makes orb web construction an attractive model for answering general questions about complex behavior by a "simple" animal (Simpson & deBivort, 2021). New techniques of recording and analyzing automated high resolution digital recordings permit recognition of the behavior of individual legs during construction behavior (Corver et al., 2021), and pS6 RNA techniques (e.g., Baran & Streelman, 2020) could allow identification of areas of the nervous system that are active during orb construction. Also available to answer a new generation of questions are the simple experimental manipulations that have already yielded important insights, including altering the direction of gravity by rotating the frame that supports the web (LeGuelte, 1966; Peters, 1937; Vollrath, 1986, 1988), removing and adding web lines (Eberhard, 1987, 2020; Hingston, 1920; Peters, 1937; Reed, 1969), altering leg lengths and removing legs (Vollrath, 1987; Witt et al., 1968), inducing spiders to repair especially revealing patterns of web damage (Eberhard, 2019; Peters, 1933; Tew et al., 2015), and administering psychoactive drugs (Hesselberg & Vollrath, 2004; Witt et al., 1968).

In sum, this review of many otherwise esoteric details of orb designs and spider behavior can provide a user's guide for asking exciting new questions of general importance concerning the control and coordination of higher-level behavioral processes, using a small, and relatively "simple" animal. A better appreciation of the behavior of such "lower" organisms is crucial to understand the relation of humans to the natural world (Chittka & Wilson, 2019; Griffin, 1981).

Acknowledgments

I thank Mary Jane West-Eberhard, Matjaž Gregorič, Thomas Hesselberg, Glauco Machado, and Samuel Zschokke for many helpful comments on preliminary versions of the manuscript, and STRI and the Universidad de Costa Rica for continued support.

References

Ades, C. (1986). A construção da teia geométrica como programa comportamental. *Ciência e Cultura, 38*, 760–775.

Ades C., Da Cunha, S. S., & Tiedemann, K. (1993). Experience-induced changes in orb-web building. In *23 International ethological conference.* Torremolinos, España.

Anotaux, M., Marchal, J., Châline, N., Desquilbet, L., Leborgne, R., Gilbert, C., & Pasquet, A. (2012). Ageing alters spider orb-web construction. *Animal Behaviour, 84*, 1113–1121.

Baran, N. M., & Streelman, J. T. (2020). Ecotype differences in aggression, neural activity and behaviorally relevant gene expression in cichlid fish. *Genes, Brain, and Behavior, 19*, e12657.

Barrantes, G., & Eberhard, W. G. (2012). Extreme behavioral adjustments by an orb-web spider to restricted spaces. *Ethology: Formerly Zeitschrift fur Tierpsychologie, 118*, 438–449.

Barth, F. G. (2002). *A spider's world: Senses and behavior.* Berlin: Springer Verlag.

Bays, S. (1962). A study of the training possibilities of *Araneus diadematus* Cl. *Cellular and Molecular Life Sciences, 18*, 423–424.

Bizzi, E., & Ajemian, R. (2015). A hard scientific quest: Understanding voluntary movements. *Daedalus, 144*, 83–95.

Blamires, S. S. L., Chao, I.-C., & Tso, I.-M. (2010). Prey type, vibrations and handling interactively influence spider silk expression. *Journal of Experimental Biology, 213*, 3906–3910.

Braitenberg, V. (1984). *Vehicles: Experiments in synthetic psychology.* Cambridge, MA: MIT Press.

Bristowe (1941). *The Comity of Spiders Volume II.* London: The Ray Society.

Buskirk, R. E. (1975). Coloniality, activity patterns and feeding in a tropical orb-weaving spider. *Ecology, 56*, 1314–1328.

Calvin, W. H. (1983). *The throwing Madonna.* New York: McGraw-Hill Book Company.

Chittka, L., & Niven, J. (2009). Are bigger brains better? *Current Biology, 19*, 995–1008.

Chittka, L., & Wilson, C. (2019). Expanding consciousness. *American Scientist, 107*, 364–369.

Christiansen, A., Baum, R., & Witt, P. N. (1962). Changes in spider webs brought about by mescaline, psilocybin and an increase in body weight. *Journal of Pharmacology and Experimental Therapeutics, 136*, 31–37.

Coddington, J. A. (1986). The genera of the spider family Theridiosomatidae. *Smithsonian Contributions to Zoology, 422*, 1–96.

Coddington, J. A., Agnarsson, I., Hamilton, C. A., & Bond, J. E. (2019). Spiders did not repeatedly gain, but repeatedly lost, foraging webs. *PeerJ, 7*, e6703. https://doi.org/10.7717/peerj.6703.

Corver, A., Wilkerson, N., Miller, J., & Gordus, A. (2021). Distinct movement patterns generate stage of spider web building. *Current Biology, 31*, 4983–4997.

Crews, S. C., & Opell, B. D. (2006). The features of capture threads and orb-webs produced by unfed *Cyclosa turbinata* (Araneae: Araneidae). *Journal of Arachnology, 34*, 427–434.

Da Cunha-Nogueira, S. S., & Ades, C. (2012). Evidence of learning in the web construction of the spider *Argiope argentata* (Araneae: Araneidae). *Revista de Etología, 11*, 23–36.

Dukas, R. (2004). Causes and consequences of limited attention. *Brain, Behavior and Evolution, 63*, 197–210.

Eberhard, W. G. (1969). Computer simulation of orb web construction. *American Zoologist, 9*, 229–238.

Eberhard, W. G. (1971). Senile web patterns in Uloborus diversus (Araneae: Uloboridae). *Developmental Psychobiology, 4*, 249–254.

Eberhard, W. G. (1982). Behavioral characters for the higher classification of orb-weaving spiders. *Evolution; International Journal of Organic Evolution, 36*, 1067–1095.

Eberhard, W. G. (1987). Effects of gravity on temporary spiral construction by *Leucauge mariana* (Araneae: Araneidae). *Journal of Ethology, 5*, 29–36.

Eberhard, W. G. (1987). Effects of gravity on temporary spiral construction by *Leucauge mariana* (Araneae: Araneidae). *Journal of Ethology, 5*, 29–36.

Eberhard, W. G. (1988a). Behavioral flexibility in orb web construction: Effects of supplies in different silk glands and spider size and weight. *Journal of Arachnology*, 295–302.

Eberhard, W. G. (1988b). Memory of distances and directions moved as cues during temporary spiral construction in the spider *Leucauge mariana* (Araneae: Araneidae). *Journal of Insect Behavior, 1*, 51–66.

Eberhard, W. G. (1990). Imprecision in the behavior of *Leptomorphus* sp. (Diptera, Mycetophilidae) and the evolutionary origin of new behavior patterns. *Journal of Insect Behavior, 3*, 327–357.

Eberhard, W. G. (2007). Miniaturized orb-weaving spiders: Behavioural precision is not limited by small size. *Proceedings of the Royal Society of London B: Biological Sciences, 274*, 2203–2209.

Eberhard, W. G. (2012). Cues guiding placement of the first loop of the sticky spiral in orbs of *Micrathena duodecimspinosa* (Araneidae) and *Leucauge mariana* (Tetragnathidae). *Arachnology, 15*, 224–227.

Eberhard, W. G. (2014). A new view of orb webs: Multiple trap designs in a single structure. *Biological Journal of the Linnean Society, 111*, 437–449.

Eberhard, W. G. (2017). How orb-weavers find and grasp silk lines. *Journal of Arachnology, 45*, 145–151.

Eberhard, W. G. (2018). Modular patterns in behavioural evolution: Webs derived from orbs. *Behaviour, 155*, 531–566.

Eberhard, W. G. (2019). Adaptive flexibility in cues guiding spider web construction and its possible implications for spider cognition. *Behaviour, 156*, 331–362.

Eberhard, W. G. (2020). *Spider webs: Function, behavior and evolution*. Chicago: University of Chicago Press.

Eberhard, W. G. (2021). Sub-units in the webs of *Dictyna meditata* (Arachnida: Dictynidae): Implications for studies of spider web evolution. *Journal of Arachnology, 49*, 167–184.

Eberhard, W. G. (2022a). Biological challenges to conclusions from molecular phylogenies: Behavior strongly favors orb web monophyly, contradicting molecular analyses. *Biological Journal of the Linnean Society, 137*, 389–408.

Eberhard, W. G. (2022b). Frame repair behavior by *Micrathena duodecimspinosa* (Araneae, Araneidae). *Journal of Arachnology, 50*, 181–190.

Eberhard, W. G., & Barrantes, G. (2015). Cues guiding uloborid construction behavior support orb web monophyly. *Journal of Arachnology, 43*, 371–387.

Eberhard, W. G., & Gonzaga, M. (2019). Evidence that *Polysphincta*-group wasps (Hymenoptera: Ichneumonidae) use ecdysteroids to manipulate the web-construction behaviour of their spider hosts. *Biological Journal of the Linnean Society, 20*, 1–43.

Eberhard, W. G., & Hesselberg, T. (2012). Cues that spiders (Araneae: Araneidae, Tetragnathidae) use to build orbs: Lapses in attention to one set of cues because of dissonance with others? *Ethology: Formerly Zeitschrift fur Tierpsychologie, 118*, 610–620.

Eberhard, W. G., & Opell, B. D. (2022). Orb web traits typical of Uloboridae (Arachnida, Araneâe). *Journal of Arachnology, 50*, 351–384.

Eberhard, W. G., & Wcislo, W. T. (2011). Morphological and behavioural correlates of brain size in miniature spiders, insects, and other invertebrates. *Advances in Insect Physiology, 60*, 155–214.

Edelman, G. M., & Tononi, G. (2000). *A universe of consciousness.* New York: Basic Books.

Fabre, J. H. J. H. (1912). *Social life in the insect world.* London: Fisher Unwin.

Foelix, R. F. (1970). Structure and function of tarsal sensilla in the spider *Araneus diadematus. Journal of Experimental Zoology, 175*, 99–123.

Foelix, R. (2011). *Biology of spiders.* Oxford: Oxford University Press.

Gonzaga, M. O., Kloss, T. G., & Sobczak, J. F. (2017). Host behavioral manipulation of spiders by ichneumonid wasps. In C. Viera, & M. O. Gonzaga (Eds.). *Behaviour and Ecology of Spiders: Contributions from the Neotropical Region* (pp. 417–437). New York: Springer.

Gotts & Vollrath. (1991). Artificial intelligence modelling of web-building in the garden cross spider. *Journal of Theoretical Biology, 152*, 485–511.

Gotts & Vollrath. (1992). Physical and theoretical features in the simulation of animal behavior: The spider's web. *Cybernetics and System, 23*, 41–65.

Gould, S. J., & Lewontin, R. C. (1979). The spandrels of San Marco and the Panglossian paradigm: A critique of the adaptationist programme. *Proceedings of the Royal Society of London B: Biological Sciences, 205*, 581–598.

Gregorič, M., Kostanjšek, R., & Kuntner, M. (2010). Orb web features as taxonomic characters in Zygiella s.1. (Araneae: Araneidae). *Journal of Arachnology, 38*, 319–327.

Griffin, D. (1981). *The question of animal awareness: Evolutionary continuity of mental experience.* New York: Rockefeller University Press.

Heiling, A. M., & Herberstein, M. E. (1999). The importance of being larger: Intraspecific competition for prime web sites in orb-web spiders (Araneae, Araneidae). *Behaviour, 136*, 669–677.

Hénaut, Y. S., Machkour-M'Rabet, & Lachaud, J.-P. (2014). The role of learning in risk-avoidance strategies during spider–ant interactions. *Animal Cognition, 17*, 185–195.

Herberstein, M. E., & Tso, I.-M. (2011). Spider webs: Evolution, diversity and plasticity. In M. E. Herberstein (Ed.). *Spider behaviour: flexibility and versatility* (pp. 57–98). Cambridge: Cambridge University Press.

Hesselberg, T. (2010). Ontogenetic changes in web design in two orb-weavers. *Ethology: Formerly Zeitschrift für Tierpsychologie, 116*, 535–545.

Hesselberg, T. (2014). The mechanism behind plasticity of web-building behavior in an orb spider facing spatial constraints. *Journal of Arachnology, 42*, 311–314.

Hesselberg, T. (2015). Exploration behaviour and behavioural flexibility in orb-web spiders: A review. *Current Zoology, 61*, 313–327.

Hesselberg, T., Simonsen, D., & Juan, C. (2019). Do cave orb spiders show unique behavioural adaptations to subterranean life? A review of the evidence. *Behaviour, 156*, 969–996.

Hesselberg, T., & Vollrath, F. (2004). The effects of neurotoxins on web-geometry and web-building behaviour in *Araneus diadematus* Cl. *Physiology and Behavior, 82*, 519–529.

Hingston, R. W. G. (1922). The snare of the giant wood spider (*Nephila maculata*). Part II. *Journal of the Bombay Natural History Society, 28*, 911–917.

Hingston, R. W. G. (1929). *Instinct and intelligence.* New York: Macmillan Company.

Hingston, R. W. G. (1920). *A naturalist in Himalaya.* London: H. F. & G. Witherby.

Jacobi-Kleemann, M. (1953). Über die Lokomotion der Kreuzspinne Aranea diadema beim Netzbau (nach Filmanalysen). *Zeitschrift für Vergleichende Physiologie, 3*, 606–654.

Japyassú, H. F., & Ades, C. (1998). From complete orb to semi-orb webs: Developmental transitions in the web of *Nephilengys cruentata* (Araneae: Tetragnathidae). *Behaviour, 135*, 931–956.

Kloss, T. G., Gonzaga, M. O., de Oliveira, L. L., & Sperber, C. F. (2017). Proximate mechanism of behavioral manipulation of an orb-weaver spider host by a parasitoid wasp. *PLoS One, 12*, e0171336.

König, M. (1951). Beiträge zur Kenntnis des Netzbaues orbiteler Spinnen. *Zeitschrift für Tierpsychologie, 8*, 337–504.

Krink, T., & Vollrath, F. (1999). A virtual robot to model the use of regenerated leg in a web-building spider. *Animal Behaviour, 57*, 223–232.

Kulkarni, S., Kallal, R. J., Wood, H., Dimitrov, D., Giribet, G., & Hormiga, G. (2021). Interrogating genomic-scale data to resolve recalcitrant nodes in the spider tree of life. *Molecular Biology and Evolution, 38*, 891–903.

Kuntner, M., Čandek, K., Gregorič, M., Turk, E., Hamilton, C. A., Chamberland, L., ... Bond, J. E. (2023). Increasing information content and diagnosability in family-level classifications. *Systematic Biology, 72*, 964–971.

Kuntner, M., Coddington, J. A., & Hormiga, G. (2008). Phylogeny of extant nephilid orb-weaving spiders (Araneae, Nephilidae): testing morphological and ethological homologies. *Cladistics, 24*, 147–217.

Le Guelte, L. (1966). Structure de la toile de *Zygiella x-notata* Cl. (Araignées, Argiopidae) et acteurs qui régissent le comportement de l'Araignée pendant la construction de la toile. *Université de Nancy, Faculté des Sciences, France.*

Le Guelte, L. (1967). La structure de la toile et les facteurs externes modifiant le comportement de *Zygiella x-notata* Cl. (Araignées, Argiopidae). *Revue du Comportement Animal, 1*, 23–70.

Le Guelte, L. (1969). Learning in spiders. *American Zoologist, 9*, 145–152.

Li, D., & Lee, W. S. (2004). Predator-induced plasticity in web-building behaviour. *Animal Behaviour, 67*, 309–318.

Liao, C.-P., Chi, K.-J., & Tso, I.-M. (2009). The effects of wind on trap structural and material properties of a sit-and-wait predator. *Behavioral Ecology, 20*, 1194–1203.

Lopardo, L., Giribet, G., & Hormiga, G. (2011). Morphology to the rescue: Molecular data and the signal of morphological characters in combined phylogenetic analyses—A case study from mysmenid spiders (Araneae, Mysmenidae), with comments on the evolution of web architecture. *Cladistics: The International Journal of the Willi Hennig Society, 27*, 278–330.

Mayer, G. (1952). Untersuchungen über Herstellung und Struktur des Radnetzes von *Aranea diadema* und *Zilla x-notata* mit besonderer Berücksichtigung des Unterschiedes von Jugend- und Altersnetzen. *Zeitschrift für Tierpsychologie, 9*, 337–362.

Monaghan, P., Charmantier, A., Nussey, D. H., & Ricklefs, R. E. (2008). The evolutionary ecology of senescence. *Functional Ecology, 22*, 371–378.

Mulder, T., Mortimer, B., & Vollrath, F. (2021). Dynamic environments do not appear to constrain spider web building behaviour. *The Science of Nature, 108*, 20.

Müller, G. B., & Wagner, G. P. (1991). Novelty in evolution: Restructuring the concept. *Annual Review of Ecology and Systematics, 22*, 229–256.

Nakata, K. (2007). Prey detection without successful capture affects spider's orb-web building behaviour. *Die Naturwissenschaften, 94*, 853–857.

Nakata, K. (2010). Attention focusing in a sit-and-wait forager: A spider controls it prey-detection ability in different web sectors by adjusting thread tension. *Proceedings of the Royal Society B, 277*, 29–33.

Nakata, K., & Mori, Y. (2016). Cost of complex behaviour and its implications in anti-predator defence in orb-web spiders. *Animal Behaviour, 120*, 115–121.

Nakata, K., & Zschokke, S. (2010). Upside-down spiders build upside-down orb webs: Web asymmetry, spider orientation and running speed in *Cyclosa*. *Proceedings of the Royal Society of London B: Biological Sciences, 277*, 3019–3025.

Opell, B. D., Schwend, H. S., & Vito, S. T. (2011). Constraints on the adhesion of viscous threads spun by orb-weaving spiders: The tensile strength of glycoprotein glue exceeds its adhesion. *Journal of Experimental Biology, 214*, 2237.

Pasquet, A., Anotaux, M., & Leborgne, R. (2011). Loss of legs: Is it or not a handicap for an orb-weaving spider. *Die Naturwissenschaften, 98*, 557–564.

Pasquet, A., Marchal, J., Anotaux, M., & Leborgne, R. (2013). *European Journal of Entomology, 110*, 493–500.

Peters, H. M. (1933). Kleine Beitrage zur Biologie der Kreuzspinne *Epeira diademata* Cl. *Zeitschrift für Morphologie und Ökologie der Tiere, 26*, 447–468.

Peters, H. M. (1937). Studien am Netz der Kreuzspinne (*Aranea diadema* L.). II. Über die Hersellung des Rahmens, der Radialfäden un der Hilfsspiral. *Zeitschrift für Morphologie und Ökologie der Tiere, 33*, 128–150.

Peters, H. M. (1939). *Probleme des Kreuzspinnen-Netzes. Probleme des Kreuzspinnennetzes.* Berlin, Heidelberg: Springer-Verlag, 179–266.

Peters, H. M. (1954). Estudios adicionales sobre la estructura de la red concéntrica de las arañas. *Comunicaciones, 3*, 1–18.

Peters, H. M. (1969). Maturing and coordination of web-building activity. *Integrative and Comparative Biology, 9*, 223–227.

Petrusewiczowa, E. (1938). Beobachtungen ber den Bau des Netzes der Kreuzspinne. *Travaux de l'Institut de Biologie Gemirale de l'Universite de Vilno, 9*, 1–25.

Quesada, R., Barrantes, G., & Eberhard, W. G. (2021). Complex plasticity in miniature spiders: Webs built in constrained spaces by small spiderlings of *Leucauge argyra* (Araneae: Tetragnathidae). *PLoS One, 16*(6), e025919.

Ramírez, M. J., Wolff, J. O., Jäger, P., Pavlek, M., Pérez-González, A., Magalhaes, I., & Michalik, P. (2023). Geometric regularity in webs of non-orb-weaving spiders. *Ecology and Evolution.* https://doi.org/10.1002/ece3.9839.

Rawlings, J. O., & Witt, P. N.1973). Appendix: Preliminary data on a possible genetic component in web building. In J. R. Wilson (Ed.), *Behavioral genetics simple systems, symposium held at the University of Colorado.*

Reed, C. F. (1969). Cues in the web-building process. *American Zoologist, 9*, 211–221.

Reed, C. F., Witt, P. N., & Jones, R. L. (1965). The measuring function of the first legs of *Araneus diadematus* CL. *Behaviour, 25*, 98–118.

Reed, C. F., Witt, P. N., Scarboro, M. B., & Peakall, D. B. (1970). Experience and the orb web. *Developmental Psychobiology, 3*, 251–265.

Roth, V. D., & Roth, B. M. (1984). A review of appendotomy in spiders and other arachnids. Bulletin of the British Arachnology. *Society, 6*, 137–146.

Sandoval, C. P. (1994). Plasticity in web design in the spider *Parawixia bistriata*: A response to variable prey type. *Functional Ecology, 8*, 701–707.

Shettleworth, S. J. (2010). *Cognition, evolution, and behavior.* Oxford: Oxford University Press.

Simpson, J. H., & de Bivort, B. L. (2021). Orb weavers: Pattern in the movement sequences of spider web construction. *Current Biology, 31*, R1467–R1469.

Soley, F., Rodríguez, R. L., Hoebel, G., & Eberhard, W. G. (2021). Insightful behaviour in arthropods? *Behaviour, 158*, 781–793.

Tew, E. R., Adamson, A., & Hesselberg, T. (2015). *The web repair behaviour of an orb spider. Animal Behaviour, 103*, 137–146.

Toscani, C., Leborgne, R., & Pasquet, A. (2012). Behavioural analysis of web building anomalies in the orb-weaving spider Zygiella x-notata (Araneae, Araneidae). *Arachnologische Mitteilungen, 43*, 79–83.

Tso, I.-M., Chiang, S.-Y., & Blackledge, T. A. (2007). Does the giant wood spider *Nephila pilipes* respond to prey variation by altering web or silk properties? *Ethology: Formerly Zeitschrift fur Tierpsychologie, 113*, 324–333.

Tso, I.-M., Wu, H.-C., & Hwang, I. R. (2005). Giant wood spider *Nephila pilipes* alters silk protein in response to prey variation. *Journal of Experimental Biology, 208,* 1053–1061.

Vollrath, F. (1986). Gravity as an orientation guide during web-construction in the orb spider *Araneus diadematus* (Araneae, Araneidae). *Journal of Comparative Physiology A: Neuroethology, Sensory, Neural, and Behavioral Physiology, 159,* 275–280.

Vollrath, F. (1987). Altered geometry of webs in spiders with regenerated legs. *Nature, 328,* 247–248.

Vollrath, F. (1988). Spiral orientation of *Araneus diadematus* orb webs built during vertical rotation. *Journal of Comparative Physiology A: Neuroethology, Sensory, Neural, and Behavioral Physiology, 162,* 413–419.

Vollrath, F. (1992). Analysis and interpretation of orb spider exploration and web-building behavior. *Advances in the Study of Behavior 21,* 147–199.

Vollrath, F., Downes, M., & Krackow, S. (1997). Design variability in web geometry of an orb-weaving spider. *Physiology & Behavior, 62,* 735–743.

West Eberhard, M. J. (2003). *Developmental plasticity and evolution.* New York: Oxford University.

Wiederman, S. D., & O'Carroll, D. C. (2013). Selective attention in an insect visual neuron. *Current Biology, 23,* 156–161.

Witt, P. N. (1965). Do we live in the best of all worlds? Spider webs suggest an answer. *Perspectives in Biology and Medicine, 8,* 475–487.

Witt, P. N., Reed, C., & Peakall, D. B. (1968). *A spider's web: Problems in regulatory biology.* New York: Springer-Verlag.

Witt, P. N., Scarboro, M. B., Daniels, R., Peakall, D. B., & Gause, R. L. (1977). Spider web-building in outer space: Evaluation of records from the skylab spider experiment. *Journal of Arachnology, 4,* 115–124.

Wu, C.-C., Blamires, S. J., Wu, C.-L., & Tso, I.-M. (2013). Wind induces variations in spider web geometry and sticky spiral droplet volume. *Journal of Experimental Biology, 216,* 3342–3349.

Zschokke, S. (1993). The influence of the auxiliary spiral on the capture spiral in *Araneus diadematus* Clerck (Araneidae). *Bulletin of the British Arachnological Society, 9,* 169–173.

Zschokke, S. (1997). Factors influencing the size of the orb web in Araneus diadematus. *Proceedings of the 16th European Colloquium of Arachnology, 329,* 329–334.

Zschokke, S. (2011). Spiral and web asymmetry in the orb webs of *Araneus diadematus* (Araneae: Araneidae). *Journal of Arachnology, 39,* 358–362.

Zschokke, S., Countryman, S., & Cushing, P. E. (2021). Spiders in space—orb-web-related behaviour in zero gravity. *The Science of Nature, 108*(1).

Zschokke, S., & Nakata, K. (2015). Vertical asymmetries in orb webs. *Biological Journal of the Linnean Society, 114,* 659–672.

Zschokke, S., & Vollrath, F. (1995). Unfreezing the behaviour of two orb spiders. *Physiology & Behavior, 58,* 1167–1173.

Zschokke, S., & Vollrath, F. (2000). Planarity and size of orb-webs built by *Araneus diadematus* (Araneae: Araneidae) under natural and experimental conditions. *Ekológia (Bratislava), 19,* 307–318.

Further Reading

Eberhard, W. G. (2021). Small details in a large spider: Silk manipulation and spinneret and cheliceral morphology in *Trichonephila clavipes* (Araneae, Nephilidae). *Journal of Arachnology, 49,* 384–388.

Franck, D. (1974). The genetic basis of evolutionary changes in behaviour patterns. In J. H. F. Van Abeelen (Ed.). *The genetics of behaviour* (pp. 119–140). New York: American Elsevier.

Hesselberg, T. (2013). Web-building flexibility differs in two spatially constrained orb spiders. *Journal of Insect Behavior, 26*, 283–303.

Hesselberg, V. (2012). The mechanical properties of the non-sticky spiral in *Nephila* orb webs (Araneae, Nephilidae). *Journal of Experimental Biology, 215*, 3362–3369.

Opell, B. D., Lipkey, G. K., Hendricks, M. L., & Vito, S. T. (2009). Daily and seasonal changes in the stickiness of viscous capture threads in *Argiope aurantia* and *Argiope trifasciata* orb-webs. *Journal of Experimental Zoology Part A: Ecological Genetics and Physiology, 311*, 217–225.

Quesada, R., Triana, E., Vargas, G., Douglass, J. K., Seid, M. A., Niven, J. E., ... Wcislo, W. T. (2011). The allometry of CNS size and consequences of miniaturization in orb-weaving and cleptoparasitic spiders. *Arthropod Structure & Development (Cambridge, England), 40*, 521–529.

Sensenig, A. T., Agnarsson, I., Gondek, T. M., & Blackledge, T. A. (2010). Webs in vitro and in vivo: Spider alter their orb-spinning behavior in the laboratory. *Journal of Arachnolgy, 38*, 183–191.

Stowe, M. (1986). Prey specialization in the Araneidae. In W. A. Shear (Ed.). *Spiders: Webs, behavior, and evolution* (pp. 101–131). Stanford, CA: Stanford University Press.

Wolff, J. O., & Herberstein, M. E. (2017). Three-dimensional printing spiders: Back-and-forth glue application yields silk anchorages with high pull-off resistance under varying loading situations. *Journal of the Royal Society Interface, 14*, 20160783.